The Porcelain Art

of

EDWARD MARSHALL

BOEHM

EDWARD

The Porcelain Art of
MARSHALL BOEHM

Reese Palley

Harrison House
New York

To Max and Anne Palley—besides being
my parents, a most remarkable couple

This 1988 edition is published by
Harrison House
distributed by Crown Publishers, Inc., 225 Park Avenue South
New York, New York 10003
All rights reserved. No part of the contents of this book may
be reproduced without the written permission of the publisher

Printed and bound in Japan

Library of Congress Cataloging-in-Publication Data
Palley, Reese.
    The porcelain art of Edward Marshall Boehm.
    Reprint. Originally published: New York:
H. N. Abrams, 1976.
    Bibliography: p. 312
    1. Boehm, Edward Marshall, 1913-1969—Catalogs.
2. Porcelain, American—Catalogs.   3. Porcelain—20th
century—United States—Catalogs.   I. Title.
NK4210.B6A4   1988   738′.092′4   87–17818
ISBN 0–517–65361–3

h g f e d c b a

Contents

NOTE TO THE READER

RPC stands for Reese Palley–Catalog and denotes sculptures created and executed by Edward Marshall Boehm. RPS stands for Reese Palley–Studio and denotes pieces completed after Boehm's death in 1969.

ACKNOWLEDGMENTS

I wish to take this small space to try, however inadequately, to thank the people who made this book possible.

Needless to say, my own staff—in particular Min Friedberg, Mike Pred and Doris Idakitis—worked untiringly to provide us with literally tons of material from which this work slowly took shape. My son, Gilbert Palley, zipped around the East Coast producing photographs of pieces of whose existence we had not even guessed. To Dr. Robert Schwartz, who made his own unique contribution both to the book and his own world of porcelain, a special word of thanks.

To the many collectors and Boehm dealers whom we contacted and who generously allowed us to pick their minds and photograph their collections—Alan Zell of Oregon; Syracuse University; the Philadelphia Academy of Natural Sciences; O. H. Delchamps; the late Raymond Tyo; T. C. McClure, Jr., and others too numerous to mention—a special "thank you." On those many occasions when we were ready to retreat in frustration, Mr. Frank Cosentino, president of Edward Marshall Boehm, Inc., came to our rescue with the information we needed, whenever he had it.

AND

very special love and gratitude to the glorious little Roman.

REESE PALLEY

Introduction

There are large revolutions and small revolutions... there are large philosophies and small, and it will not be claimed that Edward Marshall Boehm caused a revolution in the world's thought or the world's politics.

But viewed historically, Ed Boehm did make his own *little* revolution. He achieved the one hallmark of all successful revolutions. He left the world in a somewhat altered condition than he found it. He left an irreversible and ineradicable imprint on the attitudes, fortunes and ideas of a substantial number of people in the world of porcelain and porcelain collectors.

There have been similar revolutions in recent history, even in fields closely related to Ed Boehm's own. Men like Minton's Solon, of pâte-sur-pâte fame, men like Louis Tiffany, who imposed his vision on glass, men like Fabergé, who made even more unreal the fantasy of Czars. The hands of these men changed common materials so that they never can be viewed as they had been in the past. Solon changed our understanding of slip application; Tiffany our understanding of glass; Fabergé our understanding of combining precious media.

In a like manner, no one can ever again view achievements in porcelain as they were viewed until 1955. No one can ever again judge the accomplishments of porcelain sculptors other than by comparing their work with the startling 15 years' work of Edward Marshall Boehm. He shook up his world no less thoroughly than larger movements shake up theirs. Ed Boehm *changed* the world. This ability to change marks the seminal man, the creative man, the revolutionary man.

We know *what* Ed Boehm did by looking at his work and by looking beyond his work at the energies which he released from his imitators, his competitors, his detractors. We know that processes which were considered impossible before Ed Boehm showed the way are now executed on a daily basis by others.

It is easy to see *what* he accomplished. This book is really about all that. I have expended considerable labor in documenting, describing and photographing *what* he did. When we speak about *what* Ed Boehm did, we are speaking of history. That is, for the most part, factual reportage. As such, it is not difficult to avoid opinion and advocacy. However, as soon as we step away from the simple listing of the pieces and our knowledge of them, then we get into an area of *how* Ed Boehm did things and the even more problematical question of *why* he did them.

The *how* is a middle ground between *what* and *why*. In order to understand *how* Ed Boehm accomplished what he did in the few short years of his fruitful work it is necessary to understand something about the technical nature of the problems that he approached and the techniques he developed in solving these problems.

Boehm was essentially a *natural* man. That is, his methods of arriving at conclusions were instinctive and gut. Depending on an enormous capacity to observe the way life functioned, Ed Boehm was able to arrive at intuitive, instinctive and immediate understanding of basic organic processes.

Before he would begin a bird sculpture, he had to know from his own personal observation what the bird did, how the bird lived, how the bird reacted, what the breeding process was, and what the "personality" of the bird was in general. Ed Boehm was an iconoclast and as such he not only destroyed idols but he accepted practically no existing authority. He was much happier with a bird than with a book about a bird, and he was convinced that observations made by those before him were, if not incorrect, at least incomplete.

Ed Boehm didn't believe in partial answers. The entire problem had to be clear to him. He had to have the complete circle, the entire gestalt, laid out in front of him before he was satisfied with his own understanding. Long before any less intuitive mind would have been able to piece together the nature of a problem, Ed's mind leaped over thought processes and intel-

lectual steps, which most of us would have had to struggle through, to an instinctively correct answer. That answer was always congruent with Ed Boehm's understanding of the basic laws of nature and the behavior of animals. He *always* solved problems in the same manner that nature solves them and with the same straightforward, illuminating clarity.

Ed Boehm had that marvelous ability to reason back from the problem to the cause. Too many of us, in solving problems, tend to reason forward from the problem. If faced with a flat tire, most of us replace the tire. Ed Boehm, faced with a flat tire, would first go into the problem of why the tire was flat, the kind of rubber that went into the tire, the air pressure and abuses that the tire had suffered. This ability to reason backward from result to cause is the best insight I can offer into Ed Boehm's mind.

With animals, the sure knowledge on Ed Boehm's part that natural process has its own unavoidable logic, that there is an organic reality, an organic development, behind any final effect made Ed Boehm the great naturalist and the great problem solver that he was.

Ed Boehm did not think of himself as a teacher: he was, in his own eyes, a doer. However, he taught constantly throughout his whole life but only those who would take the time and the patience to observe Ed as carefully as Ed was observing his problems. His students were his closest collaborators. They worked with and learned from Ed Boehm for over 10 years. They were trained to solve problems as Ed had. Some of the work which the studio has completed since Ed Boehm's death reveals Boehm as a better teacher than any of us suspected.

RPC-1043-01 AMERICAN REDSTARTS on
Flowering Dogwood

Ed could be peremptory and bad-tempered about both the smallest and the largest matters. He was blinded by prejudice in important political and social areas of his culture. He was, however, never blind in his observations of natural phenomena. Most scientists start from a point of view about how nature works. Not Ed Boehm. Ed Boehm's starting point was that nature *does* work and that all one has to do is find out how it works. Above all he avoided prejudgments about nature. This ultimate clarity was all he needed in order to arrive at satisfactory conclusions involving any organic process.

I don't mean to give the impression that Ed's ability to solve problems was based solely on an exceptional ability to observe phenomena. That he indeed did have. But unless this ability is reinforced by other talents, the observer is left with only a mechanical recording facility and not the ability to synthesize and solve.

The ability to observe carefully and with clarity in an unprejudiced way is granted many people. But the additional talent, the additional gift of *intuition*, is something which is granted few. Based on his observations, Ed Boehm was able, intuitively, to arrive at viable organic solutions. In some cases the intuition was so overwhelming, the insight was so clear and correct and leaped so many barriers, that it took on the appearance of revelation.

Incredibly stubborn, very, very bright, capable of extended and dogged hard work, with a pure 18th-century, almost religious, belief in natural phenomena and a mind which worked backwards from effect to cause in a deceptively simple linear way, Ed Boehm

turned his talents to a thousand riddles. And solved them.

This then was *how* Ed Boehm solved his problems. I don't believe that even Ed himself knew much about the processes of his mind. He only knew that he was driven to do certain things in a certain way. This leads to the third part of the mystery of Ed Boehm: *why*.

Why, indeed, was Ed Boehm driven to use his talents? Most of us have God-given talents which we are never motivated to use. What then was the peculiar set of drives, the emotional history, the personality and family factors, which caused Ed Boehm to use these powers to the fullest?

Why did Ed Boehm do what he did? Before we go into that, let me tell a little story. I only saw Ed Boehm cry once. It is uncomfortable to see any man cry, but to see this tight, accomplished and powerful man choke with tears and run away was a shattering experience. I provoked the tears and I never knew why until many years later. My provocation was without intent and it was only when I found out what lay behind the tears that I began to get a better insight into Ed Boehm's personality.

It happened one lovely spring afternoon in Washington Crossing. Ed was working with a shovel in the earth, which he dearly loved to do, and I had come out on a number of errands, one of which was to show him a small thoroughbred horse with a jockey which I had just acquired from another dealer. It was an unimportant but not an undistinguished piece. It was small and fashioned with a good deal of understanding and

RPC-1022-02 CERULEAN WARBLERS on Wild Rose

love. I held it out to Ed. He recoiled, and it was at that moment that his eyes filled with tears and without saying a word, without touching the piece, he turned on his heel and left me. I was puzzled but too embarrassed to go into the matter at the moment. It wasn't until many years later that the clue to his distress came to my hands.

I had been negotiating for the purchase of the collection of Edward D. Boehm (Ed Boehm's father) for many years and sometime shortly after Ed's death the senior Mr. Boehm and I were going over the inventory of his collection. Mr. Boehm mentioned, just in passing, that he had disposed of a number of pieces, one of which was a small thoroughbred and jockey on a base. I still didn't make a connection, but later when I mentioned the piece to Helen Boehm she questioned me closely, and it was then that she told me that Ed had made that sculpture as a special gift to his father. Obviously the thought that his father, who was never in need of money, would sell his gift was the thought that brought tears to Ed Boehm's eyes. I am not a Freudian and I don't believe in Freudian analysis, and yet in this story and in Ed Boehm's personality lies an almost classically defined Freudian relationship between a son and his father.

Mr. Boehm, Senior, was a proud, stiff, formal man much involved in his own life and accomplishments. When he found himself with a motherless child, he turned away from supplying the softness of a mother as well as the direction and guidance of a father. Ed was placed in an institution. Ed Boehm and his father were separated, at the father's insistence, during the most formative time of Ed Boehm's life. Ed subsequently spent the whole of his creative life, unconsciously perhaps, trying to capture the attention, the affection and the respect of his father. Every accomplishment, every newspaper article, every victory, every success, was laid at his father's feet in the hope that this further proof of the son's abilities and remarkabilities would open the gates of affection and recognition which Ed Boehm so badly needed. However, to the day of Ed Boehm's death there was little evidence of returned affection.

That stiffness, that withdrawn quality, that inability to become involved with a creative son carried over even after Ed Boehm's death. I saw the senior Mr. Boehm at Ed Boehm's funeral. At that time he was well over 80 and one would think softened a little by the years. My observation, however, was that the detachment and stiffness were still there. The sense of nonparticipation in the funeral of his own son was to me a shocking reaffirmation of my understanding of the relationship between Ed and his father. To me, Ed's father seemed an uninterested spectator at the funeral of his only son.

People are what they are. This is no condemnation of the elder Mr. Boehm. He lived his life and he built his relationships as he found he had to. He was no more "wrong" than had he been the other kind of father and smothered Ed's creativity in a bathetic attempt to replace a dead mother. Quite possibly the accomplishments which Ed Boehm left behind are, in no little measure, traceable to this rejection by his father. The tragedy of this strange relationship was Ed Boehm's own personal agony. But perhaps it is only out of agony of one sort or another that the creative drive emerges.

That, then, is my understanding of Ed Boehm. Fragmentary, incomplete and perhaps jejeune. Nevertheless it is, for me at least, a workable understanding of this complex, driven man. Driven to undertaking enormous tasks. Blinded by the emotional turmoil of an unresolved relationship with his father and suffering physical and emotional agony during every moment of his waking life, Ed Boehm was Samson Agonistes, sightless and with his own strength bringing his world crashing down upon himself.

REESE PALLEY
January 26, 1976

Portrait of Edward Marshall Boehm

Who Was Edward Marshall Boehm?

Edward Marshall Boehm, a man of abundant talent, perhaps even of genius, revolutionized American porcelain sculpture and raised it to a level of technical and artistic achievement which it had never before attained. His contributions to the study of the genetics of birds and animals, though not as well known as his work in porcelain, were in many ways even more remarkable. Largely self-taught in both art and ornithology, he succeeded in all that he tried except in learning how to live with himself and his fellow man.

His life was often difficult. Severe emotional turmoil in his earliest years—the divorce of his parents, his mother's early death, rejection by his father—all combined to sour him on the world, on himself and on relationships with other people. The trauma of his tortured childhood extended in bitterness and suspicion even to those who loved and respected him most. His psychological pain left its mark physically, and throughout his life he suffered from a painful and debilitating colitis that would not respond to medical treatment.

Most of those who felt Ed Boehm's boorishness or were the target of his bad temper forgave him. They knew from what deep wells the acrimony rose. Four years after his birth, in Baltimore, on August 21, 1913,

his parents were divorced—at that time a most excruciatingly embarrassing social disaster. Divorce just did not happen in a "nice" family. There was a smell of sin, a suggestion of evil and a whisper of immorality about divorce. Boehm seldom talked about his childhood, even to his wife, but it was evident in later years that as a youngster he had felt that in some ways his mother had been stigmatized by divorce. And, as if divorce were not dreadful enough, she had worked as a model, a somewhat disreputable occupation for a woman in that age of lingering Victorianism.

In 1920, when young Boehm was seven, she died —the ultimate rejection for a child—leaving him virtually alone. His father seemed to want little to do with the boy. This added rejection was to anger, puzzle and embitter Boehm throughout his life. He did not really meet his father until he was in his middle twenties, and the father-son relationship was, even from that point on, at best tangential. Most of what has been written about their relationship tends to characterize the father as having a curious and unloving detachment, even after Ed Boehm became internationally known. Boehm often sent gifts and made approaches which never resulted in a solid friendship. Yet the elder Boehm, in the months that preceded his death in the spring of

1975, confided to friends that he was enormously injured by the biographies that suggested that his son was an orphan.

Perhaps the truth of the matter is that Ed Boehm—despite his need to establish contact with his father—was never really able to forgive him for the early rejection of both his mother and himself.

What made this rejection all the more difficult to bear was Ed Boehm's wholehearted belief in genetic predestination. "You can only be as good as your inheritance will allow," was a maxim that he used frequently when judging a person's potential. By that he did not mean simply that inheritance *affected* one's ability to achieve, or that it was *one* of the factors. It was everything. And here was his own father—a man who like himself dealt in luxury items for the wealthy (he owned a Cadillac dealership in Manhattan) and who understood animals well enough to qualify as a judge for dog shows—disowning him.

What the lack of family stability and love meant to Boehm was demonstrated three years before his death when an executive of the Coca-Cola Company, learning that Boehm's mother had been one of the famous "Coke" girls whose picture had appeared in turn-of-the-century advertising for the company, resurrected a portrait showing her to have been a beautiful woman of soft and gentle face. Boehm's delight with the photograph was childlike. Some of his associates felt that this reawakened memory of his mother brought about such a change that even in his drive for perfection he began to show some tolerance of the frailties he discovered in others.

It can be argued that the traumas of his childhood

were the wellsprings of Boehm's later drive and energy. Perhaps. But while his difficult childhood lent fanatic strength to his creative activities, the creative ability was in his genes, just as he so often said. That marvelous and synoptic quality of his mind, his ability to see into organic structure, would have emerged even without the impetus of a desperate childhood.

After his mother died, a neighbor arranged to have young Boehm sent to the McDonogh School, an excellent institution in rural Baltimore County which in those years was dedicated to the care of homeless boys. McDonogh offered an agricultural program, and it was here that Boehm began to develop his great love and understanding of animals. It was at McDonogh, too, that his artistic talents were nurtured. Watercolor paintings that survived his school years show clearly that by the age of nine Boehm was already a sophisticated draftsman with a remarkable grasp of color and form. That he was pugnacious is indicated by his favorite school sport, boxing. He was good enough to fight as a semi-professional in his late teens. His school years obviously were a time of achievement as well as of learning, but he rarely mentioned them. His loneliness overshadowed all else.

Frank Cosentino, for many years Boehm's administrative assistant and currently president of Edward Marshall Boehm, Inc., wrote a sympathetic biography of Boehm in 1970 which is valuable in understanding the forces that drove him. Cosentino writes:

He wanted to blot out the early years because they were empty and unhappy. He never experienced the love and warmth of family life, the uninhibited expressions of laughter and tears between parents and child, the dependence on parental example and guidance. His was a sterile existence, he was dependent upon his own developing character and wits. Personal relationships could not influence his direction. Emotion could not interfere with his desire. In his mind, aggressiveness and determination became honed to the competition of his society. To survive in a world he found difficult to accept, he had to be equipped properly. To influence or in some way change that world he had to set goals and let nothing deter him from them.

His pent-up love and care found expression in God's "other world" of nature and her creatures, so much so that to see, study, and understand wasn't enough. He loved God's natural world with a passion that overflowed from him into artistic expression.

But while Boehm "loved God's natural world," he had little time for God. Nature was sufficient Deism for him. What, if anything, stood behind nature was not his concern. He was ever filled with wonder at the utter logic of natural process. Process was his God. Ends and beginnings bored him.

Boehm left McDonogh at sixteen and worked as a farmhand for a time before entering the University of Maryland to study animal husbandry. In 1934, when he was only twenty-one and already the breeder of a grand champion bull, he went to work as manager of Longacre Farms on the Eastern Shore of Maryland. Longacre was the home of one of the finest herds of Guernseys in the country. He spent six of what were the most formative years of his life living close to the animals, untouched for the most part by involvement with human beings. Boehm turned naturally and logically from human relationships to associations with animals. "Animals," he said, "are reliable, truer in their affections, predictable in their actions." In short, animals never betrayed him.

He might have remained there for the rest of his life, capable, brilliant, perhaps even famous in the field of animal husbandry, but World War II intervened. Boehm entered the Army Air Force and was assigned as a therapist to a convalescent center in Pawling, New York. His job was to help restore shattered and disturbed airmen by teaching them to raise cattle and plants. His own spare time was spent in shaping clay into the animals he knew so well.

On a Sunday morning in a hotel lobby in Pawling, he met a pretty girl from Brooklyn named Helen Franzolin, who had come to visit her brother in the hospital. She managed to reach Boehm in a way that no other person had ever been able to do. Helen wore a red carnation behind her right ear and Ed, in an uncharacteristic burst of sensibility, asked if it meant that she had not been spoken for. Before the day was over she had invited him home to meet her family. The household in Bensonhurst, a thoroughly Italian neighborhood in Brooklyn, was unlike any Ed had known. The Franzolins—there were eight brothers and sisters and innumerable members of the clan visiting—were easygoing and gregarious. Helen's mother, though she spoke almost no English, "talked" with the lonely soldier for hours. This shy, aloof man had found a family to love—one that gave of its love freely. He became an ardent swain and constant visitor.

The personalities of Ed and Helen could hardly have been more different, but they recognized in each other the diverse strengths that were to make them a unique team. Throughout his career, while Ed worked in his studios or with his live birds, Helen masterfully built an empire around his work. There is simply no way the Boehm enterprise could have succeeded had there been no wedding, though Ed's inner torments nearly kept it from coming about.

The date had been set for a Sunday just two months after their first meeting. Invitations had been sent and Ed had actually converted to Catholicism. On Saturday Ed phoned Helen and told her he loved her but that there might not be a wedding because his unit had been alerted for shipment overseas and he might be confined to base. In retrospect, there is great doubt that any such alert took place. More likely, Ed was torn between the need for family and security and the terrible fear of making himself vulnerable to another human being. In any case, Ed told Helen to keep the faith and to be at Grand Central Station at 11:30 that night. Helen was there and Ed had fought his devils and won. He got off the train and the next morning this unlikely couple was married.

After the war, Boehm discovered that Longacre Farms and its prized Guernsey herd had been destroyed by fire. So in 1945, Ed and Helen Boehm moved to Great Neck, Long Island, where he obtained a job as assistant veterinarian to Dr. Michael Berliner. Boehm was a difficult assistant but Berliner remembers keeping him on because of his unique understanding of animals and the extraordinary sense of communication he had with them. The Boehms' small apartment quickly became a menagerie for dogs, fancy fowl and tropical fish, and these in turn became models for the sculpture that increasingly fascinated Boehm. He felt particularly challenged by the most difficult of all materials to work in, hard-paste porcelain. At the point when he decided what his medium would be Boehm began the career that significantly altered the history of American porcelain.

How It All Began

Ed Boehm's choice of the medium of hard-paste porcelain to bring his vision to the world was, in retrospect, both daring and arrogant. He was aware that no American had ever really conquered hard-paste sculpture, but saw no reason why he should not be the first.

His attraction to porcelain is easy enough to understand. He was, as we have noted, a man determined to make his art imitate life. Porcelain, when employed in a manner that is unsentimental and unromantic, is the art material most akin to "reality." Furthermore, porcelain neither fades nor ages, and in Boehm's mind he was dealing with the Future.

Porcelain was first produced by the Chinese more than 1,000 years ago from a mixture of special clays and minerals which could be fired at tremendous temperatures (up to 2400°F) and emerge in delicate yet strong shapes. The Chinese guarded their formula carefully, and it was not until the 18th century that Western chemists solved the riddle.

A royal collector—history's most conspicuous porcelain consumer—was responsible for the secret being discovered by the West. Augustus the Strong, Elector of Saxony and King of Poland, was such a passionate admirer of the Chinese art that he once bartered an entire regiment of dragoons for forty-eight porcelains to add to his royal collection.

In 1701 Augustus took as a protégé a fanatical nineteen-year-old German alchemist named Johann Friedrich Böttger. Böttger had, in rash moments, made certain claims regarding his ability to turn ordinary metals into gold. His claims exceeded his abilities, of course, but, clever devil that he was, he turned his attention to solving the riddle that most fascinated his benefactor: how is porcelain made?

In 1708, Böttger began firing certain "secret" ingredients at extremely high temperatures and succeeded in producing a red stoneware that was very hard and impervious to acid and flame. He began a desperate search for the substance that he knew must change his dense, heavy, opaque stoneware into light, translucent, almost mythically beautiful porcelain. He stumbled across a white powder that was used to dust fashionable wigs. The material was called "kaolin" and it proved to be the missing link. "Kaolin" is, in fact, a derivative of a Chinese word meaning "high ridge."

The porcelains that resulted from Böttger's discovery were called "Meissen" for the place where they were made, and by the mid-1730's their technical achievement was so great that they were being shipped

RPC-305-01 PERCHERON STALLION

all the way to Constantinople for sale to the potentates of the East. When Saxony fell to Frederick the Great in 1756, more than 700 artisans were employed at Meissen producing incredible treasures of porcelain. Those magnificent "Royal Saxon" porcelains form the backbone of the collections of Europe's great museums.

The United States does not have a strong tradition of hard-paste porcelain, a fact that makes Boehm's venture both typical and remarkable. Hard-paste requires extreme technical skill and most of the ware produced in the United States was soft-paste, fired at low temperatures.

The Trenton-Philadelphia area has been, since Colonial days, the hub of America's porcelain-making activities. The raw materials are there, as are the men with the requisite technical skills.

The first American company to produce porcelain was established in Philadelphia in 1771 by Gousse Bonnin and George Morris. It was an abortive attempt that lasted only three years. Very few of their pieces survive today. The modern era of American porcelain manufacturing actually began in 1863 when the Etruria Works opened in Trenton. The artist Isaac Broome was employed to create busts in Parian ware for the 1876 Centennial Exhibition in Philadelphia, including the now famous models of Ulysses S. Grant and Cleopatra. In 1882, Etruria had the good fortune to attract a William Bromley and his son, two recent immigrants from Ireland. They brought with them the expertise needed to manufacture iridescent glazed porcelain. This allowed the porcelain body to be cast very thin, resulting in light, fragile, highly translucent objects covered with an iridescent glaze. Their expertise quickly spread to other firms in the area.

One notable graduate of the Etruria Works who went on to higher things was Walter Scott Lenox, who, in 1896, founded his own company called Lenox, Incorporated. Lenox, of course, is still in business today and is one of the finest producers of dinnerware.

There was very little production of artistic porcelain in the Trenton area between World War I and II. The Polish artist Boleslaw Cybis came to New York in 1939 to do the art work for the Polish Pavilion at the World's Fair. Prevented from returning home by the outbreak of war, he moved to Trenton in 1942. A recognized artist in many media, Cybis experimented in the creation of porcelain bodies and glazes. He made religious porcelain until the early 1950's when —perhaps nudged by the success of his young Trenton competitor, Ed Boehm—his work widened into other, more contemporary, images. After Cybis's death in 1957, the studio continued to operate under his name and in his tradition, producing porcelain sculptures of birds, people, flowers and animals.

Boehm knew the history and background of his medium from days of poring over books on porcelain and touring museum and studio collections of porcelain. He made frequent trips to Trenton to talk to old-timers in the business and he knew that while there wasn't much happening in the way of artistic porcelain-making, the materials and technical skills still were there, waiting for that rare spark of creative activity.

Finally, he was ready. In 1949, he quit his job with Dr. Berliner (not before taking on the good doctor as his initial partner—the first of several) and with $1,000 and an experienced potter as an assistant opened a studio in a basement in Trenton. His confidence was staggering. The company was called "Champions on Parade."

Boehm began transferring his first sculptures of Herefords, Percherons and dogs into hard-paste porcelain. Sales were slow, however, and Dr. Berliner dropped out of the venture. What followed was a seemingly endless succession of partners, most of whom left in anger. Boehm was simply not the kind of man who could work in partnership. Partners were

The Moon Gate, Entrance to the Japanese Garden on the Boehm Estate, Washington Crossing, New Jersey

too close, had too much control over him and could not understand his drive for perfection. Most of all they were people, and people were enough to ruin any relationship.

The first five or six years, the Boehms had to struggle greatly merely to keep the venture afloat. His first porcelains were inexpensive gift shop items—cute animals, mischievous satyrs, vases and ash trays—none of them very good. But he kept working 70 and 80 hours a week and constantly experimenting with the techniques of his craft. These crude early pieces, while no great artistic achievement, are in great demand today as collector's items.

Persistence against all odds was one of Boehm's prime characteristics. He did not believe there was a problem that could not be solved. There was, for example, the time Boehm was building a Japanese gate on his estate near Washington Crossing (this was, of course, after he became successful). The gate was to have a thatched roof and thatchers were hard to find. The builders of the gate undertook to thatch the roof themselves but soon found it beyond their skills. They fumbled and agonized for days. As they fumbled, Boehm became more and more angry. He would come out and shout at them that they were stupid and inept and that he had to get the gate finished quickly. Finally, the foreman threw his tools on the ground and declared the job simply could not be done. One almost suspects that Boehm had set the poor man up. He told the foreman that he—Boehm—could do it easily. He turned on his heel, jumped into a small pickup truck and drove off to Trenton. Three hours later he returned, having visited every supermarket, hardware

RPC-310 POLO PLAYER

RPC-402-04 HEREFORD BULL

store and grocer in Trenton and bought up their entire supply of brooms. Triumphantly he sawed the handles off the brooms and quickly nailed the straw onto the roof. Within two hours there was a beautifully thatched roof, which remains there to this day. It is a small matter but an example of the kind of mind that can see into the use of material and structure. It is also an example of the need Ed Boehm had to dominate and triumph over his fellows. Instead of offering help, he allowed the affair to become a contest of wills, well knowing ahead of time that he had the answer.

While Boehm struggled with his sculpture, Helen Boehm continued to work—for the first couple of years —as an ophthalmic dispenser at E. B. Meyrowitz, Inc., a large New York optical company. She enjoyed the work and was good at it. To this day, unable to shake her early training, she often surprises visitors to her office by offering suggestions as to how their glasses might be better fitted.

During her lunch hours in New York, Helen took her husband's work to shops and galleries, but soon found that the buyers were interested only in imported porcelains. So Helen Boehm devised a new tactic. She approached cattle breeders with her husband's Herefords, horsemen with his thoroughbreds and show-dog owners with his collies and boxers. They began to buy and to tell their friends.

The event that first brought Boehm to wide public attention was orchestrated by Helen in January 1951, less than two years after he had cast his first porcelains. She phoned the Curator of the American Wing of the Metropolitan Museum of Art, Vincent Andrus, and asked if she could show him examples of what she called the greatest of American art porcelain. Andrus scoffed that there was no such thing as great American porcelain but he agreed to look. He was impressed enough to add a Boehm Hereford and a Percheron to the Met collection. The news of the Met's purchase soon turned up in the *New York Times*, thanks to Helen. Armed with the clipping from the *Times*, she was able to talk Black, Starr and Gorham, the Fifth Avenue silversmiths and jewelers who made trophies for the Westminster Kennel Club Show, into exhibiting some Boehm dogs with their silver cups and plates. The window display, called "Champions on Parade," was Ed Boehm's first exhibition.

Helen Boehm had a flair for public relations that was as inborn as her husband's sculpting ability. Instinctively she knew that there is far more to public relations than a knack for getting publicity. As Bergdorf Goodman, Bonwit Teller, Neiman-Marcus, Marshall Field and other specialty shops for the rich began to display the porcelains, they saw Helen Boehm more frequently. She would not just visit with the buyers and managers, but would personally thank the salesgirls for their help, dropping selling hints at the same time. The clerks in turn supplied her with the names of the people who bought the porcelains, and a thank-you note would be sent to these customers along with the clipping from the *Times*. She spent up to 10 months of the year on the road, and maintained correspondence with hundreds of collectors.

In 1954, she wangled a visit to the White House to present the Eisenhowers with a Hereford Bull. That visit paved the way for another Boehm triumph when Queen Elizabeth and Prince Philip came to the United States in 1957. The Eisenhower presentation gift to the royal couple was a porcelain of Prince Philip on a polo pony. The story and picture made the front page of the *Times* and other newspapers across the country. Within days, thousands of Boehm collectors received the new *Times* clipping and a note from Helen.

By the late 1950's, things were coming together for the Boehms. The early struggle had been difficult but collectors were now responding in a manner unprecedented in the annals of *objets d'art*. Helen was able to turn over the legwork to others and concentrate on administering the company, Ed to spend the greatest portion of his time with his beloved animals and birds. Just as several years earlier he had turned their small apartment in Great Neck into a wildlife sanctuary, he now did the same in his beautiful new home on River Road in Washington Crossing. Helen was never certain when she came home exactly what sort of creature she might find crawling, leaping or flying around the house. Boehm remained, in success, the same man he was in poverty.

RPC-1013-01 GOLDEN ORIENTAL PHEASANT

The Mature Years

Ed Boehm could never have been an entrepreneur. The necessary aggression was there but it was not weighted with the balance and judgment that lead to what economists like to call the maximization of profit principle. A good entrepreneur operates in the short run. His interests are in the bottom line. He builds his reputation and his activities in small accretive steps. Boehm was concerned with the long run. He wanted to make his mark with a depth and clarity that could not be argued. He always took quantum leaps. When he found himself in a situation that promised profit and success, he would quickly tire of the project and, with an expansive and expensive sweep of mind, turn to one that had no foreseeable profitable

At the very beginning of his career, Boehm had decided to design and decorate the Oriental Pheasant. The piece was difficult to make. The tail was long and heavy and had to be fired unsupported. The price, although quite modest at $350, was a little high for his collectors at that time. The Oriental Pheasant had another disadvantage as far as the early collectors were concerned. It was not particularly pretty. The bird itself has garish, raucous colors and Boehm was trying to match the loudness and vulgarity of nature in this specific case. He achieved his goal. But the birds did not sell. In the long run, of course, they added gloriously to his reputation, bringing prices as high as

$15,000 to $18,000. These escalations in price were among the factors that helped establish the popular acceptance of the value of his work and the "inevitability" of its increase in value.

Another time, in 1964, Boehm undertook to create a work of such grand proportions that it boggles the mind. The Ivory-Billed Woodpeckers, which stand almost five feet high without the base, were larger than anything Boehm had so far attempted, possibly larger than anyone had ever attempted. The technical problems that had to be met and defeated went beyond the plausible. His decision to do the Ivory-Billed stemmed both from the fact that the bird was on its way to extinction and from his desire to build a porcelain monument to himself. After the Ivory-Billed was made —only four of them were cast—it was sold for very little but went on to become the single most expensive piece of modern porcelain ever traded. One example, broken and repaired, recently brought more than $100,000. These irrational, improbable, unsound projects were what built Boehm his reputation. Had he been less unsound, less improbable, he would have been less of an artist.

New products and experiments were fundamental to Boehm's life. Just as his curiosity was constantly whetted by the infinite possibilities of breeding and crossbreeding, so it was also nourished by investigations of new techniques and technologies in his art. He sought to imbed porcelain into glass. He attempted to fire colors which had never been fired before. He even tried to catch in the most intransigent porcelain the most fleeting of life forms, the brilliant fish of the tropical seas.

Just before Boehm died he completed the Fondo Marino, a work of immense technical scope and academic scholarship. The Fondo was only the forerunner of a much more sensitive group which Boehm would have worked on had he lived. It was almost as if Boehm knew his time was limited. He seemed to need to jam the entire world of tropical fish into one piece. The Fondo Marino was not typical of the way he worked. Boehm would usually start organically, slowly developing a collection of animals. There would be single animals, experimental pieces that pressed the feel and rhythm of the animal into his hand, and then, suddenly, the irrational productions such as the Ivory-Billed Woodpeckers. In the case of the Fondo Marino, the irrational came before anything else. It just had to be done and it just had to be done at that moment.

Boehm was subtle, and profound, and accomplished. The emotional parameters within which he worked were enormously wide. But the checks and balances, the cautions and precautions within which most of us function, did not exist in Boehm's makeup. They were short-circuited. The temper was too violent. The laughter was too shrill. The volume of his voice when he wanted to attract attention rose to a level which he seemed unable to control. But that same lack of control which made Boehm socially unattractive allowed him to exceed the limits of accomplishment of more disciplined and controlled men.

Boehm was addicted to practical jokes, the childish sort of humor that quickly palls. He was fond of jokes involving telephones and telegrams, and one of his favorites was a telegram bearing the message: "Ignore first telegram."

Boehm had nothing but scorn for anything popular, whether it was opinions or attitudes or fashions. He was convinced that people seldom looked, and, if they did, never understood what they saw. His political and social attitudes were, if not Neanderthal, then certainly reactionary. He was opinionated, prejudiced and unforgiving of his fellow men. On the other hand, his feeling for and understanding of organic structure and natural law was so brilliant and full of insight that his companions and most of his colleagues were prepared to forgive him anything.

The Ed Boehm who was at peace with himself, if that were ever really so, was to be found at Duncravin Farm, 150 acres near his studio and atelier in Trenton. A few miles up from Washington Crossing, on the banks of the Delaware River, a visitor comes upon a curiously classical Palladian building stretching 200 yards across the brow of a hill. Just below is a small formal American garden, to the right a comfortable, old, very American house, and beyond that a Japanese garden. Somehow this man of remarkably catholic tastes and talents had made this jumble of sensations, eras, and places fit together without clashing. The Palladian structure, entered through the classical broken pediment, was a long narrow building divided into small heated cages filled with bright flashes of nervous tropical birds. Behind the building and its cages was a tropical jungle enclosed by acres of plastic sheeting 50 or 60 feet high. These were Boehm's remarkable aviaries.

RPC-1069 IVORY-BILLED WOODPECKERS

Boehm's absences from the Trenton studios became more frequent after he purchased the farm in 1964. And the name Duncravin tells why, although the significance escaped everyone until he explained that he had invented the name by combining two words: done craving. Ed Boehm's lifelong dream of owning a farm of his own had been fulfilled.

The great horse barn on the farm actually became a center of Boehm social life. The executives of the fine stores and galleries which handled the Boehm porcelain attended annual two-day new-collection conferences at the farm, and more than once found themselves dining in the barn. No one would mind—the cocktails served from the stalls were excellent and the gingham-covered dining tables were properly catered—until, midway through the evening, Boehm got carried away with the beauty of his livestock. The music, and conversation, too, were expected to stop while Boehm, proud as any doting father could be, paraded his champion cows and bulls and horses through the barn, one by one, explaining at great length and in technical detail what made each animal unique. Once when conversation among the restless guests began to pick up just as Boehm arrived with a young bull, he shouted: "Will you all stop throwing the bull for a minute and take a look at a real bull!"

Barn dances were held with surprising frequency, at least in part because Boehm took great pride in his ability to "call" the square-dance tunes. The old-fashioned, simple things in life held a true appeal for Boehm.

Admired by many, Ed Boehm had only a small circle of intimate friends, all of whom remember him fondly. He was very friendly with Lester Perlstein, who runs Frank Perlstein & Son, a Trenton plumbing concern. It was Perlstein, in fact, who installed the first aviary.

"One Saturday morning he called me up and said, 'We're going to Philadelphia,'" Perlstein recalls. "We went down to the zoo and into the aviary and Ed said, 'Build me one like this.' So, we did."

Perlstein first met Ed Boehm when Boehm bought the current studio on Fairfacts Street and he became the artist's favorite plumber ever after. Perlstein had done the original work in the studio which—when Boehm bought it—was being used as a warehouse for a department store. Today, Perlstein has an extensive collection of Boehm sculpture, Ed Boehm's early way of paying for the things he needed.

"Ed was quite a character," Perlstein says. "Sometimes, when he knew that Helen had arranged for some group like the Congressional wives to visit, he would call me and ask me to go with him to Philadelphia to buy some birds or supplies. When we'd get back my wife would say, 'Where the hell have you two been? Helen's been frantic looking for you.'"

As he did with so many of his friends, Boehm insisted that Perlstein involve himself with animals and he gave him his first dog, a miniature schnauzer. Perlstein was lucky. More often Boehm would announce to a friend that they were now "partners" in one champion or another and send him a bill.

Schnauzers brought Bill and Olive Moore, who own a travel agency in Trenton, into the animal kingdom of Ed Boehm.

On the Boehm Estate, at Washington Crossing:
The Ravine, the American Garden, the Japanese Garden

"We thought we were only buying a pet," Olive Moore remembers, "but, of course, that wasn't enough for Ed. He said he would sell us a dog but we had to breed it at least once and he would get the pick of the litter. Naturally, he picked one that I really loved—Champion Twister's Triumph—and the dog did terrifically well in his first three shows but in his fourth he failed to finish—he needed one point. Ed brought him over to the house and said, 'Here, you can have him back. I don't want him.' Well, of course, he was a terrific dog and we finished him right away but Ed was such a perfectionist and all of his animals had to be the best and meet a certain timetable for doing so."

As a result of their friendship with Boehm, the Moores became deeply involved with animals, particularly dogs, which they still breed and show. Since they were in the travel business, they handled many of the arrangements for Boehm's shipments of birds from Africa and South America.

"Sometimes we'd be on the phone at three and four o'clock in the morning trying to track down a missing shipment and when it did arrive we'd go over to his place and help him unload the birds and wash them," Olive says. "I loved that and I miss being able to help him with his animals."

Boehm helped the Moores with their breeding and showing efforts from the beginning but he was a tough taskmaster. "We'd groom a dog and think we'd done a pretty good job and take him over and show him to Ed and he'd say, 'No. No. That's all wrong' and he'd do a whole side and say, 'Now, take him home and match what I've done.' He had such an instinctive feel for animals. He knew exactly what to do with them."

The Moores were likely recipients of Boehm's impulsive but infrequent generosity, sometimes in the form of a sculpture simply shoved into their hands with a "Here, I thought you might like this," and—on one occasion—a whole group of live dogs. "He simply lost interest in his schnauzers," Olive recalls. "Perhaps he got involved with his horses or his cows or perhaps he was disappointed with the dogs in some way. In any event, he just called up one day and said he was sending his whole bunch over—there were about 12—and he did."

Like so many of his friends, the Moores miss Boehm's unannounced visits for breakfast or dinner and his middle-of-the-night phone calls. "He was an artist and genius and a terrific man," Olive says. "We all miss him a lot."

People Boehm was fond of were required to learn to love animals. He insisted on it. Harold Coleman, Boehm's attorney, was no animal lover but his client changed that. Boehm decided that the best way to arouse Coleman's interest was to make him part owner of a really good animal. Coleman finally gave in when Boehm called to tell him about an outstanding cocker spaniel he wanted to share. The lawyer was taken aback by the size of the bill for half ownership, $750, but the dog turned out to be a real champion. Among its more than 50 blue ribbons was the best in show in 1963 at the Trenton Kennel Club All Breeds Show and Obedience Trials, with 2,500 entrants, the first local winner in some 30 years. There remains some suspicion that the bill for "Holl" was indeed the whole cost of the animal. In retrospect, and chiefly because of Boehm's instinct for excellence in animals, the price

RPC-1093 FONDO MARINO

was a cheap one. In recalling Boehm's special distaste for all professionals—doctors, accountants and lawyers—the bill might just have been a device to get some of his legal fees back. If so, it backfired in this case.

Barbara Hanley, one of the first Boehm collectors, once tried to turn down a gift of a schnauzer from Boehm because it would be too difficult to keep where she lived. He shipped it anyway, collect.

Boehm enjoyed giving animals to young children—even over the objections of their parents. Frank Cosentino tells of the time shortly after he went to work for Boehm when the master decided that the Cosentinos' three-year-old should have a pet. He arrived at their little suburban home with a registered, unweaned nanny goat. After three days of trying to protect the goat in their unfenced yard from an army of neighborhood youngsters, Cosentino persuaded Boehm to take the nanny back. "I always felt he never quite forgave us for not accepting his gift," Cosentino says.

On the farm, in the final five years of his life, Boehm raised and assembled one of the country's finest herds of Holsteins, a string of champion saddle horses and standardbreds, a number of prizewinning schnauzers and an outstanding collection of tropical fish. He also grew varieties of trees and flowers that were not supposed to survive New Jersey winters. But most of all he bred rare birds, birds that never before had laid eggs for an aviculturist, university or zoo. As the critic Paul Richard said, "All living things obeyed him. Boehm resembled nothing half so much as an independent, secular, free-enterprise St. Francis."

One of Boehm's favorite animals was his prize Holstein cow, King's Arctic Rose, which in 1966 was named Supreme Grand Champion at the Dairy Cattle Congress in Waterloo, Iowa, and Grand Champion of Holsteins of the International Livestock Exposition in Chicago. That year, with three milkings a day, she produced 35,276 pounds of milk and 1,319 pounds of fat, the world's record. After Boehm's death, Helen sold Rose to a cattle breeder and, for the first time since reaching maturity, Rose failed to produce a calf. Helen bought her back and, of course, home again Rose quickly became happily pregnant.

Boehm collected his birds in Kenya, New Guinea and Ecuador. He maintained a steady correspondence with aviculturists on three continents and wrote extensively about his findings for ornithological publications. He bred 21 species of insect-eating birds—the Australian white-browed wood swallow, the African white-cheeked touraco, the bird of paradise from New Guinea—for the first time in North America in his aviaries, many of them for the first time anywhere in captivity.

"Our birds of paradise," he wrote in the journal of The Academy of Natural Sciences of Philadelphia, "are gourmands. They consume a formula of chopped bananas, ground apples, ground oranges, ground grapes, ground carrots; plus a mix of liver meal, fish meal, bone meal, middlings, whole-wheat flour, hard-boiled eggs; to which are added toasted bread crumbs and a caroteinoid oil. In addition to the above they are fed fresh ground beef hearts twice a day. Also, each receives 25 to 30 mealworms twice a day, plus half a dozen crickets (raised here at the aviaries), and, as a tidbit, twice a week, a small hairless white mouse."

Boehm's birds were not fed just plain mealworms.

To protect baby birds from rickets, a bone disease that makes it impossible for them to perch or fly, he developed a method of rubbing the mealworms he raised with cod liver oil and dusting them with a mixture of steamed bone meal and calcium carbonate.

When new birds arrived, Boehm would disappear from the studio for days on end. Some birds, such as paradise flycatchers, for example, had to be fed on the wing with mealworms, crickets and moths every two hours for three or four days until they could be gradually drawn down to the feeding dishes.

Charles Everitt, an English-born aviculturist who joined Boehm's staff in 1959 as curator of the aviaries, says, "Basically he was a lover of nature in all its forms, be it animal, vegetable or mineral. Reticent by nature, at times so intensely preoccupied that his manner resembled boredom when in company, you could be sure that in every waking moment he was just thinking of some way in which he could get even closer to nature."

Anyone interested in knowing the character of Ed Boehm should consider the following vignettes drawn from my experience of having known and watched him.

Let us say you go looking for him at his home but you do not know what he looks like. Nobody you ask seems to know where he is. Everybody waves you along. "Try down by the pond." "Ask at the house." You come across a workman hip deep in the mud of a trench throwing dirt up over his shoulder. You wait until he breaks his rhythm and ask if he has seen Ed Boehm around and he looks up and says, "Ain't seen him for a few days. I think he's sick." He goes back to shoveling. Later you discover that the man in the ditch was Boehm. He had learned from his birds to take on protective coloration to satisfy his compulsive need for privacy.

Or perhaps you are a social lady in an elegant Southern town. The center of life in your community is the Garden Club, which has come to represent the values and virtues of the Old South. A year and a half before, you had written to Helen Boehm and asked if Mr. Boehm would speak to the club at its annual meeting attended by 300 to 400 well-to-do ladies. Mrs. Boehm writes that her husband would be delighted to appear and you start your preparations. You advertise. You prepare the club to show its best for a man whose achievements with nature are unrivaled in our time. You hear he is a little difficult so you try to make everything easy. You provide a private plane and a limousine from the airport. And an hour to talk with the local cattle breeder (Boehm's favorite pastime). The morning of the affair is bright and sunny, the plane has been dispatched and a telegram arrives, "Sorry Mr. Boehm ill." You are, of course, disappointed, but there is no arguing with illness. You quickly make other arrangements and write Mrs. Boehm again concerning another visit for a later time because your ladies are very disappointed. Mrs. Boehm is happy to be able to inform you that her husband will be pleased with another date. That date arrives, the plane is again dispatched, the telegram arrives, "Sorry Mr. Boehm ill."

Boehm accepted commitments and promised speaking engagements, but when the hour, the very minute arrived, he often found himself incapable of honoring them. That overwhelming need for privacy overcame him when he was about to get into the car or take the plane, or even at the very moment of mounting the podium.

It is three o'clock in the morning, the phone rings. You sleepily pick up the receiver and a voice comes through already in the full flood of conversation. It is Ed Boehm, often sleepless as he endlessly relives the problems and activities of the day. In spite of his need for privacy, he reaches out for an audience, any audience. You get a lecture on animal morphology or the logic of birds and illogic of man. You are not expected to contribute. You are expected to listen carefully because at the end of the listening he tests you. At five-thirty, as quickly as the rush of conversation started, it stops. Boehm says "good night" and leaves you a tattered sleep, sure in the knowledge that you have been in touch with a tortured genius.

One day you turn a corner unexpectedly on the Boehm estate and surprise two figures sitting alone on a fallen log. The classic definition of a school—a log with a teacher at one end and a student at the other. It is Boehm and a child deep in conversation, surrounded by drawings scratched into the earth. You quietly skirt them so as not to disturb the flow of teaching. You come back two hours later and they are still there, the child fresh in his curiosity and the teacher still full of enthusiasm for the hunger of his student. You saw this same man just the day before, in the studio in Trenton, bellowing impatiently at a craftsman twice his age and with five times his experience. You saw him pick up an iron pole and smash expensive sculptures to prove his point—that the best could be done better. The same man who could patiently sit for hours teaching a child was incapable of two minutes of quiet explanation to the adults he worked with.

Often there was a strange logic to these contradictions. For three years running, this man who hated committees and public events and dressing up served as a judge at the Miss America Pageant in Atlantic City. Why would such a man, with his abhorrence of people, choose to subject himself to so social and public an event as the most ballyhooed of all beauty pageants? Helen Boehm says she talked him into it as a way of getting him better known. There had to be more to it than that. I do not believe it is possible to understand Boehm unless you understand his involvement with the science of genetics. He believed that genetics was the answer to all human activities. And to most human problems. As a geneticist he was as interested in the breeding of women as he was in the breeding of animals. I am sure he looked upon the women with the same critical breeder's eye that he turned on his cherished Guernseys and Holsteins. After the three terms as a Miss America Pageant judge—and one at the Junior Miss Pageant in Alabama—he declined to don his tuxedo again. In a four-page critique to the Pageant Committee, he argued that too many of the judges were theatrical people who leaned toward girls with theatrical talents. More importance should be given to shape, he wrote, with the finalists selected primarily on their points of conformation—just as one would select a champion dog or horse or cow!

The contradictions were caused at least in part by his inability to judge between a noble act and one of self-destruction. This lack of judgment was more damaging to himself than it was to others, and in the end I believe contributed to his death.

RPS-9005 BARN OWL

I do not know what happened to Ed Boehm in the last few hours of his life, but from my knowledge of the man I think I can reconstruct the way it had to happen. He trusted doctors even less than he did ordinary people because he believed that too many physicians functioned by the book or superficially rather than with a deep understanding, such as he himself had, of the organic processes of sickness and health. For Boehm to go to a doctor at all (on the last day but one of his life) there must have been severe pain in his chest and it must have frightened him. The physician was not a specialist, and the electrocardiograms must have showed little. This perhaps lulled Boehm a bit, but he knew his own body intimately and knew that its processes were not working well. So he must have compromised, settling for a night in the hospital. He must have suspected that he had gone through a heart attack of some seriousness. Yet he felt that his compromise, his presence in the hospital, would be enough. Never mind nurses around the clock. Never mind monitors. Never mind the attention that a cardiac patient should have. He would be all right. He would pull through by strength of will alone. He had survived before. He did not need the "know nothings" and the "fools" around him. So he lay quietly in the room and sometime early in the morning of the day after he sought help, when no one was around, Ed Boehm quietly and needlessly died of a heart attack. Out of his inability to reach out and take a helping hand, out of his deep rejection of comradeship and compassion and people, Ed Boehm died futilely on that morning of January 29, 1969, within call of techniques that might have saved him. Survival was just out in the corridor—a thump on the chest, a shot of adrenalin or a jolt of electricity had pulled thousands of others

through. Ed Boehm was not the man to allow that closeness that would have saved his life. He died almost by his own will.

Boehm was just reaching the height of his powers when he died. The collections he presented in 1967, 1968 and (posthumously) 1969 were the most interesting work he had ever done, had ever been done by anyone. Those of us who were involved at the time could not help but feel, as I am sure his craftsmen felt, that the Boehm enterprise was finished, that any new work produced at the studio would not be as important as those pieces produced prior to Boehm's death.

To everyone's surprise, the new work that emerged from Trenton after 1969 retained the vitality and the excitement of the Boehm originals. Evidently, he had taught his staff well, and evidently the energy and inspiration needed to create the new pieces were now coming from Helen Boehm. Within a year or two the new Trenton Studio, without Ed Boehm, had made its mark on porcelain collectors around the world.

By 1970 or 1971, Helen Boehm had begun to recognize that Ed Boehm's contributions had been essentially image concepts and techniques. She now felt that somewhere in Europe as well as in Trenton there must be technically trained people who could be taught to use those techniques and those images. She turned to England and built a studio at Malvern. After the usual initial missteps the Malvern Studio quickly began to provide an almost miraculous marriage of the human and technical skills of the Old World and the techniques and images of the New. Today Boehm porcelains come about half from Trenton and half from Malvern.

Growth as an Artist

During the brief span of his mature career, Edward Marshall Boehm produced a large and varied body of work. Thousands of prototype sculptures were made, of which some 400 to 500 finally came into production. It is inevitable that some of the pieces he created were less artistically and commercially successful than others. Boehm, at one point or another in his career, produced pieces on such subjects as dogs, horses, livestock, wildlife, religious objects, figurines and accessories of both a useful and a decorative nature.

Although his reputation is based largely on his bird sculptures and indeed it seems likely he would have been just as successful if he had done only birds —they were by no means his favorites. Boehm loved all animals and brought to each subject a measure of that love. I suspect that his attention narrowed and focused on birds because of the enormous range of color they allowed for experimentation. Pragmatically, the birds are the aspect of his art that first and most strongly captured the fancy of the collecting public, also.

Boehm's personal favorites may well have been the horse subjects. His earliest sculpture, Percheron Mare and Foal, modeled in 1944, was one of the first pieces he cast in porcelain when he acquired his own studio in 1950. One of his last works, the Adios Portrait, was brought out in 1969 and is one of the unquestioned masterpieces of sculptural portraiture of horses.

Boehm experimented with dogs over a 10-year period beginning in the early 1950's but somehow never developed a passion for them as serious works. During that same period, he also produced a number of livestock subjects, which were of higher quality than the dogs but of less importance than the horses. With the maturing of the birds, he abandoned the cattle subjects in 1959. The cattle were neither an aesthetic nor a commercial success.

Wildlife is one of the areas to which one wishes Boehm had paid more attention. He displayed a rare sensitivity to the nature and beauty of wild animals in the few such pieces he produced. One of the areas to which he might well have paid less attention was religious subjects. Boehm was not himself a conventionally religious man. He rarely, if ever, went to church or took part in formal religious ceremonies. One has to assume that Helen Boehm, a devout Catholic, was instrumental in influencing Boehm to undertake the various pieces of religious sculpture which he produced. Seen now, the pieces are oddly out of context with the man and his art.

Helen Boehm recalls one Sunday morning when she was preparing to go to Mass and was, perhaps, prodding Ed a bit about his failure to do likewise. Boehm was getting a little frustrated in his attempts to

RPC-301-01 PERCHERON MARE AND FOAL

RPC-311-02 ADIOS

RPC-720-06 BEAU BRUMMELLS II

RPC-1073-02 PARULA WARBLERS with Morning Glories

explain his position when a suddenly a beautiful male Cardinal alit in a big spruce next to the window. "There," Boehm said, pointing to the bird with a note of triumph in his voice, "that's my religion."

Boehm produced a few sculptures of people throughout his career, only some of which were of high quality. His Beau Brummells, however, compare favorably with any done in Europe, which has, of course, a much longer tradition of figural porcelain sculpture.

Boehm's accessories—both useful and decorative —occupy a much smaller place in the total Boehm experience than his other sculpture. Yet these pieces are still avidly sought, mainly because they represent early examples of his work and because they bear much of the grace and elegance of his more important works.

It is in his birds, however, that Ed Boehm achieved his highest level of technical, artistic and financial success. He made 94 basic bird sculptures, but, adding together the various decorations of each, there are at least 220 different sculptures. The birds were a challenge—an endless series of technical problems to be solved. How to reproduce this wild and endless range of colors? Are the wings too delicate for shipping? These were among the many crucial questions and challenges. Collectors and dealers loved the birds, to the detriment of Boehm's other work. From their introduction in 1952, when he first discovered the marketability of birds, the demand grew, as did the pressure on Boehm to produce more.

If there was one quality Boehm shared with all true artists, it was a sense of the perverse. Time and again I have seen young artists struggle to achieve a recognizable product, only to abandon it the moment it became commercially viable. Ed Boehm could have

RPC-1063-01 ROBIN with Daffodils

RPC-1056-01 LESSER
PRAIRIE CHICKENS

45

RPC-1019-01 SONG SPARROWS with Tulips

RPC-1058-01 MEARNS QUAIL with Cactus

RPC-1024-01 DOWNY WOODPECKERS on Trumpet Vine

made a great deal of money doing only "pretty" birds like Blue Jays and Robins and Song Sparrows. But, perversely and characteristically, he went to enormous trouble to produce difficult, unappealing birds like Lesser Prairie Chickens and Mearns Quails. True, he was motivated by a concern for birds that were on the verge of extinction, but at the same time the perversity was there. To Ed Boehm, the different parts of nature

RPC-1025-01 AMERICAN EAGLE

RPC-1075-01 GREEN JAYS with Black Persimmon

RPC-1021-01 **BLACK TAILED BANTAMS**

RPC-1039-01 **MOURNING DOVES**   RPC-1042-01 **NONPAREIL BUNTINGS** on Flowering Raspberry

were equally beautiful and if dealers and collectors did not understand that, that, in Boehm's words, "was their problem."

Boehm often disagreed with the popular consensus on his work. His own favorites included such less popular pieces as the Downy Woodpeckers, Prairie Chickens, Parula Warblers and Green Jays.

It is difficult to choose the masterpieces. Certainly the Song Sparrows touched a deep and responsive chord with collectors. The Ivory-Billed Woodpecker is a magnificent piece of work that stands alone among technical achievements in American porcelain-making and, indeed, in porcelain-making in all places and times. Although it never became a limited edition, Boehm's American Eagle is without parallel in the annals of porcelain production. Its strength and vitality, and its lack of sentimentality, set this eagle apart from all others.

As one might imagine, Boehm produced some pieces that were less than successful commercially. The Black-Tailed Bantams, for example, were discontinued after only 57 pairs had been made. Collectors simply did not rally to the Black-Tailed Bantams although Boehm's was an interesting rendition of a lackluster bird.

There were also problems with the Cardinals. Boehm found himself trying to reproduce a red color that was unobtainable through the processes available to him. He wanted a dull, complex, more lifelike finish, but in attempting to achieve something akin to the color of the live bird he wound up with an unpleasant glossy finish.

The Cardinals had other problems, too. The piece marked the first time importance was given to the foliage in the composition and hence is something of a landmark. However, the male bird is mounted in an extremely awkward way. If one looks at the back of the piece one sees that the bird is supported by a branch that thrusts itself right into its back. This kind of configuration obviously could not happen in nature, and as Boehm became more sophisticated in his techniques this kind of lapse disappeared from his work. But the Cardinals sold, and the edition was completed even sooner than those of some of the better pieces.

There are two other Boehm failures worth noting. With the Nonpareil Bunting, the problem was not that the bird was done badly but rather that it was done too well. In real life, the Nonpareil Bunting looks as if somebody with a poor sense of color had taken a paint brush and splashed it with very strong colors. The poor bird gets by with this in nature, but in porcelain it just looks silly.

Another piece which ran into collector resistance was the Mourning Dove. For one thing, the name of the bird is unfortunate and puts people off. For another, this Dove has, in reality, a silky, almost fabric-like feather covering. In nature, this is very beautiful. In porcelain, it looks as if somebody was too lazy or too careless to sculpt the detailing.

But, in the total context of Ed Boehm's work, these are quibbles. Boehm was a perfectionist and most of what he did—particularly in bird subjects—came close to being perfect.

It is impossible to discuss the extraordinary quality and variety of Boehm's work without some reference to his final piece, Fondo Marino. By far the most ambitious project bearing his name, the piece was a fitting climax to the career of an artist whose confidence in his own ability to create miracles never flagged. Had he lived, the Fondo would have matured and developed under his hands. I am sure that Boehm considered the Fondo unfinished. Yet, finished or unfinished, it was his last work and contains the fullest measure of his technical experience. A seascape of startling and quiet beauty, it is an elegant testament to Ed Boehm's courage to face new challenges right up to the end of his life.

RPS-1095-01 MUTE SWANS (Bird of Peace)

The Boehm Future

The Boehm Studio in Trenton seems oddly out of place in its neighborhood. Surrounded by chain-link fences, rust-covered railroad tracks and storage tanks, the gleaming black-and-white Colonial-style buildings of Boehm form an odd oasis in a desert of urban blight.

Inside, the place has the strange feel of a small hospital. Workers, mainly women, wear white technicians' coats. There is order here and a sense of purpose. That is the way Ed Boehm liked things done and that is the way they are still done today.

In a downstairs gallery visitors are given a tour of Ed Boehm's major works with a reverent, almost religious narration. "Mr. Boehm said this." "Mr. Boehm liked that." His ghost pervades the Studio.

Boehm collectors travel thousands of miles just to see the Studio. They feel they are members of a very exclusive club. They want to be where he was, to feel his presence.

Sitting at her desk, behind a sea of paperwork and with the accompaniment of an endlessly ringing telephone, Helen Boehm looks formidable and prosperous. Large and handsome, she exhausts those around her with her prodigious energy. It has been a long time since she traveled the country by Greyhound bus persuading stores to handle her husband's work, but she still devotes the same passionate attention to detail that built the Boehm empire.

Her talk these days is of the many organizations that want to make her Woman of the Year and her 20 racehorses. Next year there will be other projects and other passions, equally demanding of her total concentration. After Ed Boehm's death, Helen disbanded the aviaries, feeling no doubt that nobody could run them as successfully as Ed. The birds were given to five zoos.

"I found it hard to let go of the nature part of my husband's life," she says, in the same reverent tone that Ed Boehm is always spoken of on these premises. "I just couldn't let go of the horses and the beautiful plantings, though. They were so much a part of his life. They were what we stood for."

She smiles warmly. She is an open, friendly woman who also happens to be one of the shrewdest businesswomen this nation has produced.

There are those who said the Boehm empire was finished when Ed Boehm died. There were predictions of doom. Without the iron hand of the master, the reasoning went, quality would decline. People simply would not buy Boehm sculpture that had never felt the touch of Ed Boehm.

The doomsayers underestimated the strength of Helen Boehm, of her ever-present companion in the business, Frank Cosentino, and of the British sculptor Maurice Eyeington.

Privately held and extremely profitable, the Boehm Studios today gross $8 to $10 million annually. The Trenton Studio, where 100 of the concern's total staff of 235 are located, produces half of the 25,000 pieces turned out each year. The rest are made in the British Studio at Malvern, not far from Stratford-on-Avon. A small studio nearby that paints one-of-a-kind handmade plates was also recently opened.

With barely a glance backward, and a nearly religious fervor, Helen redoubled her promotion efforts. She opened the Malvern Studios and introduced new products of extremely high quality—most notably paintings on hard porcelain and painted presentation plates. Ed Boehm might not have quite approved of the porcelain paintings or plates. He might have altered some of the small animals that the Studios are turning out now, but they have become enormous commercial and technical successes.

The main part of the Boehm legacy—the birds—are as good as they ever were, and some have even surpassed the earlier work. Ed Boehm, for example, never saw the huge pair of Mute Swans that President Nixon took to China but they are superb pieces of work. They were designed by Eyeington, who worked and trained with Boehm, and whose contribution to the vision of Ed Boehm must certainly be acknowledged.

The inspiration for the piece grew out of a comment by former President Richard Nixon that he wished someone would come up with an alternative to the traditional "hawks" and "doves" symbolism. Helen took this desire seriously, with the result that ten of Ed Boehm's handpicked artisans spent a year and a half making one of the truly monumental porcelain sculptures of this, or any other, century. The head sculptor estimates that there are more than 60,000 individually carved barbs in the featherwork alone. No other studio in the world could even conceive an undertaking on this scale. When Nixon made his historic visit to China in February of 1972, his personal gift to Mao Tse-tung was a pair of Mute Swans from the Boehm Studio. Eloquently, it served notice on the world that American porcelain could hold its own even in the country that created porcelain, and that Boehm's work would continue beyond his lifetime.

"Mr. Boehm hated to get dressed up," Helen says. "He looked like a farmer most of the time and he didn't care. Putting on a tuxedo and appearing before some women's group was like sticking pins in his body. He simply could never get too far from nature. Right here where we're sitting we once had fancy leghorn chickens breeding. Right here in the office. He was never much of a desk man. Putting him behind a desk was like putting him in prison. Once in a while he would spend an hour here writing to bird people or cattle people but most often he was in the studio or out on the farm. He hated to travel because it took him away from his animals."

Helen Boehm smiles at some distant recollection. "We used to have animals all over the house," she says. "We dined for six months with a little baby ape named Lulu that he was training for a friend."

The phone rings and Mrs. Boehm picks it up. It is a silver phone. "Sure, come in," she says. A moment later, her secretary enters.

"Dorothy," she says, "we were talking about whether Mr. Boehm traveled. Tell him about the stack of cancelled tickets we had every year. He was always

RPS-8504 THE NYALA

Nyala
Boehm Of Malvern

going to a show or somewhere and at the last minute he was busy."

"And even when he started off he didn't always make it that far," Dorothy Kay adds. "Remember that time he was going for the television interview and it was a beautiful spring day and he stopped along the way and never made it?"

The two women laugh. Ed Boehm may often have behaved like a naughty little boy, but it is obvious that he was always forgiven.

Helen's success as a saleswoman depended on her ability to understand Ed. "I don't think there's any training for public relations," she says. "It's just a God-given talent. You must remember that when I represented Ed I was not just representing a man or a sculptor. I was representing my husband. I believed in what he was doing. I think that may be the secret. You have to believe in what you're selling."

The depth of Helen Boehm's belief is obvious. Boehm is the Rolls-Royce of the limited edition porcelain market and she knows it. She knows that a half dozen imitators have come along in the past two decades, several of them in Trenton. But none of them turn out products of the Boehm quality, nor is it likely they ever will.

If she is aware of the fact that in the realm of modern art and modern art criticism her husband's work is ignored, it does not seem to matter. Helen Boehm has known presidents and kings. Many people are passionately involved in Ed Boehm's sculpture and that is all there is to that.

"We started from rock bottom," she says. "Ed never visited another porcelain studio in his life. In terms of art, he admired Leonardo da Vinci, and people like Norman Rockwell and Andrew Wyeth and Wyeth's son Jamie. He admired Audubon although I think it bothered him that Audubon had to kill so many birds to do his work. He understood why he had to do it—there wasn't the photography there is today. But, I think it bothered him. He couldn't accept the death of any animal."

One of the highlights of Mrs. Boehm's recent life was a visit she paid to China in December of 1974. The invitation came after the presentation of the Mute Swans to Chairman Mao Tse-tung, who reportedly said at the unveiling, "Why is President Nixon bringing us stuffed birds?" It was the kind of compliment that Ed Boehm would have liked.

The Chinese liked Helen Boehm, too. In her red pants suit and white mink coat, she presented a striking contrast to the conservative appearance of diplomats' wives. And, the press reports, she was forever bestowing bear hugs on happy children.

As the afternoon wears on, the talk shifts back to her husband and she rambles on pleasantly. It is a subject of which she never seems to tire.

"Ed hated to lose at anything," she says, as if making a summation. "He was a very poor loser, but he believed firmly that you should give to life more than you take out of it and he did that. He brought pleasure to so many people. To them, you know, Mr. Boehm isn't dead. They still talk about him as if he were alive. That's the kind of man he was."

How Is Boehm Sculpture Made?

The creation of sculpture in hard-paste porcelain is an enormously complicated task involving countless processes and great care. There are too many things that can go wrong to allow for even a moment's carelessness. Ed Boehm was a man who believed nothing was impossible, and a hallmark of his career was that he always challenged the technical limits of his craft, always made the game a little tougher for himself.

Most art, whether painting or sculpture, begins on paper. So, indeed, it began with Ed Boehm. Once he had selected a subject, a bird, for example, he would often sketch from the live birds in his aviaries or from photographic studies he had made of them. From this basic design he would model a rough study in clay. Using these models, Boehm and his assistants would spend days discussing the technical problems. Sometimes a project would be abandoned as unfeasible at this point. But once Boehm had made the decision to go ahead, it was virtually impossible to turn him back, no matter how difficult unexpected problems might become.

The next step in the making of hard-paste porcelain is to break down the approved and modified model into its component parts so that plaster-of-paris molds can be made. It is rather like a three-dimensional jigsaw puzzle, and the degree of difficulty—that is, the number of separate parts—is determined by how intricate the original design is. The Western Bluebirds were dissected into 91 components of base, branches, leaves and birds. The Fondo Marino required hundreds of components.

Each of the component parts has a mold constructed around it, and this process, in the case of more complicated sculptures, can take from six to nine months. This set of molds is then duplicated in plaster because modeling-clay is too fragile to be carved and refined. Details that would crumble in clay can be worked into plaster.

Once the plaster model is refined, the moldmaking process continues, using the individual plaster model parts. The negative impressions made in the molds at this point contain exactly the finished detail of the refined parts. These molds, called block or master molds, are not used for casting, however, but to make a new positive model which, in turn, is used to make a duplicate set of the master molds. This assures the craftsmen that they will not have to go back to the original plaster model for remolding, a process that is not easy to repeat. The final negative molds are the ones in which the casting of model parts is done. For a single small porcelain sculpture, these block molds can in the aggregate weigh several thousand pounds.

Only about 25 castings can be taken from a set of replica molds before they begin to deteriorate. At this point a new set is made from the duplicate positive molds and the process continues. This assures that

Figs. 1 and 2 .

All porcelain sculpture begins with a creative artist. Above we see Ed Boehm sketching in his aviaries, which were his living collection of the birds and flowers he was to render in clay. The bird itself is sketched from life. The ultimate problems of making the Sugarbirds sculpture were already being considered. In the original sketches, future problems of molding, modeling, firing and propping, of painting and color application and the pure engineering of the piece to make it a viable whole, were already being anticipated in the artist's mind.

details remain sharp throughout the edition.

The material poured into the molds to form the hard-paste sculpture is liquid clay called slip. Since the clay ingredients from the earth have a wide chemical variance, a chemist mixes and test-fires a small quantity of each batch to see how it will turn out.

After this test, the slip is made. Kaolins, feldspar and other hard-paste-formula ingredients are poured into a ball mill which is one-quarter filled with golf-ball-sized quartz pebbles. Water is added and the mill is rotated for 72 hours. This grinding action reduces the clay particles to the smallest size possible, an important process since the finer the particle, the smoother the eventual porcelain. The slip that is created by this process is then stored in stainless steel

The making of fine porcelain sculptures is an ancient art. Knowledge, skill, experience and a good deal of love and affection for the material must be part of the maker's resource. Without a deep respect for porcelain as an art medium, the maker oftentimes is led to compromises which are not permissible in high-temperature-fired art porcelain. Each stage must be considered as important as the one before and the one after, and no stage may be skipped.

Achieving consistent results becomes difficult, since the material is subject to so many vagaries. In fact, porcelain is subject to self-destruction in the making process due to factors which are often beyond the control of even the most sophisticated maker. Colors run wrong. Pieces fire incorrectly. Clay runs or sags, cracks appear. Shrinkage is uneven. Any of a thousand problems such as these can arise, and unless the porcelainist has enormous foresight and skill, creating complicated pieces becomes impossible. Small, simple pieces which undergo no great stress in the firing and cooling processes are not subject to such problems. As a piece becomes larger and more complex, the difficulties mount out of all proportion to the increase in size.

The following series of pictures, which shows the making of the Sugarbirds, is not a definitive discussion of porcelain-making. Rather, it is meant to increase the reader's understanding of the difficulties involved, and of the need for the hand of a master porcelainist at every stage.

tanks that have paddles that automatically stir the slip every 15 minutes to keep it from settling. Several tons of slip may be mixed at a time. Only a pound or two is used in each individual sculpture.

Next the slip is poured into the replica molds and thus the model's sections are made. Each mold has a pouring hole and each caster must pour the slip carefully to make sure that no air bubbles are trapped inside. Boehm and his craftsmen were very clever about locating pouring holes at the point where joints come together.

When the slip comes into contact with the plaster mold, a thin clay lining builds on the inside lining of the mold. In other words, a positive image begins to form within the mold. A knowledgeable caster can control how thick the piece becomes by pouring off the excess slip once he is confident that the cast piece can support itself. In this way, he can stop the hardening process at a point where parts that have volume (like

Figs. 3 and 4 . From the sketch, the artist turns to modeling the clay. Every last detail is put in at this stage, for whatever is left out now can never be put in. At left we see a section of the Sugarbirds in raw clay and the meticulous and careful modeling which must take place at that point. At right we see a curious destruction of the model. Once the piece has been completed in soft clay, it is cut apart into smaller sections so that molds can be made of them. Decisions about where to cut are as important as are the decisions of a diamond cutter when he cleaves a raw stone. This step in making a porcelain requires enormous experience if one is to know how a particular piece will fire and how the pieces can best be reassembled after firing.

Fig. 5 . Here we see just a few of the many pieces—and each piece represents a whole new set of molds. The total number of pieces into which the clay model was cut was approximately 600, and each of these requires sets of both master and block molds, from which case molds are later taken. What started out as a single sculpture very rapidly becomes many individual sculptures, each of which requires many separate molds and each of which requires the same care and thought as the whole.

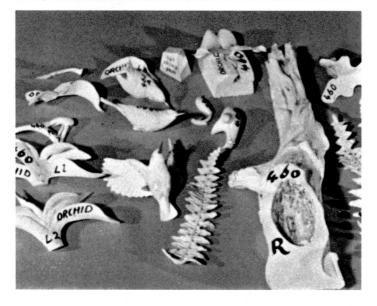

the body of a bird) are still hollow inside. This is important because otherwise each finished sculpture would become thick, heavy and difficult to fire. In fact, the hardening process slows down to the point where it is virtually impossible to solid-cast a large mass. The smaller pieces are cast solid, making them awkward to fire but providing needed strength.

The castings that result from this process are immediately stored in a damp room where moisture in the air is held at saturation. The parts must remain wet and all must retain about the same degree of moisture or they will not join together later.

These cast clay sections are called greenware; the next stage of the process is joining them together to form the design of the original model. This is perhaps the most nerve-rackingly delicate of all the steps. Beginning at the base and working up and out, artisans

Fig. 6 . Now an entirely new process commences—the pouring of the molds. These become the original molds from which subsequent molds are made. The process of replicating the porcelain in a clay mold eventually diminishes the quality of the mold; therefore many sets of molds are ultimately made. After a master set of molds is made and another set is made from that master, at most eight or ten perfect sculptures can be taken from a complicated mold. The mold must then be thrown away and the process begun all over again. Above we see the original master mold being poured. The great skill involved in pouring and emptying the mold can rarely be taught; it is something some people come to have in their hands almost intuitively. The understanding of what can and cannot be done with clay is nowhere more apparent than here, at the stage where a bucket of slip (liquid clay) takes on the exact form required by the master.

Fig. 7 . After the slip has been allowed to harden, the final master molds are produced. Each must be carefully preserved, for it is from these molds that the second level of molds—the case molds—are taken. From the case molds are taken the final pieces of soft clay, greenware, which will become parts of the Sugarbirds sculpture.

Fig. 8 . A few of the hundreds of pieces which go to make up the Sugarbird sculpture. The ware is soft, wet and fragile before it dries and must be quickly assembled into the final whole.

join the castings together by coating matching areas with a gelatinous mixture of slip, which is a natural porcelain adhesive. The castings are held together by hand until they adhere and then each joint is worked with water and wooden tools called pegs until the clays meld and the seams disappear. If they are not melded properly, the joints will come undone when the piece is fired, a not infrequent event. The parts to be joined are kept in a damp box alongside the artisan while he works.

Once all the parts are joined together, there is another hazard to be faced. As the piece dries, it becomes increasingly fragile. The slightest vibration or movement can cause the model to shatter. There is no way the piece can then be reclaimed. One must start all over from scratch with new parts.

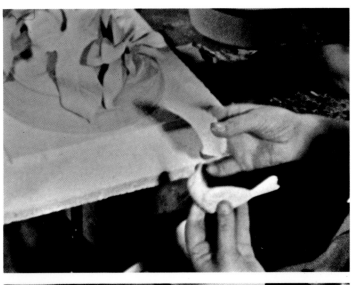

Fig. 9   The assembly begins as the artist starts putting all the pieces of this incredible jigsaw puzzle back together again. At this stage a new creation of the original clay takes place. The artist must be totally aware of every attitude, every connection, every detail of the original work.

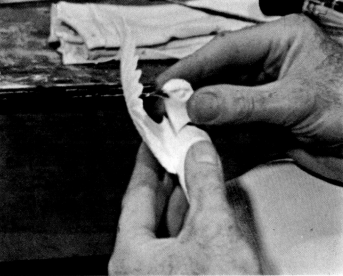

Fig. 10   One of the five Sugarbirds on this piece being meticulously reassembled.

Fig. 11   Finally the entire piece is assembled. It is now in a soft stage which must be supported in the kiln, and the artist and an assistant prepare it for the first and most dangerous of its many plays of heat in the kilns. In order that the sculptured piece be fired correctly and not emerge a warped and cracked mass of useless clay, the process of supporting—one of the most difficult and demanding processes of all—takes place. Ed Boehm carefully places clay supports to assure that, as the heat builds, the unbalanced weight of the sculpture will not cause it to sag or crack. Once a piece is propped, it is almost impossible to move it, so the great kilns are moved on rails into position over the piece. From the very beginning the artist had to anticipate this moment; in his original sketches Ed Boehm was already thinking through this crucial problem. While a piece of greenware (soft unfired clay) is in the kiln there is one precise moment when it is transformed from soft clay to hard porcelain. At this moment the whole piece wants to liquefy and sag, and only the consummate art of the kiln master can prevent its destruction.

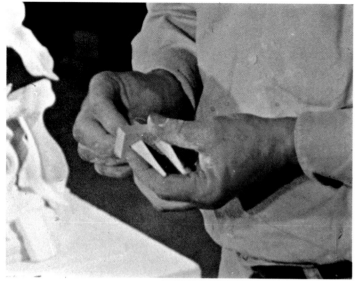

Before it is placed in the kiln—a special clay-baking oven—the greenware is trimmed, sponged and inspected for flaws. Clay crutches are made to support the model while it is in the kiln, always of the same slip so that shrinkage will be uniform. In those areas where the supports touch the model they are coated with a nonfusible material so that they do not become fired to the sculpture. Boehm always worked with his kiln master at this point, because a disaster here is final.

Propping is done on bisque loading beds, each about three feet wide and high and five feet long. These beds remain stationary and the huge kiln itself is rolled on steel rails over the greenware instead of the greenware being loaded into the kiln. This is to avoid the slightest movement of the fragile clay. The doors are then closed and the firing is begun. It takes 13 hours for the kiln to reach the proper "cooking" temperature of 2400°F.

Once the piece is fired, about two days of cooling are required before the doors of the kiln may be opened. Everyone awaits the opening of the doors rather like expectant fathers awaiting the birth of a child. If every step has not been perfect to this point, this is where errors appear. Each fired piece is in-

Figs. 12, 13 and 14

At left we see the ancient method of using cones to determine the exact heat and exact removal moment of the piece. In the center picture the cone has started to tilt, sag and melt, proving that the firing is at the right temperature and must be stopped. At right, everything has worked correctly. The piece is hard. It is finished. It is perfect. It is porcelain. The artist's smile, rare for Ed Boehm, testifies to the relief always attendant upon a successful greenware firing. This is the crucial step. The piece now needs only the artist's word that it replicates his original intentions and is ready to enter the next stage.

spected carefully for defects. Those not perfect are destroyed—on the spot—with a hammer.

Among the discouragingly long list of things that can go wrong are cracking due to faulty joining, collapsing due to prop slippage, excessive heat, too little heat, uneven heat, improper kiln loading, improper cooling, premature opening of the kiln or simply breakage in handling.

Perfect pieces are sanded to prepare an absolutely smooth surface for the critical stage of hand-painting. Artisans with years of experience mix and apply the proper paints. These paints present a very special artistic problem. The cold state in which they are applied is never the color to which they will fire. Therefore the decorator must paint in his "mind's eye," as it were, so that he will anticipate the changed hues which will emerge from the kiln. Lighter colors are applied first, then deeper colors, and finally the most sensitive reds and oranges, the bêtes noires of the kiln master.

Fig. 15   On the right is the original soft bisque piece before it was fired and on the left the same piece after it was fired. Note that substantial shrinkage has taken place. Almost 15 to 20 percent of the entire mass has seemingly "disappeared." This shrinkage makes the clay dense and hard and tough. It can also lead to the distortions that are the despair of artists and kiln masters. Unless everything is thought through ahead of time—during sketching, modeling, propping and temperature control—the piece, in the process of shrinkage, can distort and destroy itself.

Fig. 16   The artist prepares for the coloring of the sculpture. He knows that his colors will change in the course of firing, and that he must anticipate the manner and the degree in which each one will change, so that after the firings the colors relate to one another precisely as originally intended. All the colors are hand-ground, and all have been tested a thousand times. Although color firings do not represent a real threat, they have been known to destroy porcelain sculptures.

Fig. 17   The painting process itself is very straightforward.

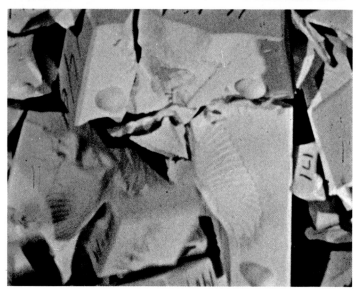

After each of many painting phases the pieces are refired at temperatures ranging from 1280° to 1450°F in decorating kilns, the temperature varying precisely according to the requirements of each of the colors. Boehm avoided creating such birds as the Baltimore Oriole and the Scarlet Tanager because he felt that the true colors, reds and oranges again, were not available and could not be mixed. This insight may have grown out of his experience with the Cardinals, which are, in terms of color, among his least true-to-life creations.

These are the major steps in creating hard-paste porcelain and one might well argue that no matter how many sculptures were created in an edition, each one is an original. The hand-crafting and hand-painting processes make individual variations inevitable. Within these natural limitations, however, the quality control exercised by the Trenton Studio under Boehm was extraordinary. I do not believe that any collector owns a "second" or even a questionable piece of work out of Ed Boehm's Studio. The man simply had too much pride in his work for that. One might quibble over the small variations of a Boehm sculpture, but the mechanics were always maintained at a near impossible level.

Fig. 18   At this point there is still opportunity to refer back to the original life models. Here the artist holds in his right hand a live Sugarbird, studying its texture and feather structure and color.

Fig. 19   At last the piece is completely decorated and now is placed in the kiln for its final firing. Ed Boehm was a master at fixing the location of a piece in the kiln. Although not a trained kiln master himself, he knew instinctively where the heat would come from and how it would affect circulation in the firing.

Fig. 20   The ultimate moment of any limited edition sculpture, the moment when the sledgehammer is taken to the original master molds. Since the master molds are good for thousands of replications, the smashing of the molds guarantees that the Sugarbirds, of which only 100 were made, can never be made again.

1053-01 SUGARBIRDS

RPC-1087-01 YOUNG
AMERICAN BALD
EAGLE

What Boehm Costs and Why

One of the sensational and widely reported facts about Boehm porcelain has been its extraordinary vitality in the marketplace. One reads in the newspapers of the $150,000 Mute Swans or the $28,500 seascapes. Actually, prices start as low as $25 for a pussy willow, but most of the pieces are fairly expensive.

Are they worth it? It is an interesting and a reasonable question. Since the beginning, about 1950, some $25 million worth of sculptures have been sold.

Obviously, there are a significant number of people who believe the prices are fair. If one believes in free market forces and the general philosophy that luxury items—diamonds, furs, paintings and so on—are worth what people are willing to pay for them, then Boehm prices are not excessive. And if one believes in the aesthetic validity of Boehm and the historical importance of the work, then all talk of actual prices paid becomes academic.

Americans love a market. We are by nature a speculative people, delighting in the upward and downward surge of prices and in the detective work required to understand the forces that move these prices. American history is full of those suddenly made rich by speculation or venture. Speculation in land is part of our history, and certainly our broad involvement in the stock market goes beyond the experience of any other country in the world. Tens of millions of Americans turn first each day to the stock market quotations featured in every major newspaper. Even those who have no investment in the market find a curious voyeur-like pleasure in observing the movements of money.

The American collector of art and *objets d'art* is not immune to this general fever. Indeed, in the market for art, *objets d'art* and antiques, careful statistical studies have shown that greater profits have been made in the buying and selling of selected objects than in the stock market or even in land investment.

There have been few instances in the history of American *objets d'art* where the prices have risen steadily and without recession for so long a period of time as in the Boehm sculptures. Increasing prices cannot help but affect the enthusiasm both of people who own Boehm sculptures (and are benefiting by the rising prices) and of those new collectors who have recently come into the Boehm market. The established collector is encouraged by constantly rising prices to value his birds even higher. He becomes convinced that his sculptures are going to be worth more tomorrow than today. In itself, this simple conviction, this anticipation of higher prices, leads to more higher prices. And the new collector, recognizing how far prices have gone beyond original issue price, is encouraged both to join the market and to pay premiums for those closed-edition sculptures that may be for sale. So the Boehm collector, like other collectors, is caught up in that great American game of buying and selling. With the Boehm collector, however, buying predominates. The Boehm collector may be excited and pleased by the fact that his birds have gone up in price but the vast majority would consider it an act of disloyalty and a bad deal to part with their birds at whatever price. The Boehm collector has come to learn that once he sells a piece of Boehm, the money he gets for it is usually inconsequential in terms of the pleasure the piece gave. As Omar Khayyam once said: "I often wonder what the Vintners buy/One half so precious as the Goods they sell." So the Boehm collector, upon considering the alternatives open to him, usually decides that the money he may receive is not nearly as satisfying or important as the Boehm he owns.

This desire to keep and to enjoy is at the very heart of the increase in prices for Boehm porcelains. The prices have increased, not because speculators and traders have pushed up the price, but for the solid and organic reason that once a collector owns a piece of Boehm he simply does not want to part with it.

The problem of what the correct price is for any art object is an enormously complicated one. In other markets (such as the one-of-a-kind fine art market) the supply is so thin that prices are almost always determined by a peculiar, almost Eastern, face-to-face negotiation between buyer and seller. This seldom reflects a deep and active market from which buyer and seller can take experience and information on the value of a work of art. In *objets d'art*, however, where there may be more than one example (in Boehm sculpture there have been as many as 500 in an edition), prices start establishing themselves in anonymous, automatic market processes rather than in face-to-face confrontations of buyer and seller.

In the case of Boehm, a competitive market process goes to work. People who want to buy or sell a piece of Boehm will shop around. They will shop the dealers, they will shop the auction establishments and they will shop the possibility of dealing directly with private collectors. In that process of looking around and seeing what can be had, a consensus is arrived at among dealers, collectors and owners of Boehm that results in a surprisingly close range of estimates as to what price a piece should bring.

Generally speaking, the dealer's price is the highest. The justification for this is that the dealer has to acquire, display and maintain his overhead on the selection of closed-edition Boehm he offers. The higher price also is justified by the fact that the reliable dealer is also the guarantor to the buyer. He can make assurances as to quality, condition and source which auctions or private parties may not be able, or want, to do.

Purchases from private parties tend to be at lower prices than dealers' prices, although there have been many cases where private exchange of porcelain sculptures has taken place at considerably higher prices than those offered at the major dealers.

The third source for closed-edition Boehm, and one of the most interesting, is the unlimited public auction, where at times great bargains can be found. Auc-

RPC-1086-01 COMMON TERN

tions, however, are subject to a series of caveats. The pieces bid upon can be of questionable quality or source; the prices can be rigged by a bidding consortium or by the seller and auctioneer; the damage rate is high and adequate insurance compensation uncertain.

Boehm prices are variable among the kinds of product that the Studio makes. The basic reputation was made in the field of bird sculptures. This habit of thinking about Boehm has held constant, so that the prices for non-bird examples such as the early giftware, the tableware and animal pieces—dogs and horses— tend to be remarkably low compared to what people are willing to pay for examples of bird sculptures.

Another factor that affects price is the size of an edition (or, if the edition was unlimited, the number made before the edition was closed). One would think that the fewer pieces made, the higher the price. This is not true. Edition size is an indication only of what the price should be. The small edition should lead to a higher price and, generally within certain restrictive definitions, it does. However, the popularity, the beauty and the category of the piece still are the strongest factors in the establishment of price. For the sophisticated collector, great bargains can be had in those categories of pieces which are not, at the moment, popular but may well become historically important. There are certain Boehm sculptures of which only five or six examples were made which are selling for $300 to $500. When one compares this to the $5,000 to $10,000 being asked for recent Boehm birds of editions of 500, it is clear that the older and less popular pieces are great acquisitions.

Original issue prices are divided into two areas, the limited editions and the nonlimited editions. Over the years, the nonlimited pieces of sculpture have been the most modestly priced and include practically no dollar cost to the consumer for the creative activity and development put into the piece by the Studio.

Actually, the word nonlimited is a misnomer. It means only that when the piece is announced there is no defined limit placed on the number to be done. However, in practice, the Studio has ceased making hundreds of pieces originally conceived as nonlimited, thereby in effect creating a real limitation. The reason for discontinuation may be either that the Studio simply gets tired of making a particular piece, or, more likely, that the Studio's technical and aesthetic abilities have outgrown what was once an important achievement.

For these reasons, the nonlimited pieces have always been an interesting investment opportunity, being considerably underpriced compared to the limited editions. Proof of this appears again and again in auctions, where nonlimited pieces (some even still in production and available from dealers) bring prices as much as twice what the pieces are currently selling for. Also, once the nonlimited editions are closed, the multiplication in price, starting as it does from a rather low base level, takes place even more quickly than in some of the limited editions.

In general, however, the change in price for Boehm does not go smoothly. Pieces do not change in price at the same rate. Individual pieces, because of their extraordinary beauty or appeal (such as the Young American Eagle or the Tern), will leap ahead of others which take longer to catch up, if they ever do. Things tend to even themselves out, however, the slower pieces showing their strength in the marketplace after the excitement over the more exotic and sensational ones has died down.

The whole market moves at an irregular gait. There will be long periods, sometimes measured in years, when the prices of a closed edition will hold steady. During these periods there may even be a regression in the price of pieces that have been pushed too far, too fast by speculators or greedy dealers. Then, all of a sudden, without any gradual upper movement but in obvious response to an increase in demand, prices will surge to an entirely new plateau and drag upward all other prices, both for the pieces that are in high demand and for those for which the demand is more moderate.

Prices are created by the marketplace process that takes into account all the information concerning a piece's worth. It is a process that considers the level of monetary inflation, the cost of production today as against that in the past, the aesthetic qualities of a piece, the edition size, the number available and the desire on the part of collectors to hold onto their examples and the inclination of dealers to sell. It is a process that reflects dynamic market factors—for example, expectations of the future as to whether prices will rise, stay the same or fall. These expectations magnify price change both upward and downward. When all these informational bits are put into the one marketplace hat, shaken up and measured one against the other, a unique and individual price (for any given moment) appears for every piece of Boehm that has been offered for sale. These prices may vary a little from place to place but generally speaking they are spread rapidly around the country.

A most important factor in determining whether a particular price is correct is to look into the factor of *activity*. Activity means the number of sales that have taken place for a specific piece over a period of time and at what prices these pieces sold. If five or six pieces have changed hands in three or four months at approximately the price you are considering paying, then I would consider that price to be a safe and proper one. If there is no indication of activity in a piece, the price must be considered both suspect and negotiable. The best bet is to ask the seller what evidence of sales he has had at the asking price in the immediate past.

In one sense, prices for Boehm are never high enough. This may sound strange and contradictory to those who consider all the prices always too high, but if one thinks a moment of the tremendous demand for these sculptures, one must agree that any piece of Boehm available at its original issue price is considerably less costly than at its free market price.

Over the years, the Studio has based retail prices purely on the cost of production while choosing to ignore the demand side of pricing policy. A Boehm price is based not on what the market will bear but on production time, complexity, the number of pieces lost in firing and the skills of the mold makers and decorators required to make a particular piece. The price is built up from actual manufacturing costs, much as the pricing for a refrigerator or an automobile. Nowhere in the Studio formulas can one detect the costing of the enormous amount of experience, expertise, sensitivity and professionalism that goes into the conception and execution of these porcelain sculptures. The Boehm Studio has never consciously placed a price on its creative activity. This is one of the reasons why almost any piece of Boehm is underpriced on the market at the time of issue.

While prices are interesting, they should in no way become the overriding consideration in the enjoyment of collecting. A collector can easily fall into the attitude of the cynic who "knows the price of everything and the value of nothing." It is in the aesthetic, technical and historic value of an artwork that its real importance lies. It is this value, which feeds the collector's sensibilities and senses, that is important. In this sense, there is really no price at all that can be put on a work of art.

Some Terms and Definitions

The only way to avoid confusion in the world of collecting is to define one's terms. In contemporary collecting, many terms are thrown about in a loose fashion. Some people who should know better are not only careless about definitions but might even prefer not to have their terms too closely defined.

In Boehm collecting, however, terms referring to collecting and to the products themselves have always had a precise meaning. Listed here are some of the more important ones to keep in mind.

Limited Edition

An edition of a contemporary product, in which the total number of the edition is announced at the time production begins. This agrees with the New York State law on the subject, which indicates that the number to be made must be clearly stated. Limitation by the number of orders received as of a certain date is not considered a true limited edition. Other terms for limited edition are: limited issue, restricted issue and restricted edition.

Limited Issue Goal (L.I.G.)

In referring to the sculptures that were created after Ed Boehm died, the term "Limited Edition" has been replaced by "Limited Issue Goal," a term that allows the Studio to make fewer than the number announced, but not more.

Nonlimited or Unlimited Edition

An edition in which no total number is announced. It may be produced in perpetuity or may be closed at any time at the will of the producer. Nonlimited editions are sometimes the most attractive from the point of view of the collector, since they tend to be less expensive. Nonlimited editions, historically, have been closed sometimes at a very low number, making some early nonlimited pieces extremely valuable.

Open Edition

Open edition means that a limited edition is still being produced (although it may very well be completely sold out). Boehm editions have been known to stay open for as long as 20 years, for reasons best known to the Studio but usually due to technical difficulties in producing particular pieces.

Closed Edition

Closed edition can refer to either a limited or a nonlimited edition. For a limited edition it is the point at which the total edition number has been produced; for a nonlimited edition it is the number that has been produced when production was stopped.

Discontinued Edition

Sometimes there are pieces that are discontinued temporarily, rather than closed permanently. Experience has shown that discontinued pieces generally stay discontinued permanently, so there is little real difference between a closed edition and a discontinued edition.

Commemorative Edition (Special Edition)

At times, portions of a limited edition and some special objects are set aside as commemorative issues. These are identified either by markings on the base, by special plaques attached or by variations in the structure of the piece itself. An example of a special, or commemorative, edition is the 100 Fledgling American Eagles, identified by a special plaque and marking, which were sold by the Boehm Studio and from which all proceeds went to the White House Historical Society. An example of a nonlimited commemorative edition was a small edition of Cygnets made for State Department gifts. They were differentiated from the regular edition by the fact that the Cygnet's eyes are open, signifying the constant awareness which the Presidency of the United States requires.

Original Issue Price

The price placed on a piece of porcelain at the time of its announcement by the producer. This is the price at which the dealer is obligated to sell it in his first sale to a collector.

Secondary Market

A secondary market is the market which a piece of porcelain enters after its initial sale from an authorized dealer to a collector. The collector then may sell it to another collector. He may sell it back to a dealer, or he may sell it at auction. All of these represent secondary market transactions. Historically, these transactions have been at prices considerably higher than the price at which the piece was originally issued. Secondary markets develop along with the primary market, and prices in the secondary market start rising even while dealers are delivering their allocations at original issue prices.

Secondary Market Price

These are prices which are determined by the interplay of supply and demand in the marketplace.

Appraisal Price

A reliable dealer making an appraisal will try to anticipate an increase in the price of the piece he is appraising in order to protect his client against possible future loss. Experience has shown that whatever price a Boehm piece carries today, it likely will be higher tomorrow. Therefore, for appraisal purposes, prices should be somewhat higher than current secondary market prices.

Allocation

Every Boehm dealer has a rigidly set and jealously guarded allocation of Boehm. The Studio tells the dealers at the time editions are announced how many they will receive, and it is extremely rare that this number is ever increased. The allocation may be delivered over a period of four, five or six years, but every dealer always knows exactly how many pieces he will eventually receive.

Status of Editions

Twice a year the Boehm Studio publishes a list of every piece still open, the number made and the number yet to be made. This has nothing to do with the number sold; it simply indicates the numbers yet to be delivered from the Studio to the dealers. The Status of Editions also lists all closed editions and closed nonlimited and discontinued editions, and the total number made in each.

Hard-Paste Porcelain

Hard-paste porcelain is the hardest of all porcelains made and it is fired at the highest temperatures. The Trenton factory produces hard-paste porcelain.

Bone Porcelain

Bone porcelain (made almost exclusively in England) is fired at a few degrees lower than hard-paste porcelain. Its surface is somewhat softer than the hard-paste surface. This makes bone porcelain less attractive as dinnerware (knives and forks tend to scratch the bone porcelain surface). However, as a medium for porcelain sculptures, it is desirable for its malleability, acceptance of color and structural integrity, although it is often subject to a somewhat unpleasant glossiness.

Mint Condition

The words "mint condition," in the original sense, refer to a coin in the condition in which it came from the minting process, uncirculated and untouched by human hands. In the world of porcelain, mint condition refers to a piece in the condition in which it came from the kiln and was delivered by the studio. Any and all changes in the piece of porcelain due to breakage, repair or so-called improvement that take place outside of the studio are a departure from mint condition. Any and all activities which take place in the studio, before delivery to a dealer, go to making a piece in mint condition. Because the production of a piece of modern porcelain includes so many techniques, it takes a sophisticated and knowledgeable eye to differentiate between a mint and a nonmint piece. A nonmint piece, even though impeccably and invisibly repaired, is usually worth about half as much as a mint piece.

Makersmarks

The marks fired onto the bottom of a piece of porcelain vary from time to time and from studio to studio. An entire history of Boehm can be developed by knowing the various makersmarks.

Black Light

A form of light in the ultraviolet range, imperceptible to the human eye, under which certain materials that look similar under natural light, appear different.

Plates

RPC-103-03 RPC-103-04 RPC-103-05 AMERICAN COCKER

RPC-106-01 RPC-106-02 WIRE-HAIRED FOX TERRIER

RPC-107-02 DANE, RECLINING

78

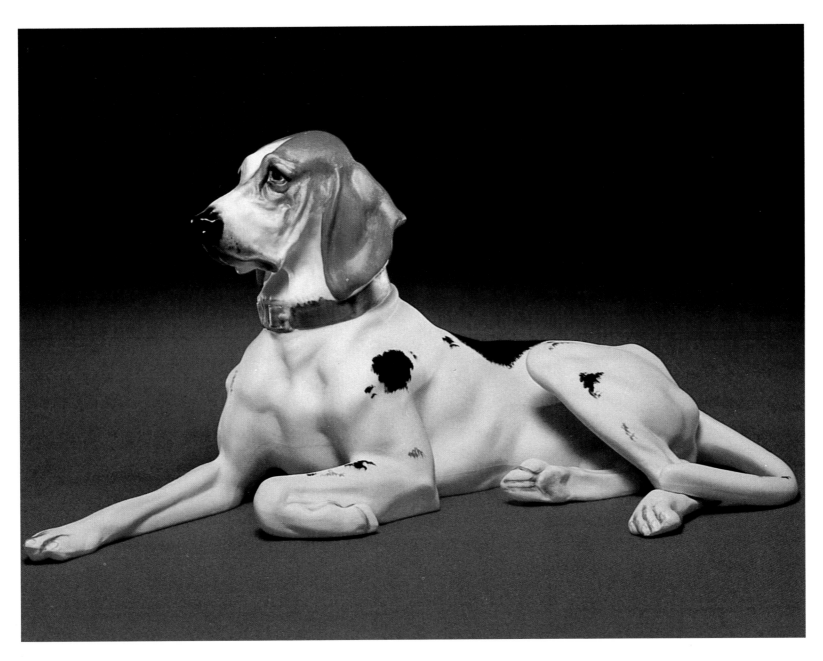

RPC-111-01 RECLINING FOXHOUND

RPC-113-02 SPRINGER

RPC-117-02 DACHSHUND

RPC-119-02 COLLIE

RPC-122-01 WHIPPETS

RPC-124-01 KING CHARLES SPANIEL

RPC-126-01 DALMATIAN "MIKE"

RPC-130 ENGLISH BULL DOG

RPC-408 LAMB

RPC-512-01 FIELD MOUSE WITH VETCH

RPC-514-01 CHIPMUNK, STANDING

RPC-701-02 SIAMESE DANCERS

RPC-623 MADONNA AND CHILD, DELLA ROBBIA

RPC-834-01 "GOLDEN-CROWNED KINGLETS" SERVICE PLATE, RPC-834-02 "GOLDEN-CROWNED KINGLETS" CUP

RPC-855-02 BUNNY BOX WITH CARROT

RPC-900 CANDY EGG

**RPC-909 EDWARD MARSHALL BOEHM
ORCHID**

RPC-962-02 ORCHID CENTERPIECE

RPC-1002-04 WOOD DUCKS

RPC-1004-02 RED-BREASTED GROSBEAKS

88

RPC-1005-01 MALLARDS

RPC-1006-02 BOB WHITE QUAIL

RPC-1007-01 CANADA GEESE

RPC-1008-03 RING-NECKED PHEASANTS

RPC-1012-01 WOODCOCK

RPC-1016-01 CARDINALS

RPC-1017-01 CEDAR WAXWINGS ON
WILD BLACKBERRY

RPC-1018-01 GOLDEN CROWNED KINGLETS with Oriental Poppies

RPC-1020-01 CAROLINA WRENS on Sugar Maple

RPC-1023-01 RED-WINGED BLACKBIRDS on Cattails

RPC-1026-01 INDIGO BUNTING, Male on
Wild Rose

RPC-1027-01 WHITE-THROATED SPARROW
on Cherokee Rose

RPC-1028-01 YELLOW-THROATED
WARBLER on Crimson-Eye Mallow

RPC-1030-01 CALIFORNIA QUAIL

RPC-1031-02 MEADOWLARK

RPC-1033-01 BABY ROBIN

RPC-1032-01 BABY BLUE JAY

104

RPC-1034-01 BLACK-CAPPED CHICKADEE,
Male on Holly Leaves

RPC-1035-01 HUMMINGBIRD,
Male on Cactus

RPC-1036-01 RUBY-CROWNED
KINGLET, on Bloodroot

RPC-1037-02 BLACK-THROATED BLUE
WARBLER, Male on Mountain Laurel

RPC-1038-01 BABY BLUEBIRD

RPC-1040-02 BABY WOODTHRUSH with Butterfly

RPC-1041-01 PROTHONOTARY WARBLER, Female with Eggs and Fledgling

RPC-1044-01 BABY GOLDFINCH with Violet

RPC-1045-01 FLEDGLING KINGFISHER

RPC-1049-01 RUFFED GROUSE

112

RPC-1050-01 GOLDFINCHES with Scottish Thistle

RPC-1054-01 BABY CHICKADEE

RPC-1052-01 MOCKINGBIRDS on Blossoming Bindweed

RPC-1055-01 PTARMIGAN

RPC-1057-01 BLUE JAYS on Strawberries

RPC-1060-01 NUTHATCH with Ivy and Moneywort

RPC-1061-01 MOUNTAIN BLUEBIRDS on flowering Magnolia

RPC-1062-01 TOWHEE with Fall-Fruiting Mushrooms

RPC-1064-01 **KILLDEER** with Bluebells

RPC-1065-01 BOBOLINK with Corn Stubble

**RPC-1068-02 FLEDGLING GREAT
HORNED OWL**

RPC-1067-01 FLEDGLING BLACKBURNIAN WARBLER

RPC-1071-01 TUFTED TITMICE with Sumac

RPC-1070-01 VARIED BUNTINGS

RPC-1072-01 CATBIRD with Hyacinth

RPC-1074-01 WOOD THRUSHES with Azaleas

RPC-1076-01 RUFOUS HUMMINGBIRDS
on Icelandic Poppy

RPC-1077-01 CRESTED FLYCATCHER on Sweet Gum

RPC-1078-01 BLUE GROSBEAK with Fall
Foliage

RPC-1079-01 NORTHERN WATER
THRUSH with Ferns and Cladonia

RPC-1080-01 FLEDGLING CANADA
WARBLER with Monarch Butterfly

RPC-1081-01 KESTRELS

RPC-1082-01 ROAD RUNNER with Horned Toad

RPC-1083-01 FLEDGLING WESTERN BLUEBIRDS

RPC-1085-01 HOODED MERGANSERS

RPC-1088-01 WESTERN BLUEBIRDS with Wild Azaleas

RPC-1089-01 VERDINS, on Thorn

RPC-1090-01 BLACK-HEADED GROSBEAK, Male on Vine Maple

RPS-1094-01 SLATE-COLORED JUNCO
on Pyracantha

RPC-1092-01 ORCHARD ORIOLE on
Blossoming Tulip

137

RPS-1096-01 FLICKER with Chipmunk
and Mushrooms

RSP-1098-02 CYGNET (Baby Bird of Peace), Presidential Cygnet

RPS-1099-01 BROWN PELICAN

RPS-1125 THE EAGLE OF FREEDOM I

Catalog

Curators' Introduction

In 1964, in connection with the First Retrospective Exhibition of Boehm porcelains conducted by Reese Palley, we first had the opportunity to attempt to list all of the pieces produced by Edward Marshall Boehm. We had hoped that our work would be both comprehensive and correct and that the assignment of specific numbers to each piece would aid in future identification. But by the time the listing was well under way, we knew that errors and omissions would be numerous. *How numerous*, we did not fully understand. The numbering system employed was inadequate to allow for new finds of old Boehm, decorations of listed pieces that had not been suspected prior to the completion of that Retrospective Catalog, and sundry unique pieces (either gifts from Mr. Boehm or experiments never carried to production) which have turned up in the intervening years.

Now, from the vantage point of 12 more years of the experience, we are going to try again.

The new numbering system is designed to allow for additions, deletions and corrections. Chronology may be disturbed should other early pieces be discovered, but at least all structurally identical pieces will be grouped together and the collector will not be required to hunt through hundreds of listings to find a particular decoration. In addition, the Decorative Accessories have been broken down into two major groupings (USEFUL ACCESSORIES and DECORATIVE ACCESSORIES), each with two sub-groupings to enable the speedy location of any piece.

Another function of the numbering system is to differentiate between those pieces done by Edward Marshall Boehm prior to his death and those completed by the Studios (both Trenton and Malvern) after his death. You will note that the pieces completed after 1969 bear the identification RPS before the number, standing for Reese Palley–Studio; RPC stands for Reese Palley–Catalog and denotes sculptures created and executed by Edward Marshall Boehm.

Each object in the catalog has a unique number and each category, as can be seen by a quick perusal, is assigned a different set of numbers:

Dogs   starts with 100
Cats   starts with 200
Horses   starts with 300
Livestock   starts with 400
Wildlife   starts with 500
Religious pieces   starts with 600
Promotional pieces   number 700 only
Figurines   starts with 701

USEFUL ACCESSORIES   starts with 800

ASHTRAYS, BOTTLES AND BOXES   starts with 850

DECORATIVE ACCESSORIES, PAPERWEIGHTS, BOOK-
ENDS AND MISCELLANEOUS PIECES   starts with 900

VASES, URNS, CANDLESTICKS AND CENTERPIECES
starts with 925

BIRDS   starts with 1000

PORCELAIN PAINTINGS   starts with 2000

ONE-OF-A-KIND PAINTINGS   starts with 3000

PORCELAIN PAINTINGS IN THE ROUND
starts with 4000

MALVERN ANIMALS   starts with 8500

MALVERN FIGURES   starts with 8700

MALVERN FLOWERS   starts with 8800

MALVERN BIRDS   starts with 9000

A collector can immediately answer the following questions from the numbers used:

1) Was it made before or after Ed Boehm's death?
2) What category of object does it represent?
3) Was the object made in Trenton or Malvern?
4) About when was the object made?
5) Was the piece done in varying decorations? In many cases the number itself will indicate this.

Please note that the "makersmark" is not related to the "Boehm Studiomark Number" listed for each individual piece. The latter is the factory number given by the Studio to each sculpture and refers to their records only. Many of the early price lists carry the Boehm Studiomark Numbers; in fact, their current yearly lists carry them still. The "makersmark" is the identifying imprint on the bottom of each piece of Boehm. There were a dozen or so marks used by Ed

Boehm in the years from 1944 on. For illustrations of all of them see Appendix A.

The "RP" number listed in parentheses after each subject refers to the number assigned to the piece in the Retrospective Exhibition Catalog published in 1964 in connection with the exhibition of Boehm's works held in Atlantic City during that year.

Some pieces in this listing do not have either a Boehm Studiomark Number or an RP number. The reason for the lack of an RP number is simple . . . the existence of the piece was not known at the time of the 1964 Exhibition. The lack of a Boehm Studiomark Number would seem to indicate that the piece was either an experimental subject or a piece made before the numbering system was introduced.

We have attempted to acquire photographs of every piece, in at least one of its decorations. We have tried thereby to remove as much of the guesswork as possible in identification of pieces. A word picture, no matter how deeply it goes into detail, cannot compare with one good photograph. At this writing, there are pieces for which no photograph exists. We hope, by publication date, to have filled these gaps.

To aid the collector who has been using the old Retrospective Catalog numbering system to make the change to this new system, we have included after each piece the "RP" number from that catalog as well as a cross-reference number chart at the end of the text (see Appendix B).

No introduction to a catalog of Boehm pieces can be considered complete without the assertion that no catalog of Boehm can be considered complete. Estimates and guesses are more often than not the *modus operandi* in the world of Boehm, especially with regard to those pieces produced prior to the extensive collection revision of 1962. In our researches we have more than once looked insanity squarely in the eye and been tempted to succumb. The alternative was to accept whatever facts we *knew* to be correct and relegate the rest to supposition and educated guesses. It has, of course, been difficult to write pages of "ifs," "possiblys" and "howevers," but we do find consolation in the knowledge that we have included within these pages more actual *facts* about Boehm porcelain than have ever been gathered before.

We are certain, however, that we have left out pieces. The problem is that we do not know which pieces we have left out. In at least one instance we have been tempted to take license and include a piece that, to all intents and purposes, may not exist at all. We are speaking of the ST. FRANCIS OF ASSISI, a beautiful piece, produced, as far as we have been able to discover, only in undecorated bisque. It seems almost incomprehensible that no decorated example of this piece existed, but from every source we received the same information: "only undecorated bisque." Against the weight of such absolute conviction from so many directions, we could do nothing but list the one we knew to exist, and omit a decorated example from the catalog. But there is always the hope that one may turn up. This Micawberish sentiment, we have discovered, can be applied to nearly all of the early pieces and makes the entire Boehm experience that much more exciting and rewarding, if not for the curator then certainly for the collector.

DORIS F. IDAKITIS
BERYL A. SILVERMAN
March, 1976

A NOTE ON THE CHRONOLOGY

Assigning the correct chronological position to the early Boehm pieces is no mean task. One would assume, at first glance, that the most obvious aid would be the Boehm Studiomark Numbers. Unfortunately, this is not the case, since these numbers were not inaugurated until the mid-1950's and, therefore, inconsistencies and errors have crept in.

Many of the early pieces which were either experimental or which were discontinued due to lack of sales were not assigned Boehm Studiomark Numbers at all, and those that were often received numbers out of sequence with their actual introduction dates.

Through the use of old price lists, studio records and studio memories, we have attempted to list the pieces in each section in as close to chronological order as possible.

Where we have found discrepancies between price lists and actual Boehm Studiomark Numbers, we have chosen to follow the price lists; therefore many of the Boehm Studiomark Numbers are out of sequence. Occasionally, other factors have entered into our decision to ignore the sequence of these numbers. Wherever possible, however, and wherever other information was lacking, we have attempted to follow them.

We are sure there are errors in our chronology. But we hope that these are few.

A NOTE ON THE WHITE BISQUE

Before proceeding to the actual catalog, we must take a moment to talk about the undecorated bisque pieces in this listing.

The early Boehm pieces were first done in a glazed finish, whether decorated or undecorated, and only later in decorated bisque. However, when an edition was discontinued, those pieces not yet decorated and still in their bisque state were often put up for sale. This explains, for the most part, the existence of the white bisque in the early years.

In the case of "Useful and Decorative Accessories," however, this rule of thumb does not always hold true, as there were pieces which were available in white bisque from the time of their introduction, and these often carried prices different from glazed and/or decorated examples of the same piece.

Thus, most early undecorated bisque pieces were leftovers. Quite often, they were not sold at all, but given away to visitors to the Boehm factory or to friends of Mr. Boehm. For this reason, it is impossible to determine the exact number left undecorated for any particular early piece.

In the mid-1950's, the studio did many limited-edition birds (including the Geese and Macaws) in all white and advertised them as such. Mrs. Hoving of Bonwit Teller was particularly fond of all white. Bob Whites, Mallards, Pheasants, Cedar Waxwings were all in limited editions up through 1958. From 1959 on, the year the Eastern Bluebirds were introduced, usually only one of each limited edition was done in white, except for an additional one of each of some pieces done for me in the early 1960's. Mr. Boehm canceled this arrangement with me after one of each of about half the collection had been delivered.

The unlimited pieces, on the other hand (with the exception of the religious pieces), were not produced in quantity in undecorated bisque after 1962, and by 1964 the production of even two or three white bisque unlimited pieces had been virtually discontinued. In this listing, therefore, unless we are definitely certain of the existence of an undecorated bisque piece in an unlimited edition, none has been included.

We sent this manuscript along to Ollie Delchamps, a major collector, for his comments and received the following note, which I find most interesting:

> You remember that Ed made this tremendously large piece—Ivory Billed Woodpecker—for Helen for her first showing of Boehm birds in England. You can talk with Frank [Cosentino]—but I know I am right. In 1962 I had to pay 10% over the list price for bisque Mocking Bird. That same year I went to New York and bought all the bisque Tiffany and Bonwit Teller had.
>
> Around about that time I got a pair of Tumbler Pigeons in bisque but Frank told me that Ed would not let any birds go out in bisque, and somewhere around 1964 they did not sell any to dealers—you can check with Frank. In your description a lot of birds which came out since 1964-65 you list in bisque as being very rare. If they did not make any how could they be very rare?

The explanation is simple: no bisque undecorated pieces were made for sale after 1964-65. However, the studio does retain one example of each sculpture in the undecorated state. That is the reason for the "very rare" description: there are none made for sale.

Works by Edward Marshall Boehm

RPC-101-01

RPC-102-01

RPC-104-01

I. The Dogs

During the 10 years that Ed Boehm produced dog sculptures, his work grew from the experimental use of commercial molds to the mature work of the late 1950's. The dog models show the change in his capacity to handle material, and, in fact, it was during this time that the "soft" bisque finish, for which he became famous, evolved.

Some of the best and the worst examples of his work show up among the dogs. With some he seems to have worked with the greatest of patience, as with the elegant Pointer; with others, such as the Reclining Poodle, there appears little of the authority which defines his great pieces.

It is curious that Ed Boehm should have paid so little attention to dogs, since he took international and American prizes for his work in the breeding of dogs. I talked with Ed Boehm shortly before his death about the possibility of his returning to the dog series and completing it. We considered together the possibility of a large number of models in the bisque finish, on a rather large scale of 10″ or 12″, covering the whole range of the popular American breeds. It is a loss that this work was never done, since the production of porcelain dogs around the world leaves a great deal to be desired.

The dogs are extremely early examples of Boehm porcelain, confined almost exclusively to pieces produced between 1949 and the late 1950's, although there is evidence to suggest that one or two pieces continued to be offered until 1961.

For the most part, the pieces are glazed and decorated with numerous variations in color for some of the examples. They bear the makersmark D (see Appendix A), the only known exception being the Basset Hound in the bisque decoration (RPC-127-02). Examples of this piece are known to exist bearing makersmark F which was first adopted by the Boehm studio for unlimited edition sculptures in 1959. Makersmark D is

generally believed to have been discontinued in 1959; however, dog subjects which are supposed to have closed later than 1959 still bear makersmark D. This may indicate that production of the dogs was actually discontinued by 1959 (with the above exception) and the pieces simply remained on the market for another year or two.

RPC-101-01 BOXER, small, glazed, decorated Fawn (RP-101) 250 made
RPC-101-02 BOXER, small, glazed, decorated Brindle (RP-102) 150 made
RPC-101-03 BOXER, large, glazed, decorated Fawn (RP-103) 400 made
RPC-101-04 BOXER, large, glazed, decorated Brindle (RP-104) 100 made

These sculptures depict the Boxer in show position (hind legs stretched back, forelegs together, head facing one-eighth left) and are grouped in the same series, even though there seems to be a subtle variation of position between the large and small pieces. The large example measures 9″ x 8½″ and carries the Boehm Studiomark Number 102. The small Boxer bears Boehm Studiomark Number 101 and measures 5″ x 4½″.

The Boxer first appears on the 1952 price list. It is quite possible this piece was actually introduced at a much earlier date: say, 1949. The Brindle decoration apparently was discontinued in 1958, while the studio continued to produce the Fawn coloration for another year.

RPC-102-01 SCOTTISH TERRIER, glazed, decorated Gray (RP-105) 10 made
RPC-102-02 SCOTTISH TERRIER, glazed, decorated Black (RPC-106) 100 made

As are most of Ed Boehm's standing dogs, the Scottish Terrier is depicted in show position with his forelegs together, ears and tail up, head forward, and his right hind leg stretched back while his left hind leg is pulled in. The piece is 6″ x 4½″ and carries the Boehm Studiomark Number 103. This, too, is an early piece, introduced in 1951.

The piece appears on the 1952 price list. The last year of production seems to have been 1957.

RPC-103-01 AMERICAN COCKER, glazed, decorated Red (RP-107) 100 made
RPC-103-02 AMERICAN COCKER, glazed, decorated Buff (RP-108) 100 made
RPC-103-03 AMERICAN COCKER, glazed, decorated Black (RP-109) 200 made*
RPC-103-04 AMERICAN COCKER, glazed, decorated Brown and White (RP-110) 200 made*
RPC-103-05 AMERICAN COCKER, glazed, decorated Black and White (RP-111) 200 made*
RPC-103-06 AMERICAN COCKER, glazed, White (RP-112) approximately 20 made

Another early example was first offered in 1951. The piece is 6½" x 5" and modeled in show position with the head turned one-quarter right. The piece carries Boehm Studiomark Number 104. The Black and Red decorations were discontinued in 1958 and the piece itself in 1959. It is interesting to note that no price list specifies the glazed White decoration, although the others are mentioned. This would lead to the logical conclusion that the White pieces were not produced in any kind of quantity, although verification of this is impossible at this time. The other decorations appear to have been made in fairly large quantity, from about 100 pieces of the Red and the Buff to 200 of the others.

RPC-104-01 LARGE COCKER SPANIEL, glazed, decorated Buff (RP-169) unique
RPC-104-02 LARGE COCKER SPANIEL, glazed, White—rare

This piece is similar in modeling to the RPC-103 series, except for its size, 8½" x 10½". It appears on no price list and it must, therefore, be assumed that this was a slow-moving piece when it was introduced and was discontinued before any quantity had been produced. The heft of this piece is quite dif-

ferent from that of the other Boehm dogs. The body seems almost solid, or at least the walls are thick, and the feel and texture are quite unlike the classic Boehm porcelain body. They were produced before there was even a Boehm Studio and they represent slip experiments by Ed Boehm when he was perfecting his body. This was therefore one of the earliest pieces. Since it was a piece developed for slip experiments, it is remarkable that it was decorated at all. We have been advised that Ed did make one as a birthday present for someone in 1945 or 1947 while working at Dr. Berliner's hospital. In any event, it is certain that the piece was decorated considerably later than it was made. No auction record has come to light. It carries the Boehm Studiomark Number 104.

I believe the decorated Buff piece was experimental and was personally modeled and cast by Ed Boehm.

RPC-105 AMERICAN COCKER WITH PHEASANT, glazed, decorated (RP-113) unique

This piece, on a rectangular, beige-colored base, depicts a Brown and White Cocker standing guard over a dead pheasant. It measures 7" x 5" and only one was produced, around 1953. It carries no Boehm Studiomark Number and was obviously not for sale.

RPC-106-01 WIRE-HAIRED FOX TERRIER, glazed, decorated White with patches of black and brown (RP-114) 150 made*
RPC-106-02 WIRE-HAIRED FOX TERRIER, glazed, White—3 made*

There seem to have been approximately 150 of the decorated example produced, although few have come onto the market. The piece measures 7" x 6¼" and depicts the Wire-Haired Fox Terrier in show position with the head turned half right and the tail up. The decorated example carries the Boehm Studiomark Number 105. The glazed

White piece is extremely rare. There may have been as few as one or two produced, although there is no way to verify this. The piece last appears on the 1959 price list.

RPC-107-01 DANE, RECLINING, glazed, decorated Fawn (RP-115) 100 made
RPC-107-02 DANE, RECLINING, glazed, decorated Brindle (RP-116) 100 made*
RPC-107-03 DANE, RECLINING, glazed, decorated Harlequin (RP-117) 100 made
RPC-107-04 DANE, RECLINING, bisque, undecorated (RP-118) 50 made

This is another early dog, produced in some quantity (approximately 100 of each decoration and 50 undecorated), measuring 10" x 5½". This sculpture depicts a reclining Dane with head up, ears erect. The left forepaw is crossed over the right forepaw. The tail is curled to the left, around and over the left hind paw. This piece carries Boehm Studiomark Number 106.

The piece was introduced in 1951. The Harlequin and Brindle decorations last appeared on the 1958 price list and the Fawn on the 1959 list.

RPC-108-01 GREAT DANE, glazed, decorated Fawn (RP-119) 75 made
RPC-108-02 GREAT DANE, glazed, decorated Brindle (RP-120) 25 made

RPC-105

151

RPC-108-02

RPC-109-01   RPC-109-03

RPC-110

RPC-108-03 GREAT DANE, glazed, decorated Harlequin (RP-121) 50 made

RPC-108-04 GREAT DANE, glazed, undecorated (RP-122) rare

This piece introduced in 1951 is also called "Noble Dane" and carries the Boehm Studiomark Number 107. It depicts a 13″ x 12½″ standing male with head up, ears pointed. The left legs are leading; the tail is down and curved over right hind leg to hock of left hind leg.

The Great Dane was discontinued in 1956. The total number made would appear to be about 150: 75 Fawn, 25 Brindle and 50 Harlequin. Again no verification is possible, and not even an educated guess could place a number on the glazed, undecorated examples, except that few were made.

RPC-109-01 DOBERMAN PINSCHER, glazed, decorated Black (RP-123) 200 made

RPC-109-02 DOBERMAN PINSCHER, glazed, decorated Red (RP-124) 10 made

RPC-109-03 DOBERMAN PINSCHER, glazed, undecorated (RP-125) less than 25 made

A standing male in show position, this 9¼″ x 9¼″ sculpture depicts the Doberman with forelegs together, right hind leg stretched back, the bobbed tail raised and the head up with ears pointed. This piece carries the Boehm Studiomark Number 108. It was first offered in 1951; the last listing was in 1957. There seem to have been approximately 200 done in Black, 10 in Red, and the number produced undecorated is not known.

RPC-110 STANDING FOXHOUND, glazed, decorated (RP-126) 200 made

Although called "standing," this is actually a walking male foxhound with right foreleg and left hind leg leading; the head is turned one-quarter left and the tail is curled up. This sculpture is 9½″ x 9½″ and carries the Boehm Studiomark Number 109. It was probably produced in a quantity of 200, from 1951 through 1958.

There is every possibility that an undecorated example of this piece exists. However, it has not yet come to light.

RPC-111-01 RECLINING FOXHOUND, glazed, decorated (RP-127) 200 made*

RPC-111-02 RECLINING FOXHOUND, bisque, decorated (RP-128) 15 made

RPC-111-03 RECLINING FOXHOUND, bisque, undecorated (RP-129) 10 made

This is the first dog to appear in a decorated bisque finish. Only 15 were produced, along with 10 undecorated bisque and approximately 200 of the usual glazed, decorated. The piece is large, 13¼″ x 6¼″, showing a foxhound reclining on right rump with his right hind leg extending under his body to the left side. His left hind leg is pulled up and resting on the inner side of his hock. His head is up and he is wearing a wide buckled collar. His right foreleg is extended and left foreleg is turned under at the knee. It carries Boehm Studiomark Number 110, and was made from 1952 to 1961.

The Reclining Foxhound is an extremely appealing dog and among my favorite pieces by Ed Boehm.

RPC-112-01 FRENCH POODLE, STANDING, glazed, decorated Gray (RP-130) 25 made

RPC-112-02 FRENCH POODLE, STANDING, glazed, decorated White (RP-131) 100 made

RPC-112-03 FRENCH POODLE, STANDING, glazed, decorated Black (RP-132) 25 made

RPC-112-04 FRENCH POODLE, STANDING, glazed, decorated Apricot (RP-133) 4 made

This well-clipped and beribboned poodle is 9″ x 7½″ and depicts a standing French Poodle with left hind leg and right foreleg leading. The dog has double pom-poms on the hind legs with single pom-poms on the forelegs and tail. The hair on the rump is clipped close and tightly curled while the hair on the forequarters is long and full. There is a ribbon and bow above the face at

*See page 79

the hairline. This piece carries Boehm Studiomark Number 111.

The Gray and White pieces are listed on the 1952 price list; they were discontinued in 1959.

RPC-113-01 SPRINGER, glazed, decorated Liver and White (RP-135) 100 made

RPC-113-02 SPRINGER, glazed, decorated Black and White (RP-136) 100 made *

The Springer is depicted in show position with its short tail horizontal and the head up and forward. The size of the sculpture is 8½" x 6¾" and it carries Boehm Studiomark Number 112. It was discontinued in 1959.

The Springer is a beautiful example of Ed Boehm's most mature work in the dogs and it was done in fairly small quantity.

RPC-114-01 BEAGLE, glazed, decorated White with Black and Tan (RP-137) 400 made

RPC-114-02 BEAGLE, glazed, undecorated (RP-138) number made unknown

Again in show position (head turned half right and tail up), this piece measures 7" x 6¼" and carries Boehm Studiomark Number 113. There seem to have been about 400 decorated, but, unfortunately, no estimate is possible of the number done in white. However, few were ever sold. The decorated piece was listed in 1952, the year of its introduction, and closed in 1961.

RPC-115-01 POINTER, glazed, decorated Liver and White (RP-139) approximately 25 made

RPC-115-02 POINTER, glazed, decorated Black and White (RP-140) approximately 25 made

This is a sculpture of a walking male pointer with left hind leg and right foreleg leading. The right hind leg extends back and to the right. The Pointer's ears droop, the head is thrust slightly forward and the tail is up and back. This piece was introduced in 1952, but made its first appearance on a 1953 price list;

*See page 80

it was discontinued in 1959. The piece is 12½" x 7" and there are records indicating that approximately 275 were made: 150 in the Liver and White decoration and 125 in the Black and White. I believe these records are wrong. For the past 10 years I've been searching for this particular model and the extreme scarcity suggests to me that no more than approximately 25 of these pieces were made. Another possibility is that more were made and shipped, but that the packing was insufficiently sophisticated to support the long straight-out tail and that most of the tails were broken upon receipt by the retailers and the dogs were disposed of. At any rate there are practically none on the market, and those collectors of dogs who have searched diligently have been unable to find more than a few. There do not seem to be any auction records for this piece. It carries Boehm Studiomark Number 114.

RPC-116-01 BULL TERRIER, glazed, decorated Brindle (RP-142) 50 made

RPC-116-02 BULL TERRIER, glazed, undecorated (RP-141) 150 made

This is a male dog in show position, with ears up and tail horizontal, which measures 9½" x 7½". It is Number 115 on the Boehm Studiomark list. Introduced in 1953, it is believed that 150 of the undecorated and 50 in the Brindle decoration were produced before the piece was discontinued in 1957.

RPC-117-01 DACHSHUND, glazed, decorated Tan (RP-143) 150 made

RPC-117-02 DACHSHUND, glazed, decorated Black and Tan (RP-144) 50 made*

RPC-117-03 DACHSHUND, bisque, decorated Tan (RP-145) 50 made

RPC-117-04 DACHSHUND, glazed, undecorated (RP-146) 25 made

A male in show position (tail curved down and ears drooping), this piece is 9" x 5" and was the second dog figure to have been produced in a bisque decoration. It was introduced in 1953; the Black and Tan was discontinued in 1959 and the other decora-

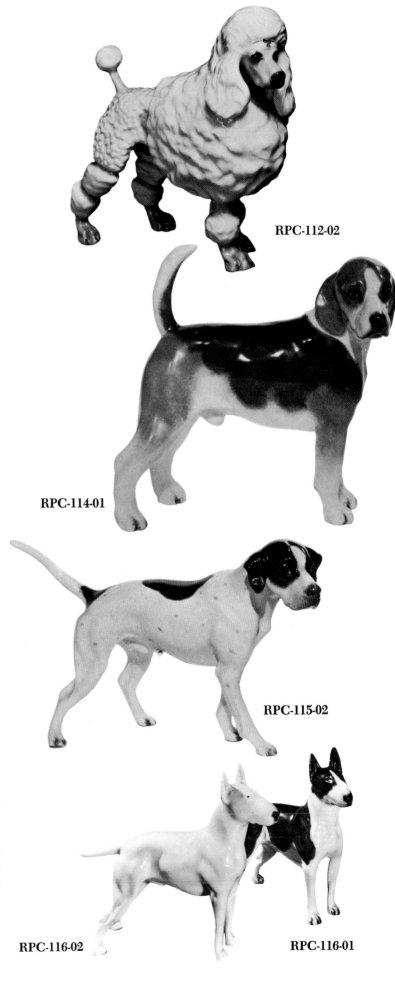

RPC-112-02

RPC-114-01

RPC-115-02

RPC-116-02   RPC-116-01

RPC-118-02

RPC-120

RPC-121

tions by 1961. The piece carries Boehm Studiomark Number 116 and there seem to have been about 150 with the glazed Tan decoration, 25 undecorated and 50 of each of the other two finishes.

RPC-118-01 LABRADOR RETRIEVER, glazed, decorated Black (RP-167) 100 made

RPC-118-02 LABRADOR RETRIEVER, glazed, decorated Lemon (RP-168) 25 made

This is a standing male with forelegs together, right hind leg stretched back. The head is turned half right and the tail is horizontal. This piece was introduced in 1953. It is 9″ x 6½″ and carries Boehm Studiomark Number 117. There seem to have been about 25 done in the Lemon decoration, which was discontinued in 1957, while approximately 100 were done in the Black and that decoration was continued until sometime in 1959. I have never personally seen a decorated Lemon Labrador Retriever, and it is quite possible that my estimate of 25 produced is quite high.

RPC-119-01 COLLIE, glazed, decorated Gold (RP-148) 25 made

RPC-119-02 COLLIE, glazed, decorated Tri-Colored (RP-149) 125 made*

RPC-119-03 COLLIE, glazed, undecorated (RP-151) less than 25 made

RPC-119-04 COLLIE, bisque, undecorated (RP-150) less than 25 made

The Collie is depicted in show position (with head up, ears turned down at tips, tail down) and was introduced in 1954. It measures 10″ x 8½″ and carries Boehm Studiomark Number 118. There is no way to determine how many of the undecorated pieces (either bisque or glazed) were produced. However, of the decorated, it is believed that approximately 25 were done in Gold and 125 in the Tri-Colored decoration.

RPC-120 GREYHOUND, RECLINING, glazed, decorated (RP-147) 10 made

*See page 80

There is little information available on this piece; it is 9″ long and there were only about 10 made. It carries the Boehm Studiomark Number 119 and appears only on the 1956 price list. However, our information places the date of its introduction at 1954.

RPC-121 WHIPPET, on base, bisque, undecorated (RP-152) unique

This is a one-of-a-kind piece. It is believed to have been sculpted in 1953, and the quality and design are exceptional. The piece is 12″ x 18″ and depicts a male standing, hind quarters in half crouch, left hind leg forward. The head is turned half right, ears back, tail curled down behind the left hind leg above the hock. The Whippet wears a collar. Although similar in position to the female of the RPC-122 series (see below) and carrying the same Boehm Studiomark Number (120), it has definite modeling differences. The base, too, is different, being oval with a textured surface. During the years that Walter Hoving was actively directing Tiffany's in New York, he became interested in Boehm and it is known that this large Whippet graces his office.

There is some evidence to indicate that this piece and the RPC-122 series were not sculpted by Ed Boehm or the Boehm Studios. Some years ago, I was shown a bronze Whippet sculpture which appeared identical to RPC-121 and RPC-122 except in size. Since it is quite possible to take a mold of a bronze, my belief is that the bronze I saw was the sculptural origin of the Whippets. Furthermore, the Whippet differs aesthetically from all of Boehm's other dogs. The Whippet is a mannered, decorative piece; Ed's own work is more natural.

RPC-122-01 WHIPPETS, pair, glazed, decorated White (RP-154) 8 made*

RPC-122-02 WHIPPETS, pair, bisque, undecorated (RP-153) 240 made

Male and female on individual bases, the sculptures measure 7¾″ x 5½″ and were introduced in 1954. The male is standing, hind

*See page 80-81

quarters in half crouch, left hind leg forward. The head is turned half right, ears back, tail curled down behind left hind leg above hock. The Whippets both wear collars. The female is standing, left foreleg drawn up and bent at the knee. Left hind leg is forward, and the head is turned over left shoulder. The female's ears are horizontal with tips drooping. Her tail curls down behind left hind leg above hock. She also wears a collar. The glazed and decorated examples were discontinued in 1957, while the bisque, undecorated pieces continued in production until 1961. Eight pairs of glazed, decorated were made, and 240 pairs of bisque, undecorated. The Boehm Studiomark Number is 120.

A pair of the Whippets was presented in 1958 by then President and Mrs. Eisenhower to the Prime Minister of Canada and is now in the collection of the Royal Ontario Museum.

RPC-123 POMERANIAN, glazed, decorated (RP-155) 25 made

In show position (with tail draped over back), the piece measures 4″ x 4″. We understand that it was first introduced in 1954. It carries the Boehm Studiomark Number 121, and it is believed that only 25 examples of this sculpture were produced.

RPC-124-01 KING CHARLES SPANIEL, glazed, decorated (RP-156) 5 made*
RPC-124-02 KING CHARLES SPANIEL, glazed, undecorated (RP-170) 2 made
RPC-124-03 KING CHARLES SPANIEL, bisque, undecorated—2 made

This is an extremely rare piece, only five having been done of the glazed, decorated and one or two each of the other decorations. The size is 3¼″ x 3″ and it carries the Boehm Studiomark Number 122. The only mention of this appealing little dog in any of the records is a listing in 1956. It is obvious that the piece was discontinued shortly after its introduction in 1954, even though

*See page 81

examples were still being merchandized in 1956. The location of one undecorated, glazed piece is known, in a private collection. Two of the glazed, decorated are also in a private collection.

RPC-125 SKYE TERRIER, glazed, decorated (RP-157) 5 made

This is another rare dog. Only five examples of this 3½″ high piece are known to exist and it is mentioned on only one price list, incorrectly identified as a Yorkshire Terrier, in 1956. The dog is depicted in show position and carries Boehm Studiomark Number 125. It is quite possible that an undecorated example, most likely glazed, may exist.

RPC-126-01 DALMATIAN "MIKE," glazed, decorated (RP-158) 400 made*
RPC-126-02 DALMATIAN "MIKE," bisque, decorated (RP-159) 200 made

"Mike" is the Anheuser-Busch mascot and this perky little 3″ x 1″ dog (seated, head up, tail curled around left leg and over paw) was originally intended to grace the seat of a model of the beer wagon drawn by the magnificent Anheuser-Busch Clydesdales. The wagon may someday be completed by Mrs. Boehm. The original molds which were made by Ed for Anheuser-Busch are still in existence. It is hoped that some day when the studio has the time and energy this piece will be produced. It is, of course, doubtful that it will ever be done commercially since the Anheuser-Busch people have an interest in this piece. When the larger work was delayed due to Ed Boehm's fanatical requirement for technical perfection, it was decided that "Mike" at least would see the light of day, and see it he did.

Nearly 600 of these pieces were sold between 1955 and 1959, the bulk of them (approximately 400) in the glazed decoration. This dog carries Boehm Studiomark Number 126. Either of these decorations is worth about the same, but for the serious collector, the bisque decoration is much to be preferred.

RPC-127-01 BASSET HOUND, glazed, decorated (RP-160) 310 made
RPC-127-02 BASSET HOUND, bisque, decorated (RP-161) 100 made

This floppy little dog is shown seated on his left hind leg with his head turned one-quarter right and his tail curled up at the tip. Its appeal is reflected in the number of pieces produced in the five years between its introduction in 1957 and its discontinuance in 1961: 100 in the bisque decoration and 310 in the glazed. The seated hound measures 7″ x 5¾″ and bears Boehm Studiomark Number 127. Examples of this piece are marked with makersmark F (see Appendix A), indicating that actual production of the Basset continued at least through 1960.

RPC-123   RPC-125

RPC-127-02

RPC-128

RPC-129-01

RPC-131

RPC-132

RPC-128 GERMAN SHEPHERD, glazed, decorated Tan and Black (RP-162) 25 made

The Shepherd is depicted in show position (with his head one-quarter right, right hind leg fully stretched, left hind leg drawn in) and stands 8″ high. It carries Boehm Studiomark Number 129. It is one of the rarer dogs, there having been only about 25 made, and it appears on only two price lists, 1957 and 1959. It is quite possible that a glazed, undecorated piece exists.

RPC-129-01 PUG, glazed, decorated (RP-163) 48 made
RPC-129-02 PUG, bisque, undecorated (RP-164) less than 5 made

This is a male dog, collared, in show position with tail curled to the left on the rump, and stands 5″ high. It bears the Boehm Studiomark Number 130 and, as with the Shep-

herd, appears on only two price lists: 1957 and 1959. Of the glazed and decorated pieces, approximately 48 were completed. The number in undecorated bisque is not known and it may well be that only one or two were left undecorated.

RPC-130 ENGLISH BULL DOG, glazed, decorated (RP-165) 46 made*

This is a standing male with head and chest thrust forward, forelegs spread and tail down. The piece is 7″ long and bears Boehm Studiomark Number 131. It shows up in 1957 and 1959 lists, and there seem to have been only 46 produced.

RPC-131 SHEEP DOG PUP, bisque, decorated (RP-166) 10 made

This pup is seated with left hind leg out, mouth slightly opened and head turned one-quarter left. It is 4½″ high and carries

*See page 81

Boehm Studiomark Number 132. This appealing work for some reason seems to have been discontinued before any quantity was made; only about 10 were produced and the piece does not appear on any price list as far as we have been able to determine. There can be no doubt, however, regarding its worth and rarity.

RPC-132 POODLE, RECLINING, bisque, decorated white with blue collar (RP-134) 2,300 made

This sculpture depicts a poodle reclining with forelegs extended, head tilted back and turned half right. The mouth is open, hair long, tail rests behind the right hind leg, curled up. This long-haired, collared poodle was obviously a popular sculpture, since almost 2,300 were produced in the three short years it was available: 1959 through 1961. It is 5″ long and bears the Boehm Studiomark Number 133.

II. The Cats

The two cat subjects were both introduced about 1956, or possibly a year earlier, and were not produced in any great quantity. Obviously, Ed Boehm preferred to devote his talent to other subjects.

As a matter of fact, there is even some doubt (especially in the case of the RPC-202 series) that these were originally sculpted by Boehm. There is reason to believe that this piece may have been done from a commercial mold, as were a number of the earlier Boehm pieces. This supposition is lent weight by the number of copies which have come to light—copies that are definitely not Boehm porcelain and definitely not decorated by Boehm, and yet appear to be structurally identical. It must be assumed that a deliberate copy would at least attempt to come closer to the quality and beauty of the original. Most of the copies of the RPC-202 are crudely done from obviously inferior materials and it does not seem that these are deliberate attempts to duplicate a piece of Boehm sculpture.

This whole question remains conjectural, as does so much about Boehm.

RPC-201-01 CAT PLAYING WITH BALL,
glazed, decorated (RP-203) 51 made
RPC-201-02 CAT PLAYING WITH BALL,
glazed, undecorated—less than 10 made

This is a crouching kitten with a ball between its front paws and measures 5½" x 3". It appears that there were 51 of the decorated produced. The piece was first introduced in 1953. The number of glazed, undecorated pieces is unknown. The Boehm Studiomark Number is 124 and the pieces are marked with makersmark D.

RPC-202-01 CAT WITH TWO KITTENS,
glazed, decorated (RP-201) 74 made
RPC-202-02 CAT WITH TWO KITTENS,
bisque, decorated (RP-202) 62 made
RPC-202-03 CAT WITH TWO KITTENS,
bisque, undecorated—less than 10 made

This piece is 5" x 4" and first appears on the 1956 price list, decoration unspecified. It is a gray and white tabby, seated, protecting two kittens, one gray and white and one orange. This piece carries the Boehm Studiomark Number 123. Approximately 74 examples were glazed and decorated and 62 were bisque, decorated. The number of undecorated pieces is unknown. Most of the pieces carry the makersmark D. However, there are a number of examples of the decorated bisque with makersmark F. This leads us to believe that the production of the glazed decoration was discontinued sometime in 1959 and only the bisque, decorated examples produced thereafter, until the piece was discontinued entirely in 1961.

RPC-202-03

RPC-201-01   RPC-201-02

157

III. The Horses

With three exceptions, all of the equestrian and equine sculptures were produced between 1950 and 1961. The exceptions are the Polo Player, which closed in 1964, the Bay Hunter, which has just closed as a limited edition and the Adios Portrait, which was brought out in 1969, the first new horse subject introduced by Boehm since 1957.

Ed's involvement with horses was lifelong: he bred them, he raised them and he raced them. There is no wonder then that the first important piece Ed Boehm ever did was a horse and it is somehow fitting that one of the last pieces he turned his hand to was the great Adios Portrait.

It is hard to imagine Ed Boehm without animals, and I never knew him to be out of touch with horses. They responded to his love for them and his mere presence would calm a frightened horse and ease the pain of a sick one.

I remember his telling me the story of how he bought a race horse one day which had never won a race, but Ed liked the horse and her genetic history was excellent. Ed went to the track and watched her race week after week until he discovered something the trainer had overlooked completely. This mare preferred to run in daylight. Her preference was due to the fact that she was frightened by the bright lights of night racing, especially the powerful lights that flashed on at the finish line. Since she was a smart horse, she quickly realized that as she approached the line these lights flashed. Therefore as she approached the line, she invariably slowed down in anticipation and lost the race. Not until Ed came along did anyone notice that this only happened at night. Ed retrained her, raced her only in the daytime, and she became one of the prides of his stable. It was this ability to observe the animals' needs and habits which surfaced again and again in all of Boehm's work.

While Boehm was capable of turning out a questionable dog, or a somewhat less than perfect bird, all of his horses were perfect. Every example listed below is a masterpiece in its own right.

RPC-301-01 PERCHERON MARE AND FOAL, on base, glazed, decorated Black Foal—possibly unique*
RPC-301-02 PERCHERON MARE AND FOAL, on base, glazed, decorated Dapple Gray Foal (RP-308) 2 made

This is the first Boehm sculpture. It was modeled in 1944. However, this piece was not cast into porcelain until 1950 and only three were produced. The sculpture is 9½" x 14", a dapple gray mare with foal. The first example of the three was decorated with a black foal and represents the beginning of the Boehm experience. The other two have dapple colts. The mare is standing, head thrust out, ears up, tail cut short, right hind leg drawn up with tip of her hoof touching the ground. The colt is standing against the right side of the mare, forelegs together, left hind leg forward, head up and turned one-eighth to the right. The mare and foal were later reproduced as separate pieces (RPC-306 series and RPC-308 series). This particular piece has been given a separate series number because of its historic value.

This, the first piece of sculpture ever modeled by Edward Marshall Boehm, deserves some comment. The date is interesting. In 1944, the United States was still at war and Ed Boehm had certainly not yet committed himself to the creation of art porcelain. It can be assumed that it was a piece of work done to escape the boredom of Army life. Since it was in that year that Helen Franzolin and Ed Boehm met in Pawling, N.Y., it is quite possible that Helen Boehm had an involvement with the Boehm experience from its inception. It took six long years until the Percheron Mare and Foal was cast in porcelain in 1950, and by that time Ed Boehm had learned what he could do with that difficult material. Only three pieces were ever produced and these three pieces now rest in major collections around the world.

RPC-302

The example with the Black Foal was done by Ed Boehm as a gift to his father, Edward D. Boehm, and for many years was in the elder Boehm's private collection. Because of its personal association with Boehm Senior and Junior, and because it can be considered the absolute first example of Ed's work, this piece, with the Black Foal, is, in my opinion, of great historical importance. There is an indication that after Ed Boehm decorated the original mare and black colt for his father another piece might have been done later on. This second example, if indeed there was one, must have been decorated at the same time that the two dapple foals were decorated. Certainly this piece which was done by the son for the father makes this example unique.

It is rare, in trying to trace the history of an artist, to be able to put your finger on precisely the point at which an experience commenced. In this case we are able to reach back and see Ed Boehm still in the Army, probably in an Army hospital, passing the time by "playing" in clay. This piece of sculpture cast a long shadow forward.

As far as value is concerned, these pieces should command a premium because they were the first pieces ever designed by Boehm. They carry an additional premium because of the beauty and authority of the work.

*See page 40

RPC-302 BELGIAN STALLION, glazed, decorated Chestnut (RP-301) 5 made

This is a prancing stallion, 15″ x 12″, produced in 1950 and marked with makersmark D. The piece depicts a massive chestnut animal,with a short tightly braided tail, with rosebuds braided into the mane. There were only about five produced in all. It is reasonable to assume that the shades of chestnut vary with each piece.

RPC-303-01 THOROUGHBRED, glazed, decorated — extremely rare, possibly unique

RPC-303-02 THOROUGHBRED, bisque, decorated — extremely rare, possibly unique

RPC-303-03 THOROUGHBRED WITH BLANKET, glazed, decorated (RP-316) extremely rare, possibly unique

RPC-303-04 THOROUGHBRED WITH BLANKET, bisque, decorated (blanket glazed) 3 made

RPC-303-05 THOROUGHBRED WITH BLANKET, AND EXERCISE BOY, glazed, decorated — extremely rare, possibly unique

RPC-303-06 THOROUGHBRED WITH BLANKET AND EXERCISE BOY, bisque, decorated (blanket glazed) extremely rare, possibly unique

RPC-303-07 THOROUGHBRED (Saddled) WITH EXERCISE BOY, glazed, decorated (RP-317) extremely rare, possibly unique

RPC-303-08 THOROUGHBRED (Saddled) WITH EXERCISE BOY, bisque, decorated (RP-318) extremely rare, possibly unique

RPC-303-09 THOROUGHBRED (Saddled) WITH EXERCISE BOY, bisque, undecorated extremely rare, possibly unique

RPC-303-10 THOROUGHBRED WITH EXERCISE BOY AND JOCKEY, glazed, decorated (RP-319) extremely rare, possibly unique

RPC-303-11 THOROUGHBRED WITH EXERCISE BOY AND JOCKEY, bisque,

RPC-303-02

RPC-303-10

RPC-303-07

RPC-303-12

159

RPC-304-01

RPC-305-05

decorated (RP-325) extremely rare, possibly unique

RPC-303-12 THOROUGHBRED WITH JOCKEY, glazed, decorated — extremely rare, possibly unique

RPC-303-13 THOROUGHBRED WITH JOCKEY, bisque, undecorated—extremely rare, possibly unique

This is a walking animal and was decorated in varying shades of bay and dapple gray. The piece is 11″ x 7½″ on an oval base with a rail fence at one side and bears the makersmark D. The number made was originally believed to be about 10 altogether; however, as more examples come to light, the estimate must be revised. At this writing we know of at least three examples of the RPC-303-04 alone. There may be more. However, because of the large number of variations in the basic sculpture, it must be assumed that examples of this are among the rarest of Boehm pieces.

There is a particularly liquid quality about the sculpture of this piece. It is a quality which was not repeated in any of Ed Boehm's later work. This is most clearly

noticed in the almost, but not quite, comical aspect of the exercise boy.

The pieces were done in 1950 and were not merchandised, with the exception of the RPC-303-07 and 08 and the RPC-303-11.

Suffice it to say that the pieces are extremely rare and extremely valuable. It can safely be assumed that no two pieces are identical in structure and coloring. In fact, the studio recalls that the horses were done in various shades of chestnut and bay, in dapple gray and at least one palomino. The blankets were plaid, mainly yellow and green, and most had a red edging. The clothing of the exercise boys varies and each piece was done with a different number on the horse and different silks on the jockey.

RPC-304-01 THOROUGHBRED, RACING, WITH JOCKEY, glazed, decorated (RP-327) unique

RPC-304-02 THOROUGHBRED, RACING, WITH JOCKEY, bisque, decorated (RP-320) unique

RPC-304-03 THOROUGHBRED, RACING, WITH JOCKEY, bisque, undecorated (RP-321) unique

With the exception of the horse's gait and the position of the jockey, this series is similar in structure to the RPC-303 series. Current information indicates only one of each decoration. It bears makersmark D.

RPC-305-01 PERCHERON STALLION, glazed, decorated Dapple Gray with roses (RP-305) 50 made*

RPC-305-02 PERCHERON STALLION, glazed, decorated with roses, blue finish, approximately 5 made

RPC-305-03 PERCHERON STALLION, glazed, decorated Dapple Gray (no roses), pink and blue ribbon on mane (RP-302) 100 made

RPC-305-04 PERCHERON STALLION, bisque, decorated Dapple Gray (RP-303) approximately 20 made

RPC-305-05 PERCHERON STALLION, bisque, undecorated (RP-304) approximately 50 made

This is a prancing stallion, 12″ x 9¼″, with braided and beribboned tail and braided mane (Boehm Studiomark Number 201). In the case of RPC-305-01, rosebuds have been

*See page 22

braided into both mane and tail. It is almost impossible to find a Percheron Stallion with roses in which one or more of the roses are not broken off. This sort of breakage is so prevalent that I tend to think of a piece with broken roses, if it is properly repaired, to be as close to mint as one can expect in this particular example.

The Stallion with roses was purchased by the Metropolitan Museum of Art in January 1951. Thus, it was one of the first pieces of Boehm to receive official museum recognition.

Production was discontinued in 1959.

RCP-306-01 PERCHERON MARE, glazed, decorated Dapple Gray (RP-306) 50 made

RPC-306-02 PERCHERON MARE, bisque, undecorated (RP-307) approximately 50 made

As previously mentioned, this sculpture is identical to the mare of RPC-301. The piece is 11½″ x 8″ and carries the Boehm Studiomark Number 202. The pieces are marked with makersmark D and there seem to have been approximately 50 produced. The makersmark would seem to indicate that production of the piece was discontinued in 1959.

In spite of the fact that the studio records indicate that approximately 50 of each were made, my feeling is that considerably fewer than that were done.

RPC-307-01 HUNTER, glazed, decorated Dapple Gray (RP-328) 5 made

RPC-307-02 HUNTER, glazed, decorated Bay—unique

RPC-307-03 HUNTER, bisque, decorated Dapple Gray (RP-323) 3 made

RPC-307-04 HUNTER, bisque, decorated Bay (RP-322) limited edition of 250

RPC-307-05 HUNTER, bisque, undecorated —unique

The history of the Hunter is extremely interesting. One of the earliest of Boehm sculptures, it is the only one of that early group (aside from the Pietà Madonna) to survive

the drastic cutback in the size of the collection that was made in 1962.

Introduced in 1952, it is 14″ x 14″, a beautiful standing, saddled horse. It carries Boehm Studiomark Number 203.

It is impossible to set an accurate figure on the number of glazed pieces produced in those early years, although it is believed that only one glazed Bay Hunter exists. The Dapple Gray decoration in bisque finish is thought to number only five in all and was offered for sale at least through 1959.

The collection revision of 1962 found the bisque, decorated Bay the only remaining Hunter, in a limited edition of 250. This number includes *all* the decorations.

Through 1959, the Hunters carried the makersmark D. In 1959, the Hunter was designated a limited edition and from that time on, carried the limited edition makersmark E.

RPC-308-01 COLT, glazed, decorated Black (RP-309) 10 made

RPC-308-02 COLT, glazed, decorated Dapple Gray (RP-311) 100 made

RPC-308-03 COLT, glazed, decorated Palomino (RP-310) 100 made

RPC-308-04 COLT, glazed, decorated Pinto (black and white) approximately 25 made

RPC-308-05 COLT, glazed, decorated Pinto (brown and white) approximately 25 made

RPC-308-06 COLT, glazed, decorated Bay (RP-326) less than 10 made

RPC-308-07 COLT, bisque, decorated Dapple Gray (RP-312) 75 made

RPC-308-08 COLT, bisque, undecorated (RP-313) less than 10 made

As mentioned at the beginning of this section, this piece is the same sculpture as the Colt of RPC-301. It is a small piece, 5¾″ x 6¼″, carrying the Boehm Studiomark Number 204 and makersmark D.

It appears to have been introduced in 1952 in the Black, Gray and Palomino decorations; it was discontinued in 1959. After 1953, only the Dapple Gray decorations were merchandized, except for the sale of the undecorated bisque remainders in 1960.

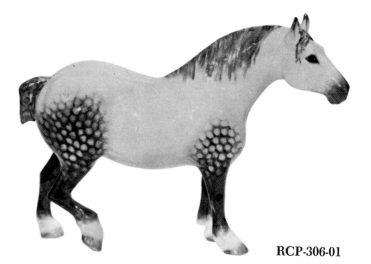

RCP-306-01

RPC-307-04

RPC-308-03   RPC-308-02

RPC-309-01 ARABIAN STALLIONS, glazed, decorated (RP-315) 48 made
RPC-309-02 ARABIAN STALLIONS, bisque, decorated—approximately 5 made
RPC-309-03 ARABIAN STALLIONS, bisque, undecorated (RP-314) 82 made

Two rearing Arabians with manes flying and tails curving are mounted on individual oval bases in this sculpture which bears makersmark D and Boehm Studiomark Number 205. Each piece measures 10¼″ x 7½″.

The undecorated, bisque examples were introduced in 1953 and were discontinued late in 1961. In 1956 and 1957 glazed and decorated examples were being made. Few were made and it may have represented one of the many experiments with that piece before the bisque decoration was abandoned. It is estimated that 82 pairs were done undecorated and 48 in the glazed decoration.

RPC-310 POLO PLAYER, bisque, decorated (RP-324) 100 made*

In 1957, then President and Mrs. Dwight D. Eisenhower commissioned Ed Boehm to design a sculpture to be presented to Queen Elizabeth II and Prince Philip of England. The result was this magnificent Polo Player, 14″ x 13½″, with the pony rearing beside a goal post and the rider holding a mallet about to strike the ball. The rider's colors and number are those of the Prince. The presentation piece was mounted on a wooden base to which was affixed a plaque bearing the Presidential Seal and the Royal Arms. It carries Boehm Studiomark Number 206. After the presentation of the prototype° the piece was designated a limited edition of 100 and offered for sale.

No one can have a really serious collection of Boehm without owning the Polo Player. It was the Polo Player which demonstrated to the English what Americans were capable

*Two prototype sculptures were made, one being presented to the Queen and the other put aside for the Studio collection. The balance of the edition, 98 pieces, was offered for public sale. It should be noted that a prototype of every limited edition was set aside for the Studio collection.

*See page 25

RPC-309-03

of in porcelain; and it was the Polo Player, through President Eisenhower, that gave Ed Boehm the encouragement to carry on.

RPC-311-01 ADIOS, glazed, decorated—unique
RPC-311-02 ADIOS, bisque, decorated (RP-329) limited edition, 130 made*

This magnificent champion standing bay, introduced as a limited edition of 500 pieces in 1969, was to be the last horse subject sculpted by Boehm. The edition finally closed in June 1974 with only 130 made. The first sculpture, the only one produced with a glazed finish, was presented by Boehm to Adios's owners, Mr. and Mrs. Delvin Miller of Pennsylvania. The remainder of the edition was completed in the bisque finish. The piece is 14″ x 15″, on a walnut base, and a biographical booklet about this great horse accompanies each sculpture sold. Adios carries Boehm Studiomark Number 400-05.

As mentioned before, this is one of the last pieces Ed sculpted. He closed his life as a porcelain maker with a horse, just as he opened it.

Boehm collectors, because they narrowly focus their attention on the birds, have overlooked the enormous accomplishment this piece represents. The demand for this sculpture was, as a result, never heavy. I believe that in the future the Adios portrait will become equal in importance to the birds.

*See page 43

IV. Livestock

With one exception, RPC-409, all of the livestock subjects were produced between 1950 and 1959. All of the examples that have come to light have borne makersmark D, although the dates of the introduction of the various pieces would seem to indicate that makersmark A, B and C must also have been used on the earlier examples.

By 1959, production of the livestock subjects had ceased; however, white bisque examples of some of the pieces were still available through 1961. These were part of the original production which had not been decorated and were offered for sale until the supply was exhausted. It is quite possible that several decorated examples were also in this category.

It must have been difficult for Ed Boehm to resist producing cattle subjects after 1959. So much of Ed's personal philosophy was built upon principles of genetic selection, involving the breeding of cattle and horses, that I am sure there were times that he wished he could go back to sculpting the magnificent specimens which he bred so successfully.

Up to the moment of his death, Ed Boehm was deeply concerned with the breeding of important race horses and high-output dairy cows. His horses and cows were always prize winners in their classes. It was an exciting event to visit the barns at the Boehm farm near Washington Crossing.

RPC-401 HOLSTEIN, glazed, decorated (RP-414) 15 made

The Holstein was the first cattle subject to be produced by the Boehm studio. It depicts a Holstein standing, his head facing one-quarter left, his left hind leg forward with his tail down over the hock of the right hind leg. It was introduced, at the latest, in 1950, and measures 16″ x 9¼″. It carries Boehm Studiomark Number 300.

RPC-402-01 HEREFORD BULL, glazed, decorated (RP-403) 36 made

RPC-402-02 HEREFORD BULL, bisque, decorated (RP-402) 36 made

RPC-402-03 HEREFORD BULL, bisque, undecorated (RP-401) 24 made

RPC-402-04 HEREFORD BULL, on base with presentation plaque, glazed, decorated (RP-416) 3 made*

This sculpture depicts a Hereford Bull walking, left hind leg leading, right foreleg drawn up with his head one-quarter left. The piece measures 10½″ x 5½″ and carries Boehm Studiomark Number 301. The number produced is assumed to run about 100 in total.

The Hereford Bull, with the Percheron Stallion, was one of the first pieces of Boehm to receive recognition as porcelain art. An example of the glazed, decorated Bull was purchased by the Curator of the American Wing of the Metropolitan Museum of Art in New York in 1951.

The Hereford was first introduced in 1950, and was discontinued in 1959. Pieces, most likely the undecorated examples, continued to be available through 1961.

Before the destruction of the mold, three examples were produced on a gold base (RPC-402-04), one of which was presented to President and Mrs. Eisenhower by the Boehms. This presentation led eventually to a number of Presidential commissions, including the Polo Player and the Whippets.

RPC-403 HEREFORD COW, glazed, decorated—unique

This piece has only recently come to light. There is only one in existence and its story is rather amusing. It seems that a gentleman from Pennsylvania appeared one day at the Boehm studio and admired the Hereford Bull. However, he wished to have a cow as well. Mr. Boehm obliged (he must have needed the money badly), performed the necessary alterations on the unfired Hereford Bull, and the cow was born, only to disappear into Pennsylvania for over 15

*See page 26

years. Happily, it has been rediscovered and can be included in this listing.

RPC-404-01 ANGUS BULL, glazed, decorated (RP-405) 100 made

RPC-404-02 ANGUS BULL, bisque, decorated (RP-404) 100 made

Also introduced in 1950, the Angus is 8¼″ x 5″ and depicts a standing bull with his head turned one-quarter left and his left hind leg forward. It carries Boehm Studiomark Number 302. There appear to have been approximately 200 made.

RPC-405 ANGUS COW, bisque, undecorated, unique

At the time this catalog was being prepared, a good deal of evidence pointed to the fact that an Angus Cow had indeed been made. Later information indicates that an Angus Cow was never made. However, it was too late to reassign the RPC number and I am not entirely convinced that sometime or other Ed did not perform the necessary surgery.

RPC-406-01 SHORTHORN BULL, glazed, decorated Roan (RP-406) 50 made

RPC-406-02 SHORTHORN BULL, glazed, decorated Red (RP-407) 100 made

RPC-406-03 SHORTHORN BULL, glazed, undecorated (RP-408) 25 made

The Shorthorn was introduced in 1951 and discontinued in 1959. The piece is 8½″ x 5″ and depicts a bull standing with his left hind leg forward and his head turned one-quarter left. It carries the Boehm Studiomark Number 303.

RPC-407-01 BRAHMAN BULL, glazed, decorated, Dapple Gray (RP-409) 50 made

RPC-407-02 BRAHMAN BULL, glazed, decorated Red (RP-411) 25 made

RPC-407-03 BRAHMAN BULL, glazed, White (RP-410) 5 made

RPC-401

RPC-402-01

RPC-403

RPC-404-01

RPC-407-04 BRAHMAN BULL, bisque, undecorated (RP-412) 10 made

The Brahman was introduced in 1953 and was available until 1961, when production was discontinued. This most marvelous piece of sculpture measures 12″ x 10″ and depicts a bull standing, his right hind leg extended and his head turned one-half right. It carries the Boehm Studiomark

Number 304. There appear to have been 100 made in all decorations, although the paucity of records for this piece, as with all the early Boehms, leaves us with no exact count.

RPC-408 LAMB, bisque, decorated (RP-413) 50 made*

This charming little sculpture (7½″ x 4¼″)

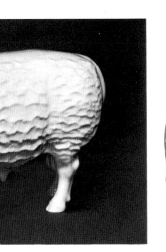

RPC-406-03

RPC-407-01

depicts a sitting Lamb with its left foreleg extended in front and bent at the knee with the right foreleg tucked under the right side, hind legs together and forward in front of the body. This piece was introduced in 1957 and appears only on two lists, 1957 and 1959. It carries Boehm Studiomark Number 305 and it has been assumed to have been produced in a quantity of about 150. However, from its merchandizing history, and from the fact that few examples of this piece have come to light, we must conclude that the 150 figure is too high and far fewer (perhaps as few as 50) were actually produced.

RPC-409 QUADRUPLET BLACK ANGUS CALVES, glazed, decorated (RP-415) unique

Designed as a gift in 1963 for Ed Boehm's friends Mr. and Mrs. Oliver H. Delchamps, whose Angus cow had borne quadruplet calves a few years before (an extremely rare occurrence), the Quads are unique both in number produced and beauty of composition. The sculpture stands on a thin slab of porcelain and is mounted on a rectangular ebony base.

Six months were required before this sculpture was successfully fired, three examples having been ruined, either in the greenware stage or in the decorating kiln.

This piece, of course, never was for sale and never will be for sale, as Mr. Delchamps has already indicated that it is being held for a museum of his choice.

Before closing this section on Ed Boehm's livestock subjects, we must say a word or two about copies. It seems that the Hereford and Brahman Bulls have been reproduced by the Japanese in plastic! And, from what we gather from the Boehm Studio, they're quite good copies. It is a compliment to any artist for someone to go to the trouble of copying his work when ready-made commercial molds of other sculptors are available. Certainly the Japanese cannot be faulted for poor taste.

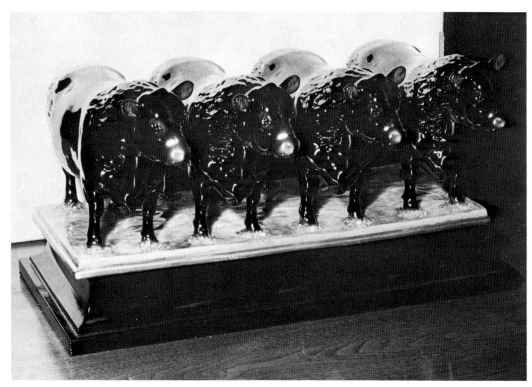

RPC-409

*See page 82

V. Wildlife

The wildlife subjects were produced in the nine years between 1952 and 1961, the last piece having been discontinued during the 1962 revision of the Boehm collection. Most of the sculptures were reproduced in fairly large quantity, and their quality, especially the bisque decorations, is exceptional. This quality has stood the test of time, as will be seen from the auction records. All of the wildlife subjects bear makersmark D, unless otherwise indicated in the individual listings.

The paucity of the wildlife collection can only be explained by Ed Boehm's involvement at the time in other sculptures. It is inconceivable that Boehm, with his deep, almost mystic, respect for animal life of all kinds and for wild animals in particular, would have skipped over the enormous amount of material which was available to him in this area. The great wild animal sculptures were the bronzes of the 18th and 19th centuries. These were more concerned with aesthetic problems than with the realistic qualities of the animal, and had Ed Boehm lived but a little longer, we might have seen his return to this fascinating subject.

In order to represent wildlife properly, one must be a great naturalist. Boehm was. It is in this field that I miss his work most acutely. From the hints and indications we have from the few pieces he did do of wild animals, the sensitivity that is displayed in birds and livestock would doubtlessly have led to a superior wildlife collection.

The Malvern collection produced after Boehm's death reinforces my belief that Ed was concerned with and planning a wildlife series. The Malvern collection, in its first year of issue, included three wildlife groups, the Foxes, the Raccoons and the Bobcats, and it is almost as if the hand of Ed Boehm were over the Malvern sculptors when the pieces were done.

As the result of Ed Boehm's general inability to relate to people, we often found him turning to nature, to plants and to animals. But the qualities of independence and predictability drew him to the wild animal. Ed Boehm believed in nature, he believed in natural selection, he believed in the process of genetic cleansing which takes place when animals are freely pitted against their environment. As a result, in his philosophy the real genetic test could only have been played out, ultimately, in a wild state.

The wild animal pieces that Ed Boehm did not live to do would have been of incredible sensitivity. This can be seen in the most elegant treatment he gave to the White Mouse Preening and the Field Mouse with Vetch, two simple little sculptures which, had Ed Boehm done nothing else, would have been sufficient to place him in the ranks of the masters.

RPC-501 COTTONTAIL BUNNY, glazed, undecorated (RP-522) 25 made

RPC-501

The Cottontail sculpture, which is a reclining rabbit with hind legs stretched back and with a hole (where the tail should be) for cotton, was Ed Boehm's first venture into wildlife subjects *per se*, although wildlife themes were used on his decorative pieces. As a matter of fact, the Cottontail may well have been originally intended as a decorative or use item. Possibly the piece was even meant to be a cotton dispenser. However, since the Boehm Studio includes this 6½" x 3¾" bunny in the listing of wildlife subjects, we will follow suit. The Cottontail bears makersmark C.

RPC-502-01 RED FOX, glazed, decorated (RP-501) 50 made
RPC-502-02 RED FOX, glazed, undecorated (RP-520) 50 made

RPC-502-01

The Red Fox was introduced in 1951, under the Boehm Studiomark Number 501. The sculpture depicts a standing fox with

RPC-503

RPC-504

RPC-505

his hind legs stretched back, chest and head up, tail sweeping the ground, his forelegs together.

Studio records show that approximately 200 replicas were made of this 6″ x 4″ piece, but it is my belief that the figure of 200 replicas is high. I have seen few and I must assume that few were made. I saw one example in our Retrospective Exhibition of 1964. Those of you with a sharp eye should search for this piece in unexpected places. If any quantity was indeed made, there should be a number of these floating unsuspectedly around in small antique and gift shops.

RPC-503 MALE BUNNY, glazed, decorated (RP-502) 518 made

This 3″ x 3″ attractive little Bunny was introduced sometime between 1954 and 1956 under the Boehm Studiomark Number 502. It depicts a seated bunny with his head and chest up and ears flat and back. It was available at $4 until 1957 and seems to have been popular, since more than 500 pieces were made. Some of the replicas, however, bear makersmark F, which was not adopted until 1959. Since the piece was not offered for sale until 1957, we can only assume that a quantity remained undecorated until after 1959 and were then decorated, with the new makersmark, and either sold or given away.

The fate of the Male Bunny and the Female Bunny in private hands is obvious. Since they were selling for $4 they could have very easily been given away as toys to children or to spruce up the Christmas tree. Anything bought this cheaply tends to disappear quickly and I am sure that of the 500 pieces made, hundreds were broken and thrown away and more hundreds are probably lost in attics and in the bottoms of trunks. My guess is that no more than 100 survive.

RPC-504 FEMALE BUNNY, glazed, decorated (RP-503) 532 made

Obviously intended as a mate for RPC-503, the Female measures 3″ x 2″. It depicts a reclining bunny with front legs curled under her chest, ears flat and back. Its history and price are identical with the former piece. Here, too, more than 500 pieces were produced and some replicas bear makersmark F. Neither of these two bunnies seems to have appeared at auction. As with the Male, few seem to have survived. (How you tell she's female—I'm not sure.)

RPC-505 FAWN, glazed, decorated (RP-504) 50 made

The Fawn, too, was introduced between 1954 and 1956, under Boehm Studiomark Number 504. The piece measures 4″ x 3″ and represents a reclining fawn on a square base with its head raised.

RPC-506-01 SQUIRREL, glazed, decorated (RP-505) 60 made
RPC-506-02 SQUIRREL, glazed, undecorated (RP-521) 25 made

The Squirrel, bearing Boehm Studiomark Number 505, measures 2½″ x 1½″ and depicts a squirrel standing with tail up and head turned one-quarter left.

I can't help wondering why Ed Boehm chose to do this ugly little piece. One explanation is that the little squirrels and the little bunnies were suggested by Ed Boehm as grandmothers' gifts to little children. Ed felt this would serve to teach children about animals. The pieces would, therefore, have to be well done and resistant to damage. Both the Bunnies and the Squirrel are made in this manner. It is interesting that this is another indication that Ed Boehm never did stop teaching about nature. This was also the motive behind the baby birds: they were to be used as a teaching aid. Of course, they have become important in themselves.

The Squirrel came fairly late (1956), at which time Ed Boehm was already making significant and beautiful pieces. It is only

RPC-506-02

2½" at its extreme measurement and the small size doesn't allow for any interest in the decoration. The nicest thing I can say about this piece is that it was only in production for a year or so and then it quietly and quite properly disappeared. However, since so few were made and since it is so atypical, it is a must for any serious collector of Boehm even though the Squirrel lies at the exact polar opposite from the Song Sparrows.

RPC-507-01 LION CUB, glazed, decorated (RP-506) 102 made
RPC-507-02 LION CUB, bisque, decorated (RP-507) 21 made

Also introduced sometime between 1954 and 1956, the Lion Cub is 5" x 4½". It depicts a seated cub with head turned one-half right and tail curled right. Boehm Studiomark Number 506 was assigned to this piece. Although it appears on price lists to 1959 only, this piece, too, has appeared with the makersmark F, as well as the more usual makersmark D. It is interesting to note that only the glazed examples have been discovered to have makersmark F. Of course, that does not mean that bisque examples with this makersmark do not exist, only that we have yet to discover one.

RPC-508 TIGER, glazed, decorated (RP-509) 14 made

Only 14 examples of this 15" x 6" piece were produced. The sculpture depicts a tiger reclining with his hind legs crossed under his body, left hind leg crossed over right, left foreleg extended, right foreleg bent in with the paw touching the left foreleg. It was introduced in 1952, under Boehm Studiomark Number 508, and discontinued in 1959. This beautiful piece is one of the best of the Boehm sculptures.

RPC-509 LIONESS, glazed, decorated (RP-508) 12 made

This is a lioness and is actually the same sculpture as the Tiger, the difference between them being only of coloration. Although the Lioness carries Boehm Studiomark Number 507, an *earlier* number than the Tiger's, it does not appear to have been offered for sale until sometime between 1954 and 1956. Since we do not have a complete price list for 1954 and 1955, the date of its introduction must remain approximate. It was discontinued in 1959; only about a dozen were produced in all.

It may well be that the piece was first conceived as a lioness (hence the early number) and that it was then decided to offer the Tiger first.

But whatever the facts of the matter were, the use of the Tiger for the Lioness displays a certain carelessness of nature which is simply not characteristic of Ed Boehm. There are so few moments in studying Boehm when one can see human frailties showing through, that many questions rush to mind. Did Ed Boehm simply take the easy way out with this piece? Was there someone else involved in the decision to offer the same pieces as the Tiger and Lioness? Was there some confusion among the decorators? Or, in fact, did Ed Boehm simply become bored and decorate a few pieces as a tiger, a few pieces as a lioness as a private joke and then drop the whole matter? It seems quite likely that these pieces were not taken seriously by Ed. It is this playfulness in the decorations that makes them so rare and so much in demand today. Both of them, the Tiger and the Lioness, are serious sculptures of great majesty in spite of the problem of the decoration.

RPC-510-01 RABBIT, bisque, decorated with flowers (RP-511) 144 made
RPC-510-02 RABBIT, bisque, undecorated with flowers (RP-510) 423 made
RPC-510-03 RABBIT, bisque, decorated without flowers (RP-523) 144 made
RPC-510-04 RABBIT, bisque, undecorated —rare

RPC-507-01

RPC-508

RPC-509

167

RPC-510-01

RPC-511-02

RPC-513-02

Almost 600 of this 5" x 4" piece were produced, under Boehm Studiomark Number 509, all between 1957 and 1961. It depicts a rabbit standing with hind legs bent in a crouch, head up, ears up and out, wearing a ribbon with flowers (or without). Interestingly enough, the undecorated, bisque seems to have been the first offered. On no list does the example without flowers on the neck ribbon appear; however, examples are known to exist.

RPC-511-01 WHITE MOUSE, PREENING, glazed, decorated (RP-512) 14 made
RPC-511-02 WHITE MOUSE, PREENING, bisque, decorated (RP-513) 455 made

Introduced in 1957 and produced in a quantity of nearly 500 pieces before its discontinuance in 1961, this appealing little 2½" high mouse is a charming sculpture. It is from the White Mouse Preening that one would have expected Ed Boehm to start his adventure into wildlife subjects. Ed Boehm understood that little mouse and it is this kind of firm personal knowledge of the animal that made Boehm great. The piece depicts a white mouse, ears back, sitting on his hind legs with his tail curled around to the left. His head and right forepaw are turned to the right and the latter rests on his back above the tail.

RPC-512-01 FIELD MOUSE WITH VETCH, bisque, decorated (RP-514) 479 made*
RPC-512-02 FIELD MOUSE WITH VETCH, bisque, undecorated (RP-524) 150 made

The Field Mouse was also produced in large quantity. Introduced in 1957, it remained in production until 1961. The piece is 4½" high and bears the Boehm Studiomark Number 511. The piece depicts a field mouse clinging with its hind legs to the side of a stump, forepaws grasping the top

of stump, tail curled around the stump to right with its head turned left and ears up.

RPC-513-01 NEWBORN RABBITS, bisque decorated (RP-515) 3 made
RPC-513-02 NEWBORN RABBITS, bisque, undecorated—unique

From the moment I saw this piece some years ago at the Retrospective Exhibition, I have been covetous of it. To my continuing chagrin, I have not yet been able to persuade any of the four people who own an example to part with it. It appears on only one price list, 1958, and for a reason incomprehensible to me was discontinued after only four were produced. I cannot understand what could have motivated the Studio to stop production of such a charming sculpture. It doesn't take an expert to discover that an enormous amount of imagination and work went into the sculpture model that preceded this piece. The idea was so great and the moment of innocence that it captured was so poignant that I am again set to wondering about the pieces that Ed Boehm would have made. My sense of loss in this particular case is great.

The piece is listed by the Boehm Studio as Boehm Studiomark Number 512. The two babies are set on an oval base measuring 8" x 4"; one is curled up asleep on its back and the other one is stretched out on its stomach with eyes closed and mouth open.

RPC-514-01 CHIPMUNK, STANDING, bisque, decorated (RP-516) 254 made*
RPC-514-02 CHIPMUNK, STANDING, bisque, decorated Red—unique
RPC-514-03 CHIPMUNK, STANDING, bisque, undecorated (RP-517) 6 made

This 3½" high Chipmunk was introduced in 1958 and discontinued in 1961. The piece carries the Boehm Studiomark Number 513 and depicts a chipmunk standing with hind legs bent in a crouch, left forepaw drawn in under chest, tail and ears up.

*See page 83

RPC-515-03   RPC-514-03

RPS-516-01

RPC-515-01 CHIPMUNK, PREENING, bisque, decorated (RP-518) 317 made
RPC-515-02 CHIPMUNK, PREENING, bisque, decorated Red—unique
RPC-515-03 CHIPMUNK, PREENING, bisque, undecorated (RP-519) 6 made

A companion piece to the Standing Chipmunk, this piece is 3″ high and bears Boehm Studiomark Number 514. The sculpture depicts a chipmunk sitting on his hind legs and tail with his tail curved up and around to left and forepaws drawn in to the chest; the head is turned one-half to the right. It was not introduced until 1959, and was discontinued in 1961.

There seems to have been a total of about 325 produced, the bulk in the decorated bisque finish. Only one was decorated with a red coat. It is probable that undecorated bisque examples of all of the wildlife subjects exist; however, those we have not actually seen cannot be listed with any degree of confidence.

RPS-516-01 GIANT PANDA CUB, RE-CLINING (6½″ x 8″) bisque, decorated, nonlimited edition still in production
RPS-516-02 GIANT PANDA CUB, RE-CLINING (6½″ x 8″) bisque, undecorated, unique

The Giant Panda Cub, introduced in 1975, was one of the first in a series of small animals done by the Trenton Studio since 1959. This piece represents Helen Boehm's gift to the children of China and is so inscribed on the bottom of the piece. The inscription reads: "To the People of the People's Republic of China from the Edward Marshall Boehm Artists and Craftsmen of the United States of America, December 1974." The inscription further reads: "In friendship, gratitude and respect for the enormous contributions of the Chinese people to the honored art of Porcelain. Presented on the visit to China of Mrs. Edward Marshall Boehm and her Studio colleagues Mr. Frank Cosentino and Mr.

169

RPS-517-01

RPS-518-01

RPS-519-01

Maurice Eyeington." The Boehm Studio-mark Number is 400-47 and the makers-mark J. The sculpture depicts a Giant Panda Cub lying on bamboo and munching bamboo shoots.

RPS-517-01 GIANT PANDA CUB, SITTING (8½" x 6½") bisque, decorated, nonlimited edition still in production
RPS-517-02 GIANT PANDA CUB, SITTING (8½" x 6½") bisque, undecorated, unique

The Giant Panda Cub, Sitting, was introduced in 1976. The sculpture carries Boehm Studiomark Number 400-54 and makersmark J. This sculpture is also referred to as the Drowsy Panda and depicts the Panda Cub falling asleep while eating his fill of bamboo shoots and leaves.

RPS-518-01 KOALA (8¾" x 9½") bisque, decorated, nonlimited edition still in production
RPS-518-02 KOALA (8¾" x 9½") bisque, undecorated, unique

Introduced in 1976, the Koala carries Boehm Studiomark Number 400-36 and makersmark J. The Koala Bear is much closer to life-size than the other Cubs and he is depicted in a eucalyptus tree, ready to pluck a leaf.

RPS-519-01 OCELOT (6" x 8½") bisque, decorated, nonlimited edition still in production
RPS-519-02 OCELOT (6" x 8½") bisque, undecorated, unique

Another 1976 sculpture, the Ocelot carries Boehm Studiomark Number 400-40 and makersmark J. The Ocelot cub is lying on its side, seemingly playing with an imaginary playmate—eyes open, ever alert. 516-519 are RPS rather than RPC because they were actually produced after Ed Boehm died, and to conform with the rest of this catalogue they must carry an RPS designation.

VI. Religious Subjects

Edward Boehm introduced his first religious piece around 1950 and continued to introduce new pieces in this category up to 1960. Even after 1962, when the cutback in the collection saw the discontinuance of nearly every category except the birds, five of the religious pieces continued in the collection as unlimited editions: the three sizes of the Madonna La Pietà and the Brother and Sister Angels. All are in undecorated bisque. As of 1970, however, all had been discontinued except the 9½" Madonna.

Several of the religious pieces were originally made from commercial molds, although in at least one of these Ed Boehm did make structural changes in the mold. Their design, however, is markedly inferior to those pieces sculpted by Boehm. The grace and beauty of the latter clearly show deep religious feelings.

Ed Boehm's religion was nature itself. He was rarely if ever seen in a church. His concern was with the relationship between man and animals rather than between man and man. It is difficult to put one's finger exactly on Boehm's involvement in religious questions. However, there is no question about the depth of religious feeling on the part of Helen Boehm. It is not difficult to conclude, therefore, that many of the explicitly religious pieces were done, if not at the instigation of Helen Boehm, certainly with her enthusiastic approval.

With few exceptions the religious pieces were made during the period when the Boehm Studio was using the makersmark D. Therefore, unless otherwise noted, the religious pieces carry makersmark D.

RPC-601 SMALL SAINT FRANCIS, glazed, ground color body Celadon (RP-634) approximately 10 made

This is an early piece, probably made from a commercial mold. Only one has come to light, although there is the possibility that others do exist. It does not carry a Boehm makersmark and, at first, there was some doubt as to whether it was actually Boehm. However, it has since been authenticated. It is marked, under the base, "OSSI-VOZANY."

The glazed celadon body is quite beautiful, considering how early the piece was made. It is smooth and soft and sensuous.

RPC-602-01 MADONNA AND CHILD, glazed, decorated—probably unique
RPC-602-02 MADONNA AND CHILD, glazed, undecorated—probably unique

This is an example of the use of a commercial mold, with a structural change made by Boehm. The original mold has no blanket. The piece was probably done in 1951 but has never appeared for sale on a price list and, therefore, we have no record of exact dates. It is possible that the piece was an experimental one and the fact that only two have come to light, one in each decoration, lends credence to this conclusion.

RPC-603-01 MADONNA BUST, MEDIUM, glazed, decorated, approximately 25 made
RPC-603-02 MADONNA BUST, MEDIUM, glazed, undecorated (RP-605) approximately 25 made

This, too, is an early piece and may also have been done from a commercial mold, although we have not been able to confirm this.

Interestingly enough, it is the only one of the Boehm Madonnas to have been done with a halo and cowl. It depicts a Madonna with her head tilted right, arms raised in prayer, and stands approximately 7″ high. The decorated example is done with gold.

Unfortunately, we have been unable to obtain a glazed, undecorated example for comparison and it is possible that these are

RPC-601

RPC-603-01

RPC-604

two entirely different pieces. However, the similarity of description we have uncovered leads us to discount this possibility and assume that the two are the same sculpture.

We have come upon only one of the decorated examples; however, our information indicates that there may have been as many as 50 in all, in both decorations.

RPC-604 MADONNA, glazed, decorated (RP-632) probably unique

Also about 7″ high, this piece is a shoulder-length bust with a fluted cowl. Our information indicates only one was produced and it is an extremely early example.

RPC-605-01 MADONNA LA PIETÀ, large, glazed, undecorated (RP-601) approximately 320 made
RPC-605-02 MADONNA LA PIETÀ, large, bisque, undecorated (RP-602) nonlimited edition, still in production

RPC-605-01

RPC-605-02

RPC-605-07

RPC-605-03 MADONNA LA PIETÀ, medium, glazed, undecorated (RP-635) approximately 50 made

RPC-605-04 MADONNA LA PIETÀ, medium, glazed, white with gold trim, approximately 50 made

RPC-605-05 MADONNA LA PIETÀ, medium, bisque, undecorated (RP-603) approximately 2,750 made

RPC-605-06 MADONNA LA PIETÀ, small, glazed, undecorated, approximately 50 made

RPC-605-07 MADONNA LA PIETÀ, small, bisque, undecorated (RP-604) approximately 3,100 made

These are grouped together because they are structurally identical (except for size and the fact that the large Madonna La Pietà is a full waist-length bust with arms). The heights are 9½", 6½" and 4½", respectively, and examples of the large glazed example have been found to carry makersmark F as well as the usual D.

The sculpture depicts a waist-length figure of a woman wearing a long-sleeved loose garment. Her head drape drops behind her left shoulder and around her left arm to front. The right side of the drape loops onto her right shoulder and drops down in back. The arms bend up at the elbows and are crossed in front of her breast; her head is slightly bent.

The piece was first introduced in the large size in 1952, under Boehm Studiomark Number 601, although it does not appear on that year's price list and must, therefore, have been introduced late in that year. After 1957 it disappears from the listings. In 1953 the medium example was introduced in bisque (Boehm Studiomark Number 605). The small Madonna La Pietà was not introduced until 1958, and bears the Boehm Studiomark Number 613. It was discontinued in 1970.

The year 1971 shows all of the religious pieces discontinued except the large Madonna in bisque (RPC-605-02), which is still being produced in an unlimited edition.

RPC-606-01 MADONNA BUST, small, glazed, decorated with gold trim (RP-606) approximately 5 made

RPC-606-02 MADONNA BUST, small, bisque, undecorated—unique

RPC-606-03 MADONNA BUST, small, glazed, blue and white garments with gold trim—unique

RPC-606-04 MADONNA BUST, medium, glazed, decorated—extremely rare

This piece carries Boehm Studiomark Number 602 and some of the examples have been known to bear makersmark F. It was introduced in 1953 and discontinued in 1957. We are unable to determine the actual quantity produced but assume it to have been a fairly small amount. The sculpture shows the Madonna's head and shoulders smoothly draped, with her head bent down to the left and with eyes closed. The RPC-606-01 has gold trim around the face on edge of drape.

RPC-607 LONG-HAIRED ANGEL, glazed, decorated—signed in gold—fewer than 10 made

This is another example of the use by Boehm of commercial molds. It seems to have been an experimental piece, as it was never merchandized and few are believed to be in existence.

RPC-608-01 SAINT MARIA GORETTI, glazed, decorated (RP-607) 32 made

RPC-608-02 SAINT MARIA GORETTI, bisque, decorated (RP-608) 201 made

RPC-608-03 SAINT MARIA GORETTI, glazed, decorated—rare

This 6½" piece was introduced in 1952 under Boehm Studiomark Number 603. The sculpture is a kneeling figure of a barefoot girl in a loose gown, wearing a headscarf, her head raised and arms crossed, holding flowers. There were well over 200 produced in all and at least one structural variation has come to light.

The variant, RPC-608-03, is a glazed and decorated piece with the feet of the figure much closer together and the flowers held out from the body. This may well have been an experimental model of the Saint Maria Goretti, which was then modified slightly and produced in quantity. If this conclusion is correct, the variation would be a unique piece.

The Saint Maria Goretti has a special place in my memory of early Boehm, since it was this very piece which first introduced me to the Boehm experience. As I recall, it was sometime in 1952. I had recently returned from schooling in England and for personal reasons found myself working in my family's jewelry business in Atlantic City. At that time we were just beginning to look at European porcelain and had no real interest in American porcelain. A lady walked into the shop, carrying two heavy suitcases on a hot summer afternoon and asked if I would like to see some porcelain figures. I said I would and asked what part of Europe they were from. When she said they were American, I told her we were not interested as we were only after quality ware. It was, of course, Helen Boehm, and she refused to take "no" for an answer. It wasn't long before there were spread out in front of me what today would have been an absolute fortune in the earliest and most elegant pieces of Ed's work. At any rate, the only piece I chose to buy was the Saint Maria Goretti. The little Saint is special for me. Were I Catholic, I would perhaps choose her as my own personal saint.

RPC-609-01 PIGTAIL ANGEL, glazed, decorated (RP-609) approximately 300 made

RPC-609-02 PIGTAIL ANGEL, bisque, undecorated—approximately 100 made

This piece showing a standing angel with her pigtails tied with blue ribbon and her wings back and folded was first introduced in 1953, under the Boehm Studiomark

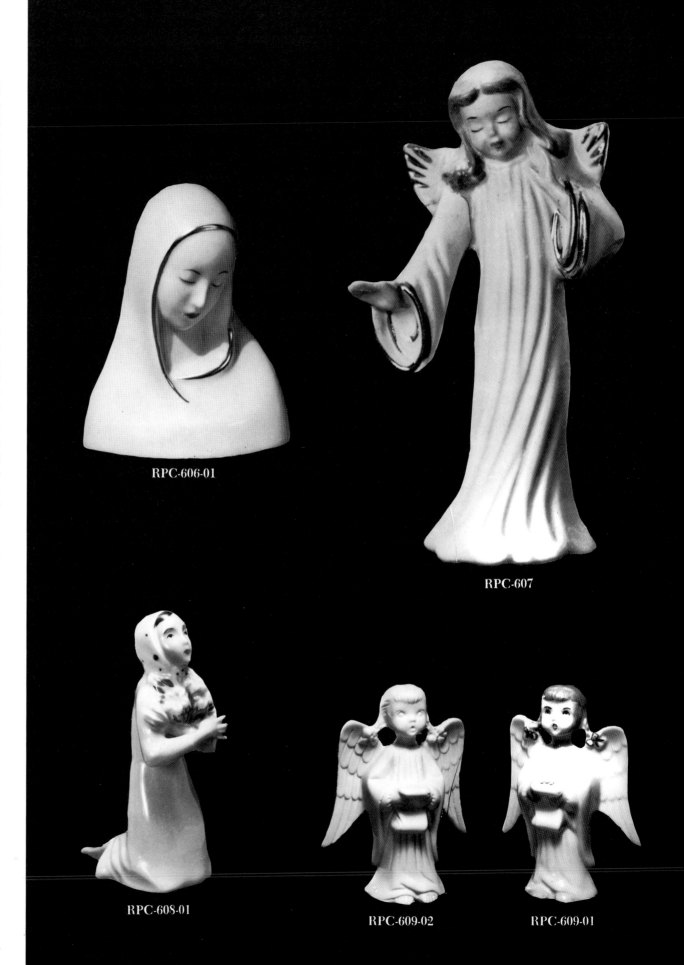

RPC-606-01

RPC-607

RPC-608-01

RPC-609-02

RPC-609-01

RPC-610-01   RPC-611-01   RPC-612-01   RPC-612-04

Number 604. It was discontinued late in 1957. This 4½″ high standing angel is believed to have been made from a commercial mold. There were well over 400 produced, several showing makersmark F.

RPC-610-01 LADY OF GRACE, glazed, undecorated (RP-610) approximately 50 made

RPC-610-02 LADY OF GRACE, bisque, undecorated (RP-611) approximately 100 made

Introduced in 1954 under Boehm Studiomark Number 606, this 11¼″ high figure of the Madonna (full-length, long-haired draped figure, head bent, arms down and outstretched) was made through 1958, when it was discontinued.

RPC-611-01 SAINT JOSEPH, glazed, decorated (RP-613) 5 made

RPC-611-02 SAINT JOSEPH, glazed, undecorated (RP-612) 5 made

RPC-611-03 SAINT JOSEPH, bisque, undecorated—extremely rare

The Saint Joseph was first introduced in 1954 under Boehm Studiomark Number 607. For early Boehm it is a large piece. This sculpture represents a full-length bearded figure standing on a base, wearing a long, loose gown, holding a child at his left and a spray of lilies in the crook of his right arm. The child's right hand rests in his lap and holds a cross.

The piece was not offered after 1956, and there seem to have been only about 15 produced, although, if we consider that the number of the undecorated bisque example is highly conjectural, the total would probably come closer to about 20.

RPC-612-01 ANGEL ON PILLOW, glazed, decorated—6 made

RPC-612-02 ANGEL ON PILLOW, glazed, undecorated (RP-615) 6 made

RPC-612-03 ANGEL ON PILLOW, bisque, undecorated—fewer than 5 made

RPC-612-04 GUARDIAN ANGEL, bisque, undecorated (RP-614) approximately 200 made

RPC-612-05 GUARDIAN ANGEL, glazed, decorated—2 made

The Angel on Pillow (Boehm Studiomark Number 608) was introduced around 1954 both glazed and decorated. There appear to have been only about six made, two each with blue pillows, purple pillows and red pillows. A similar small number of the glazed, undecorated were produced. We have no really firm information on the number of bisque, undecorated. The sculpture is a long-haired angel on a pillow, wings extended to either side, kneeling on the right knee on a small cushion. The arms are bent at the elbows, hands in prayer position at the left side of the face with the head turned one-quarter right.

In 1961, a price list from the Boehm Studio lists a Guardian Angel in undecorated bisque, and approximately 200 were produced in that finish. The only difference between the Angel on Pillow and the Guardian Angel is that, in the latter, the book on the figure's knee has been omitted. Otherwise the two are structurally identical. In recent years, the glazed undecorated Angel on Pillow has been mistakenly designated as a Guardian Angel, and was so listed in the June 7, 1969, Parke-Bernet sale. Also

RPC-614-01   RPC-613-01   RPC-614-05   RPC-613-04

misnamed at that sale was a bisque, undecorated Angel on Pillow.

The Angels are 7″ high and are quite lovely pieces. The last year of their production seems to have been 1961. They were, obviously, victims of the 1962 collection cutback.

RPC-613-01 SISTER ANGEL, glazed, decorated, narrow sleeves—approximately 25 made

RPC-613-02 SISTER ANGEL, bisque, undecorated, narrow sleeves—100 made

RPC-613-03 SISTER ANGEL, glazed, decorated, draped sleeves (RP-616) 300 made

RPC-613-04 SISTER ANGEL, bisque undecorated, draped sleeves (RP-617) 500 made

RPC-614-01 BROTHER ANGEL, glazed, decorated, narrow sleeves—approximately 25 made

RPC-614-02 BROTHER ANGEL, bisque, undecorated, narrow sleeves—100 made

RPC-614-03 BROTHER ANGEL, glazed, decorated, draped sleeves (RP-618) 100 made

RPC-614-04 BROTHER ANGEL, glazed, undecorated, draped sleeves (RP-619A) 300 made

RPC-614-05 BROTHER ANGEL, bisque, undecorated, draped sleeves (RP-619) 500 made

Introduced in 1955, these 5″ high pieces are among the most numerous of the Religious Subjects. They depict a barefoot angel kneeling, wearing a long, flowing garment, wings spread to either side, head tilted back and to the right, eyes open and hands raised in prayer.

The glazed and decorated Angels do not seem to have been offered after 1957. The undecorated bisque pieces were discontinued in 1970, after at least 500 of each had been produced.

Since these pieces were intended as pairs, there is every possibility that a Sister Angel to RPC-614-04 in the glazed, undecorated finish, does exist. However the Boehm Studio has no record of it, nor has one ever come to light.

The Sister Angel carries Boehm Studiomark Number 609 and the Brother Angel carries Studiomark Number 610. The glazed, decorated draped-sleeve examples have appeared with makersmark F, although most of the other pieces bear makersmark D.

RPC-615-01 ALBA MADONNA AND CHILD, glazed, decorated (RP-633) probably unique

RPC-615-02 ALBA MADONNA AND CHILD, glazed, undecorated (RP-621) approximately 2 made

RPC-615-03 ALBA MADONNA AND CHILD, bisque, undecorated (RP-620) 350 made

The Alba Madonna and Child, 10¼″ high on its base, depicts a full-length figure of a seated woman in a long flowing garment. The right leg is bent back and the left knee bent. The Madonna is holding a book in her left hand with her index finger marking the place. Her right arm protects the child

175

RPC-615-03   RPC-616   RPC-617-02   RPC-618   RPC-619

seated on her right leg. The child's left leg is bent at knee. The right arm is bent at the elbow and his head is tilted and turned one-quarter to the left. It bears Boehm Studiomark Number 611 and first appears on the price list of 1956.

At least one of the glazed and decorated Alba Madonnas is known to exist and it is believed that there might be two of the glazed, undecorated. The bisque, undecorated, however, continued in production through 1962, the year of its discontinuance, with an approximate total of 350 being made. It seems to have been one of the last pieces discontinued during the cutback.

RPC-616 SAINT FRANCIS OF ASSISI, bisque, undecorated (RP-622) 264 made

The Saint Francis (Boehm Studiomark Number 612) was also a piece which was produced in fairly large quantity. Introduced in 1958, this graceful 12½" figure of the Saint surrounded by his beloved animals was discontinued in 1962. The sculpture shows a full-length standing monk figure with cowl draped around his neck. A dove with outstretched wings perches on the

Saint's right shoulder. His right hand is extended forward, palm up, and his left hand touches the left ear of a standing fawn. Several examples of this sculpture have come to light with no makersmark on the bottom. This has happened from time to time.

RPC-617-01 IMMACULATE CONCEPTION, glazed, undecorated (RP-624) approximately 20 made
RPC-617-02 IMMACULATE CONCEPTION, bisque, undecorated (RP-623) approximately 80 made

This lovely 10" high sculpture depicts a full-length standing figure of a Madonna on a base, wearing a loose flowing garment with her head tilted left and her hands raised in prayer. It bears Boehm Studiomark Number 614 and was produced in a quantity of approximately 100, the majority of those having been undecorated bisque. It was introduced in 1959 and discontinued the following year.

RPC-618 INFANT OF PRAGUE, LATIN, bisque, undecorated (RP-625) 2 made
RPC-619 INFANT OF PRAGUE, BYZANTINE, bisque, undecorated (RP-626) 12 made

These two pieces were both introduced in 1959, and both carry the Boehm Studiomark Number 615. However, even though the basic structure is similar, the elaborate differences in costume, taken together with the slight modification in position, have led us to assign them as two entirely different pieces. This sculpture shows a standing boy in religious robes wearing a heart on a chain and a rosary. His right hand is raised in blessing. His left hand holds an incense burner topped by a cross. The Infant wears a crown with a cross. The whole piece is mounted on a porcelain base.

The only year of listing was 1959. Both pieces are 10" high, and we believe that approximately two in Latin robes and 12 in Byzantine robes were made.

RPC-620-01 POPE PIUS XII BUST, LARGE, bisque, undecorated (RP-630) 50 made
RPC-620-02 POPE PIUS XII BUST, SMALL, bisque, undecorated (RP-631) 1,000 made

Originally commissioned by Mrs. Mary Roebling, of Trenton, New Jersey, as a gift

RPC-620-01 RPC-620-02 RPC-621-02 RPC-622 RPC-624

to Cardinal Francis Spellman, the Large Pope Pius (11½"), on an ebony pedestal base, was introduced in 1958 as a limited edition of 50, which was completed in December of 1960. It is a head-to-waist figure of Pope Pius XII in formal vestments. His right hand is raised in blessing with his left hand resting against his chest. The smaller bust (7½") with the Pope's crest was produced for Tiffany as a special edition of 1,000 pieces.

RPC-621-01 CRUCIFIX, GUIDO RENI (finish unknown), decorated—unique
RPC-621-02 CRUCIFIX, GUIDO RENI, bisque, undecorated—3 made
RPC-622 CRUCIFIX, MODERN, bisque, undecorated (RP-627) 9 made

The Crucifix after Guido Reni was commissioned by the then Reverend Emilio A. Cardelia (now a Monsignor), pastor of Saint Joachim's Parish in Trenton, New Jersey, early in 1959. In October of that year, a replica was presented to Pope John XXIII in the Vatican and is now in the Vatican's permanent collection. In all, only four of the Guido Reni Crucifix exist and one is known to have been done in color. Although it is believed to have a bisque finish, there is no proof. Records at the Boehm Studio are incomplete and we have never been able to discover where the piece is. Wherever it is, it is a unique and valuable Boehm sculpture.

Also in 1959, another Crucifix, more modern in design, was created; it was intended as a limited edition of 30. In 1961, however, the sculpture was discontinued after only nine had been produced. This is one of the few editions of Boehm which were individually numbered. This is a figure of the crucified Christ on an ebony-finished cross. A triangular porcelain base supports the feet of the figure and the scroll above the head bears the inscription "INRI." The sculptures are 36" high and the Modern Crucifix bears Boehm Studiomark Number 619.

RPC-623 MADONNA AND CHILD, DELLA ROBBIA, bisque, undecorated (RP-628) 120 made *

This sculpture, after Della Robbia, stands 10" high and bears Boehm Studiomark Number 620. It was introduced in 1959 and was discontinued in 1960, after approximately 120 examples had been produced.

The sculpture is a waist-length figure of the Madonna holding a child on her left arm, wearing a head shawl and loose, wide-sleeved robe tied at the neck with a tasseled cord. The Madonna's right hand rests on the Child's left leg. The Child's right hand is raised, index finger extended. The Child's left hand, holding a long narrow scroll, rests on the Madonna's left wrist. The Child wears a drape around his shoulders.

RPC-624 POPE JOHN XXIII BUST, bisque, undecorated (RP-629) approximately 80 made

Approximately 80 of this 10" piece were made during its one year of production, 1960. It was the last religious figure to be introduced by the Boehm Studio. It bears Boehm Studiomark Number 621.

This sculpture is a waist-length figure of Pope John XXIII in papal vestments, on a high rectangular base, emblazoned with his crest. His arms are bent at the elbows with his fingers interlaced and thumbs together.

This is a curious piece. Its popularity is a reflection of the universal affection that Pope John enjoyed among Catholics and non-Catholics alike. There is a touch of humanity and joy in this piece which the other Pope sculptures do not have. I am only sorry that Ed Boehm never undertook to do a large head of this remarkable man.

*See page 84

177

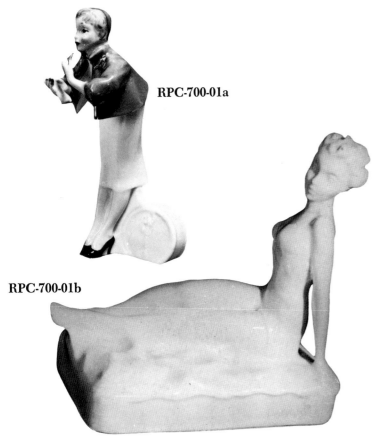

RPC-700-01a

RPC-700-01b

RPC-700-02b

RPC-700-03   RPC-700-05

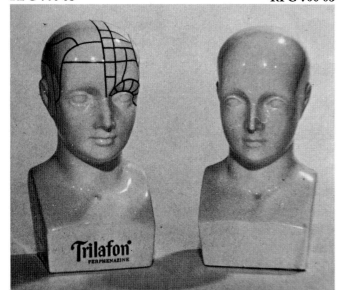

VII. Promotional Pieces

Since these pieces were special commissions never intended for sale and therefore cannot be considered part of the "collection" *per se*, we feel that they should be handled separately.

RPC-700-01a SUSIE, THE LIPSTICK GIRL, glazed, decorated (RP-737) 50 made

This well-dressed young lady (well-dressed, that is, by 1951 standards) depicts a standing model applying lipstick, with a round hat box at her left, and wearing a knee-length dress with a wide short blue jacket and a blue hat. She was commissioned by *Glamour* magazine and was produced in a quantity of approximately 50. Susie is 7″ high and bears the OSSO CERAMICS makersmark A.

RPC-700-01b BATHING BEAUTY, glazed, white, 50 made

Bathing Beauty was also done for *Glamour* magazine. She was to be the second in a series of figures, Susie, the lipstick girl, being the first. The series was discontinued after a management change at *Glamour*. Probably only about 50 of these pieces were made, in glazed white. The third figurine in the series, which was never completed, was to have been a tennis girl.

RPC-700-02a SWAN CAKE PLATE, glazed, decorated, unique
RPC-700-02b SWAN CAKE PLATE, glazed, undecorated (RP-939) unique

This is a 15½″ x 11½″ circular flat platter resting on the wings of two swans which face in opposite directions. It was commissioned by the Swans Down Division of General Foods in 1953. Since there appear to have been only two made, it is obvious that the piece was not meant for general distribution by Swans Down, but more probably as part of an advertising layout or television commercial. Neither of the pieces has appeared at auction, and the whereabouts of the decorated plate is unknown.

RPC-700-03 PHRENOLOGY HEAD, TRILAFON, glazed, decorated (RP-931) 5,000 made
RPC-700-04 PHRENOLOGY HEAD, ETRAFON, glazed, decorated (RP-981) 5,000 made
RPC-700-05 PHRENOLOGY HEAD (THE BALD MAN), glazed, undecorated—unique
RPC-700-06 PHRENOLOGY HEAD, Boehm mold only, glazed, decorated—5,000 made

The RPC-700-03 and 04 were commissioned by the Schering Corporation in quantities of approximately 5,000 each. The first was produced in 1958 or 1959 and the second in 1967. They are 5¼″ high and the later model is sectionalized by incised lines. Both bear makersmark D.

The sculpture is a bust with head divided into sections by black lines, inscribed on the front "Trilafon Perphenazine," inscribed on the right side "Schering, full-range tranquilizer" and on the left side "Schering, outmoding older concepts."

There was indeed another Phrenology Head done, but not by Boehm. This has led to a good deal of confusion and there is only one rather subtle way of detecting the difference between them. When Schering first commissioned the RPC-700-03, they ordered 5,000 pieces. The promotion for Schering was an extremely successful one and there was an immediate demand by physicians for additional pieces. Schering went back to Boehm, and at that time Boehm was not prepared to do any more and Schering turned to another Trenton house which turned out, I believe, an additional 5,000 on Boehm's

RPC-700-07

VIII. Figurines

The figurine subjects span the entire Boehm experience, except for a regrettable seven-year gap between 1961 (the last year of production of the old figures) and 1969.

It might well be asked why, after a lapse of seven years, Ed Boehm decided to take up the production of figurines again in 1969. I once had a long talk with Ed about this, as he recognized that figures were neither in his *oeuvre* nor in his area of specialization. His answer to my "Why do it?" was a curious one. Ed always sought challenges and he felt that no American had ever done a purely *European concept* in porcelain as well as the Europeans had. The Beau Brummells were an answer to this challenge and Ed indicated in his definite way that the Beau Brummells were going to teach the Europeans how to do classical European figures. This was another case of Ed Boehm's setting goals for himself which, for more ordinary mortals, would have been impossible. The Beau Brummells which were brought out in 1970 are certainly the best things of that kind ever done. Although they were not held in high esteem by Boehm collectors, the day will come when their intrinsic worth will be noted.

Unless otherwise noted, the makersmark on all the figurines is D.

RPC-701-01 SIAMESE DANCERS (pr.)
  glazed, decorated—2 made
RPC-701-02 SIAMESE DANCERS (pr.)
  bisque undecorated—2 made*

These are the earliest Boehm figures yet discovered and only four have thus far been found: two undecorated and two glazed, decorated. Of the latter, one bears makersmark A and the other makersmark B, which indicates that they were first produced in 1951. The Siamese Dancers were hobby molds. They are in native costume. The

*See page 84

female has her right hand on her head, left hand on her hip and her right knee is bent. The male's position is reversed.

RPC-702 KNEELING NUDE, glazed, white (RP-738) extremely rare

The 1964 Retrospective Catalog listed this piece as "Bathing Beauty" and could give no description. Since then, one example has been found and we feel that since it is a kneeling nude, it should be so called.

Early in Ed Boehm's career, he was asked by several well-known sculptors to cast in porcelain some of their work. There were two pieces done by two different sculptors (the Ichabod Crane and the Kneeling Nude). Neither is in Ed's style, but both display his complete control, even at that early date, over the medium in which he was working. Somewhere along the line, however, the project became bogged down and few of this work were done.

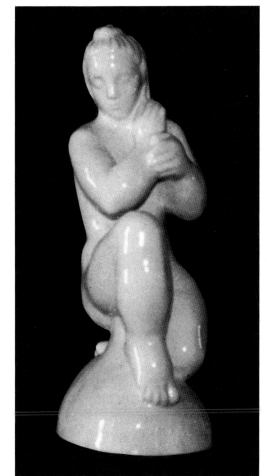

RPC-302

original molds. This is the RPC-700-06. It is difficult to tell them apart, but if they are turned upside down, the original Boehm Phrenology Head (that is, the Trilafon Head) has a slight ridge along the bottom around the base with an indentation at the center. The Trilafon Head by the other potter (RPC-700-06) has a completely flat base. The head done by the other potter has only a curiosity value, whereas the Trilafon is a genuine collector's object.

The RPC-700-05 Phrenology Head, which I have labeled above as the Bald Man, carries an interesting story. It was done by Ed Boehm as a special gift for a friend of his. The friend was, as you may have guessed, bald.

RPC-700-07 ASHTRAY, glazed, decorated, approximately 5,000 made

This ashtray was commissioned by the RCA Corporation and given as gifts to their employees. Diameter of the ashtray is 4½". Although, according to the Boehm Studio, there were about 5,000 of these made, I have seen only one.

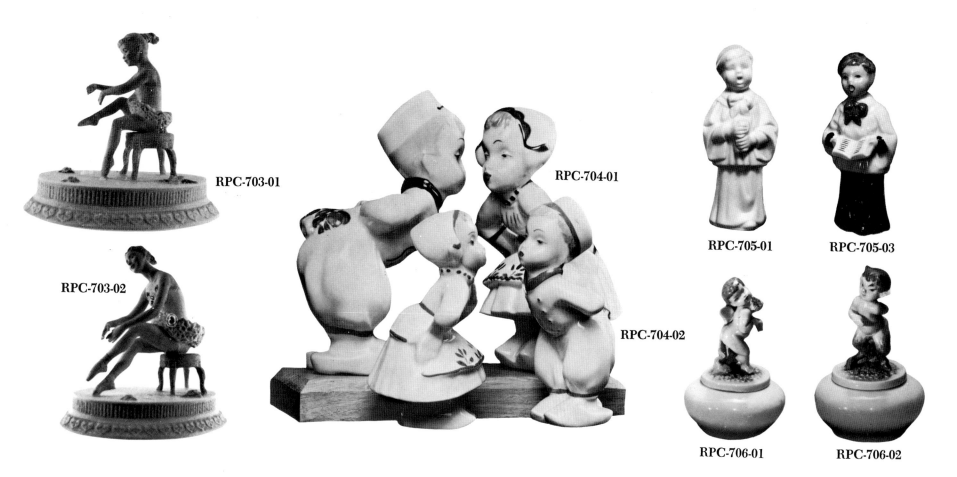

RPC-703-01

RPC-703-02

RPC-704-01

RPC-704-02

RPC-705-01   RPC-705-03

RPC-706-01   RPC-706-02

RPC-703-01 BALLERINA, "PINKY," bisque, decorated (RP-732) 2 made

RPC-703-02 BALLERINA, "PAMELA," bisque, decorated (RP-733) 2 made

These pieces, 5½″ and 6½″ respectively, depict a ballerina in a tutu seated on a round four-legged stool on an ornate oval base. They bear makersmark C, which would seem to place their introduction and discontinuance between 1952 and 1954. There appears to have been only two of each produced and their similarities indicate that they may originally have been meant as a pair. However, they do not appear to have been merchandized nor do they appear in any auction records.

RPC-704-01 DUTCH BOY AND GIRL, LARGE (pr.) glazed, decorated (RP-734) 12 made

RPC-704-02 DUTCH BOY AND GIRL, SMALL (pr.) glazed, decorated (RP-735) 12 made

RPC-704-03 DUTCH BOY AND GIRL,

SMALL (pr.) glazed, decorated—unique

These are the traditional Dutch Boy and Girl kissing figures with the Boy holding a bouquet behind his back and with the Girl's hands on her hips. They were produced from commercial molds sometime in the early 1950's.

I never really expected to see these pieces. There is an accepted opinion that 12 pairs of each were produced, but this is really a guess. There could as easily have been just two or three pairs. Since the possibility of seeing them as a *pair* is slim, it was with great joy and surprise that I ran across a pair in a collection I bought. The RPC-704-03 pair was produced as a salt and pepper shaker and the quantity made is unknown.

RPC-705-01 CHOIR BOY, glazed, decorated (RP-740) appproximately 500 made

RPC-705-02 CHOIR BOY, bisque, undecorated—approximately 500 made

RPC-705-03 CHOIR BOY, bisque, undecorated—unique

This 4½″ high sculpture, depicting a boy in choir robes holding an opened book, was produced from a commercial mold, probably about the same time as the Dutch kissing figures. The quantity is assumed to be well over 500, and possibly as many as 1,000. However, there is another example of this sculpture with the Choir Boy holding a scroll instead of a book (also bisque, undecorated), and this piece is believed to be unique (RPC-705-03). They are among the earliest examples of Boehm's work.

RPC-706-01 MISCHIEF, glazed, decorated (RP-730) 4 made

RPC-706-02 INNOCENCE, glazed, decorated (RP-731) 4 made

Although perhaps intended as use items (and probably designed for sale in pairs), the importance of these pieces lies in the charm of the figures rather than in the functional value of the simple, round powder boxes they adorn. Mischief is a faun on the cover of a round powder box with the left

180

RPC-707-01   RPC-711-01   RPC-709-02   RPC-710-01   RPC-708-01

hand bent in back above its short tail and the right hand bent near the waist. Innocence is a cherub with blue wings and drape on the cover of a round powder box; the cherub's head is tilted back and a butterfly sits on its upraised left hand.

Introduced around 1952, they were discontinued after only four of each had been completed.

RPC-707-01 NEPTUNE WITH SEA-HORSE, bisque, decorated (RP-701) 30 made

RPC-707-02 NEPTUNE WITH SEA-HORSE, bisque, undecorated (RP-702) 24 made

RPC-708-01 DIANA WITH FAWN, bisque, decorated (RP-703) 20 made

RPC-708-02 DIANA WITH FAWN, bisque, undecorated (RP-704) 22 made

RPC-709-01 VENUS, bisque, decorated (RP-705) 50 made

RPC-709-02 VENUS, bisque, undecorated (RP-706) 50 made

RPC-710-01 MERCURY, bisque, decorated (RP-707) 50 made

RPC-710-02 MERCURY, bisque, undecorated (RP-708) 50 made

RPC-711-01 APOLLO, bisque, decorated (RP-709) 30 made

RPC-711-02 APOLLO, bisque, undecorated (RP-710) 21 made

These figures represent the "Babyhood of the Gods" series introduced by the Boehm Studio in 1953. All the figures are approximately 7½" high and all are charming. The Neptune with Seahorse depicts a boy standing with his right knee bent on a stylized wave base, his head facing left. The top half of the seahorse rests against Neptune's left thigh. Neptune's legs, with knees bent, protrude on either side of the seahorse, which faces left. The boy's left hand holds a trident rising above the head of the seahorse. Diana with Fawn shows a young girl standing on an oval base, facing one-quarter right and wearing a crescent symbol on her head; her right leg is bent up at the knee. Her left arm is bent at the elbow; her left hand holds a bow. Her right hand rests on the neck of

the fawn at her right. Venus depicts a young girl standing on a round base composed of round shells. Her head is tilted to the right and her eyes are closed; her right arm is bent up and the left arm is curved down to hold a narrow swirling drape.

Mercury depicts a young boy standing on a round base wearing winged sandals and hat. His right arm is bent at the elbow; his right hand holds a caduceus. His head is tilted back and to the left. His left leg is bent up at the knee and his left arm is extended to the side. The Apollo figure is a young boy standing on a round base surrounded by stylized clouds in front of a flat round sun symbol. His left arm is bent up at the elbow while his left hand holds a lyre. His right hand rests on his hip and holds the end of a narrow drape which is pulled up to the left shoulder and across the front of his neck. They bear the Boehm Studiomark Numbers 901 through 905 and examples of all of the pieces have been found with makersmark F as well as makersmark D. The series was discontinued in 1959. The quantities produced vary: Neptune—54; Diana—

181

RPC-712-02

approximately 42; Venus and Mercury—nearly 100 each; Apollo—51.

RPC-712-01 QUAN YIN, glazed, undecorated (RP-711) 60 made
RPC-712-02 QUAN YIN, bisque, undecorated (RP-712) 20 made

Intended to suggest the Chinese figures which were carved in one piece from a single tusk of ivory, these 16″ high figures were first introduced in 1954 under Boehm Studiomark Number 906. They represent a curved Oriental figure in long flowing garments, wearing a high headdress, arms folded across the waist. Strangely enough, although the piece is believed to have been discontinued by 1956, examples of both finishes have turned up bearing makersmark F. This would seem to indicate that a number of the 80 or so examples were left over after the official discontinuance of the piece and the makersmarks were applied much later, when the pieces were finally sold or given away.

RPC-713-01 CUPID WITH FLUTE, glazed, decorated (RP-713) 19 made
RPC-713-02 CUPID WITH FLUTE, bisque, decorated (RP-715) 22 made
RPC-713-03 CUPID WITH FLUTE, bisque, undecorated (RP-714) 172 made
RPC-714-01 CUPID WITH HARP, glazed, decorated (RP-716) 14 made
RPC-714-02 CUPID WITH HARP, bisque, decorated (RP-718) 12 made
RPC-714-03 CUPID WITH HARP, bisque, undecorated (RP-717) 196 made
RPC-715-01 CUPID WITH HORN, glazed, decorated (RP-719) 12 made
RPC-715-02 CUPID WITH HORN, bisque, decorated (RP-721) 21 made
RPC-715-03 CUPID WITH HORN, bisque, undecorated (RP-720) 194 made

Just over 200 of each of the three Cupids were produced between their introduction in 1954 and their discontinuance in 1959.

They carry the Boehm Studiomark Numbers 907 through 909 and all are approximately 5″ high. The Cupid with Flute shows a figure of a young faun seated on a stylized scrolled base, right hoof raised, with head tilted right, playing a pipe. The Cupid with Harp depicts a winged cherub seated on a stylized, scrolled pedestal, head tilted, strumming a lyre held in the right hand against the right shoulder. The Cupid with Horn depicts a cherub seated on a stylized, scrolled pedestal, both knees drawn up, right hand bent up to the right shoulder, head tilted far back, blowing a short flared-mouthed horn.

RPC-716-01 BALLERINA, SWAN LAKE, glazed, decorated (RP-724) 4 made
RPC-716-02 BALLERINA, SWAN LAKE, bisque, decorated (RP-723) 12 made
RPC-716-03 BALLERINA, SWAN LAKE, bisque, undecorated (RP-722) 325 made

Introduced in 1954 under Boehm Studiomark Number 910, this lovely 7¼″ Ballerina remained in production through 1961, although after 1957 only the undecorated example was available. This sculpture is a Ballerina dressed in a tutu and wearing a tiny crown headdress. She is on point in the open fifth position, right leg leading, bent slightly forward at the waist; arms are shown in lower fifth position, left wrist crossed over the right, head forward, facing down. The Swan rests at her left with its neck curved right, touching the Ballerina's left knee.

RPC-717 ICHABOD CRANE, glazed, decorated (RP-736) 2 made

As mentioned previously, the Ichabod is not one of Ed Boehm's original sculptures, but he did cast it in porcelain. There were only two replicas made of this 7½″ high sculpture.

RPC-718-01 CHERUB ON PEDESTAL, bisque, undecorated (RP-725) 250 made

RPC-715-03

RPC-714-03

RPC-713-03

RPC-716-06

RPC-717

RPC-718-01

RPC-719-01

RPC-720-01

RPC-720-04

RPC-718-02 CHERUB ON PEDESTAL, bisque, decorated—unique

RPC-718-03 CHERUB ON PEDESTAL, glazed, decorated—unique

This decorative figure is 5½″ high and was introduced, under Boehm Studiomark Number 911, in 1957. This sculpture is a winged Cherub in flight, right side resting on a narrow, circular, rococo, four-footed pedestal. The Cherub holds a looped drape in both hands. It was discontinued late in 1958, after approximately 250 had been produced. I have reason to assume that at least one or two pieces were done in bisque, decorated or glazed, decorated condition. If so, of course, these would be extremely valuable pieces.

RPC-719-01 GAY NINETIES (pr.) glazed, decorated (RP-728) 3 made

RPC-719-02 GAY NINETIES (pr.) bisque, decorated (RP-739) unique

RPC-719-03 GAY NINETIES (pr.) glazed, undecorated (RP-729) 6 made

RPC-719-04 GAY NINETIES (pr.) bisque, undecorated—unique

These charmingly costumed figurines were introduced in 1954. The sculpture depicts a man and woman on individual bases dressed in 1890 costumes. The man is holding his hat in his left hand against his chest and the woman holds her skirt with her right hand. They appear on the 1956 Boehm Studio price list, and there seem to have been only 11 pairs produced in all, three glazed and decorated, one in the bisque decoration, six glazed, undecorated and one in the bisque, undecorated. The

only year this pair was officially merchandized was 1956, according to our records. However, it is possible that the price lists of 1954 and 1955 also carried it.

RPC-720-01 BEAU BRUMMELLS, OLD (pr.) glazed, decorated (RP-727) unique

RPC-720-02 BEAU BRUMMELLS, OLD, Male only, glazed, undecorated—unique

RPC-720-03 BEAU BRUMMELLS, OLD (pr.) bisque, undecorated (RP-726) 4 made

RPC-720-04 BEAU BRUMMELLS I (pr.) glazed, decorated (RP-741) 1 made

RPC-720-05 BEAU BRUMMELLS I (pr.) glazed, white—4 made

RPC-720-06 BEAU BRUMMELLS II (pr.) glazed, decorated (RP-742) 2 made*

RPC-720-07 BEAU BRUMMELS II (pr.) glazed, white—1 made

*See page 43

RPC-721-01   RPC-722

First introduced in 1954, under Boehm Studiomark Number 912, the Beau Brummells represent a man in daytime dress holding a walking stick and a lady in evening dress holding a nosegay. Of these early pieces, we believe only five and a half pairs were produced: one glazed and decorated, four bisque, undecorated and one male glazed, undecorated. The three "old" Beau Brummells were discontinued in 1956.

In 1968, Ed Boehm slightly redesigned the sculpture and issued Beau Brummells I (a pair in evening dress) as a limited edition of 500 pairs. The lady of this new edition is the same sculpture as the female figure of the old Beau Brummells, with some slight variations in position.

The gentleman of the old Beau Brummells shows up in the Beau Brummells II, a pair in daytime dress, introduced in 1970,

also as a limited edition of 500. The only differences are in coloration and, as mentioned previously, slight variations in position. Coin gold is used on the bases, fob and buttons of the Beau Brummells I and on the fob of the Beau Brummells II. The lady of the former sculpture also wears solid gold hairpins. The Boehm Studio decided in February, 1973, not to produce these figures. They did produce four pairs of Beau Brummells I and three pairs of Beau Brummells II. None were sold.

RPC-721-01 SHRINER, glazed, decorated (gray trousers), 10 made
RPC-721-02 SHRINER, glazed, decorated (black trousers), 50 made

This little figure is about 3¾″ high on a small round base. He is in full Shriner cos-

tume including the red fez. At the request of a friend, Ed Boehm made this sculpture in 1947 or 1948. In error he placed gray trousers on the fat little man—only about ten of these "error" pieces were made. The correction was then made and an additional 50 black-trousered Shriner figures were produced.

RPC-722 JAN AND JOHNNY, glazed, decorated—rare

This 3¾″ high pair was made from a hobby mold in the 1950's. Neither we nor the Studio have any idea how many were made except that "very few" were produced. They are in Southern antebellum costume with the young gentleman holding a bouquet of flowers and the young lady primly picking up her skirt.

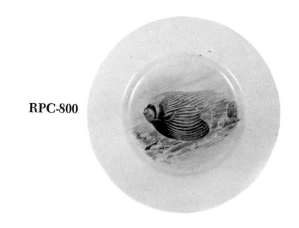

RPC-800

RPC-801-01

RPC-801-03

RPC-801-05

IX. Useful Accessories

Useful accessories that were merchandized were produced in fairly large quantities; lesser quantities usually represent pieces that were discontinued due to lack of response on the part of the buyers. Naturally, the value of these pieces today is dependent upon the number of each that have survived, the number that are available from private sources and the value each owner has placed on his piece for the resale market.

The survival rate among the accessories is low. Many Boehm collectors who instantly recognize a Boehm figure, a Boehm bird, or horse or dog seem to have little information concerning the useful accessories. For this reason much of this category of Boehm is undoubtedly lying around in antique shops and in attics while waiting to be found or waiting to be lost. Also, because of the low prices of these accessories and, at that time, total lack of recognition of the maker, the dispersal was wide and the destruction rate was high.

There are, however, a number of exceptions. There exist accessory pieces as rare and as valuable as pieces in any other category of Boehm porcelain. These are the unique (in its literal sense) pieces, designed as personal gifts by Ed Boehm, and the highly successful design experiments shelved for unknown reasons after only the first few pieces were cast.

During these early days, Ed Boehm spent a good deal of time and effort in developing the body which contributed to his recognition as a master ceramist. It was in these accessory pieces that the experimentation was done. In fact, a number of these useful accessories which were preserved, at later times would have been destroyed at the kiln as imperfect. These are the pieces which came out of the kiln flawed or warped or bent and were obviously being used by the factory in order to perfect technique and controls. From a historical

point of view, every collection of Boehm should have at least one of the accessory category.

The accessories generally carry makers-mark D, although there are exceptions, which will be noted.

DINNERWARE AND SERVING PIECES

RPC-800 SERVICE PLATE, glazed, decorated—unique

This is a 10¼″ plate, decorated with a tropical fish. Only one is known to exist.

RPC-801-01 "WILD FLOWER" SERVICE PLATE, 10″, glazed, decorated with colored flowers (RP-801) 24 made

RPC-801-02 "WILD FLOWER" DEMI-TASSE CUP AND SAUCER, glazed, decorated with colored flowers (RP-802) 14 made

RPC-801-03 "WILD FLOWER" DEMI-TASSE CUP AND SAUCER, glazed, decorated with gold flowers (RP-948) 6 made

RPC-801-04 "WILD FLOWER" TEACUP AND SAUCER, glazed, decorated with colored flowers (RP-949) 6 made

This is believed to be the first dinnerware pattern designed by Edward Boehm (although RPC-800 may possibly predate it). It was produced in 1950 and bears his signature on the reverse (similar to makers-mark D). There were 24 service plates, 20 demi-tasse cups and saucers (14 with colored flowers and 6 with gold) and one teacup and saucer produced. There are no records indicating the sale of any of these pieces.

The service plates in the "Wild Flower" pattern are round with 1¾″ rim decorated black with colored flowers. There is a black 2¾″ circle in the center, decorated with colored flowers. The demi-tasse cups with colored flowers are cylindrical with plain scroll handles. The saucers are decorated in colored flowers on a black background.

The demi-tasse cup with gold is a deep round cup, narrowing at the bottom, then widening into a circular base with an angled handle.

The teacup and saucer has a narrow circular base and rounded scroll handle. The rimmed saucer is decorated with colored flowers on a black background.

These pieces plus the 24 service plates are not widely dispersed. Only three people have them all.

RPC-801-05 "GAUDY DUTCH" DINNER SERVICE, glazed, decorated—unique

"Gaudy Dutch" Service is an absolutely unique undertaking in the entire range of the Boehm output. It is the only important set of Boehm that we know of which was not done on Ed Boehm's own body.

One of the directors of Lenox, Inc., a friend of Boehm, provided 16 place settings at Boehm's request. Ed Boehm and Franz Fenzel, the German decorator who was helpful to Ed in the early days, produced a set of the "Gaudy Dutch." The set was painted with beautiful bright colors and each piece was signed on the front by Fenzel. Fenzel's signature makes this service even more remarkable, since it is the only production of the Boehm factory I know of which bears a signature other than Boehm's. The reverse side shows a blue mark which has covered the Lenox backstamp and to one side is written in script "Boehm hand painted." This mark is rare and used only for specially decorated pieces. There were 16 five-piece place settings produced plus one platter, one creamer and one sugar. The 16 place settings are a curious number. I have a feeling that the number produced was directly related to the number of blanks acquired from Lenox. The colors are remarkable and the sureness of the decorator's hand is evident in every piece. I know of no other

"Gaudy Dutch" service done in this country with such authority and with such force.

RPC-802 AFTER-DINNER CUP, glazed, decorated white with gold trim—approximately 24 made

These 3¾" x 3" cups appear on the 1952 Boehm Studio price list. The estimate of the number made is a guess. There were no hard and fast records kept but the best approximation we can get is approximately 24.

RPC-803-01 DEMI-TASSE CUP ON BASE, glazed, decorated white with gold trim (RP-803) 6 made

RPC-803-02 DEMI-TASSE CUP ON BASE, glazed, ground color body pink (RP-804) 4 made

RPC-803-03 DEMI-TASSE CUP ON BASE, glazed, ground color body celadon (RP-805) 4 made

RPC-803-04 DEMI-TASSE CUP ON BASE, glazed, blue—extremely rare

RPC-803-05 DEMI-TASSE CUP ON BASE, glazed, decorated (handpainted) extremely rare

These cups are approximately 3¾" high on a square base. They are believed to have been produced between 1952 and 1954 and do not appear to have been merchandized. The glazed, handpainted example was done by Franz Fenzel and has the *very* rare makersmark "Boehm" in script followed by the word "Handpainted."

Generally the same thing is true of these demi-tasse cups as was true of the RPC 802 after-dinner cups. These are among the rarest bodies ever produced by Boehm in work which was entirely his own. There were other celadon pieces produced, but they were derived from commercial molds.

RPC-804-01 NUT DISH, glazed, decorated white with gold trim—approximately 36 made

RPC-804-02 NUT DISH, glazed, ground color body pink—approximately 36 made

These appear only on the Boehm Studio price list of 1952, but do not appear on the 1953 price list. Therefore we must assume that they were discontinued due to lack of response. The number produced is, at present, unknown.

RPC-805-01 LOTUS BOWL, large (7"), glazed, decorated white with gold trim—rare

RPC-805-02 LOTUS BOWL, large, glazed, ground color body pink—rare

RPC-805-03 LOTUS BOWL, large, glazed, undecorated (RP-866) 88 made

RPC-805-04 LOTUS BOWL, large bisque,

RPC-803-04

RPC-805-04

187

RPC-808-01

RPC-809-01

RPC-807

undecorated (RP-865) 70 made
RPC-805-05 LOTUS BOWL, small (4½″) glazed, decorated white with gold trim— very rare
RPC-805-06 LOTUS BOWL, small, glazed, undecorated (RP-868) rare
RPC-805-07 LOTUS BOWL, small, bisque, undecorated (RP-867) rare

This is a bowl with six flaring petal-shaped panels, each divided in the center by a vertical line similar to that which separates each pointed "petal." The large bowl is first listed in 1952. In 1958, the small glazed bowls appear, and in 1959 the large bisque appears at the same price.

The pieces all bear Boehm Studiomark Number 764 and examples of the large glazed, undecorated bowl have been found with makersmark F.

RPC-806-01 GRAVY BOAT, glazed, undecorated, very rare
RPC-806-02 GRAVY BOAT, bisque, undecorated, very rare
RPC-806-03 GRAVY BOAT, no description available (RP-978) unique
RPC-806-04 GRAVY BOAT, no description available (RP-979) unique
RPC-806-05 GRAVY BOAT, no description available (RP-980) unique

The gravy boats are believed to have been produced in 1952, although they were never merchandised. They were made of Boehm's slip but were not modelled by Boehm. These were sculptured by the Artists Studio in New York, possibly by a sculptor named Davis. In fact, Boehm did not like them.

Originally the last three were believed to be in the collection of the Philadelphia Academy of Natural Sciences. However, it now appears that the Academy has neither record nor recollection of any gravy boat ever having been in its possession. It is possible the Academy simply didn't realize the importance of the pieces which were tucked away and forgotten in one of its

cavernous attics. There are many stories of museums losing pieces for many years, and it is possible that the Academy may some day come across them. We can only wait and see if these unique pieces reappear. Further research has not yet produced any examples, and it is quite possible that, if any are found, they will turn out to be examples of one of the first two decorations listed.

RPC-807 BUNNY MILK MUG, glazed, decorated (RP-925) 93 made

This piece may have been introduced between 1954 and 1956 and carries Boehm Studiomark Number 735. It is 3″ high and it is believed that 93 were produced prior to its discontinuance in 1957. Examples are also known to carry makersmark F.

RPC-808-01 BEE BASKET, glazed, decorated (RP-827) 42 made
RPC-808-02 BEE BASKET, bisque, decorated—rare
RPC-808-03 BEE BASKET, bisque, undecorated (RP-828) 206 made

The fact that there seem to have been approximately 42 glazed and decorated examples of this 3″ x 2″ candy dish produced, leads us to believe that it was introduced around 1954. It was discontinued late in 1957.

The piece carries Boehm Studiomark Number 746 and examples of the glazed decoration have been discovered to bear makersmark F. It is a round candy dish, molded to represent a woven basket with a bee perched on the rim.

RPC-809-01 TULIP DINNER BELL, glazed, undecorated (RP-832) 250 made
RPC-809-02 TULIP DINNER BELL, bisque, undecorated (RP-831) 442 made

This 4″ dinner bell (which bears Boehm Studiomark Number 749) is a charming addition to any table setting and seems to have been quite popular, since over 650 were produced, the larger quantity (442) in bisque. The piece was probably introduced in 1955 and appears glazed in 1956. In 1958 the glazed edition was discontinued and replaced by the bisque, which was discontinued in 1960.

Glazed examples have been found bearing makersmark F. The piece is in the shape of a tulip blossom, the stem forming the handle.

RPC-810-01 MUFFINEER, glazed, decorated white with gold trim (RP-885) 21 made

RPC-810-02 MUFFINEER, glazed, undecorated (RP-883) 89 made

RPC-810-03 MUFFINEER, bisque, undecorated (RP-884) 68 made

RPC-810-04 MUFFINEER, large, 12″ high, glazed, decorated white and pink—unique

RPC-810-05 MUFFINEER, large, 12″ high, glazed, undecorated—unique

The small Muffineer (or, if you prefer, "Sugar Shaker") is 5″ high and was introduced under Boehm Studiomark Number 765, around 1955 or 1956. It is a round body on a circular base rising to a concave cylindrical neck. The body is irregularly fluted. The dome lid, pierced by diagonal curving slits, is topped by a button knob. There appear to have been 180 pieces in all produced before the item was discontinued in 1958.

The large Muffineers, although identical in design to the smaller version, were actually intended as lamp bases. For some reason, however, this project was abandoned after only two examples had been completed. Both examples are now in the collection of Syracuse University.

RPC-811-01 TULIP BOWL, glazed, ground color body pink (RP-892) 8 made

RPC-811-02 TULIP BOWL, glazed, ground color body celadon (RP-893) 7 made

RPC-811-03 TULIP BOWL, glazed, undecorated (RP-890) 200 made

RPC-811-04 TULIP BOWL, bisque, undecorated (RP-891) 10 made

The Tulip Bowl does not appear on any of the Boehm Studio price lists that we have. However, since our research indicates that over 200 were produced of the glazed, undecorated example alone, we must assume that the piece was introduced in either 1954 or 1955, years for which we have no price lists. By 1956 the piece had been discontinued. It is a round bowl molded in the shape of 12 overlapping pointed tulip petals curving out from the round base and in at the mouth. It is 7″ x 4″ and carries no Boehm Studiomark Number. Several of the first three decorations have been found with makersmark F, although the majority bear makersmark D. There were few produced in the pink, celadon and undecorated bisque, only 8, 7 and 10 respectively, and none of any decoration has appeared at auction.

RPC-812-01 ROSE PITCHER, 7″ high, glazed, decorated (RP-951) unique

RPC-812-02 ROSE PITCHER, 7″ high, glazed, undecorated (RP-900) 664 made

RPC-812-03 ROSE PITCHER, 7″ high, bisque, undecorated (RP-901) 185 made

The glazed, decorated example of this piece is unique: only one was produced and this particular decoration was never marketed. Obviously it was intended as an experiment. It is a four-sided pitcher of generally rectangular shape, rising from a square base, with a pointed spout and a rectangular scroll handle. The sides are cross-hatched and bear raised roses. In 1956, the undecorated examples were offered for general sale, the glazed from 1956 through 1958 and the bisque from 1959 through 1961.

Several of the glazed, undecorated examples have come to light bearing makers-

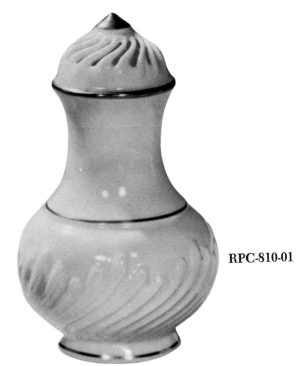

RPC-810-01

RPC-811-03

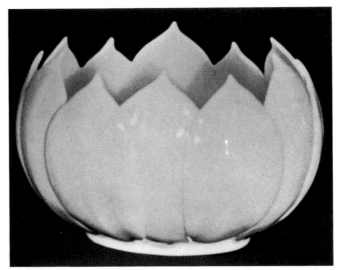

RPC-812-03

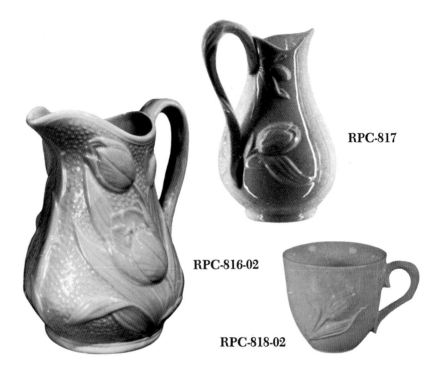

RPC-817

RPC-816-02

RPC-818-02

RPC-814-01 RPC-813-01 RPC-815-01

mark F. The piece itself, in all decorations, bears Boehm Studiomark Number 801. It seems to have been an extremely popular item, with 664 glazed, undecorated and 185 bisque, undecorated produced during the six years of its availability.

RPC-813-01 ROSE COFFEE POT, glazed, undecorated (RP-913) 25 made
RPC-813-02 ROSE COFFEE POT, bisque, undecorated (RP-914) 6 made

Although this is basically the same piece as the Rose Pitcher (the only difference being the addition of the lid) it does not appear to have enjoyed the same popularity. Its only year of activity seems to have been 1956. The piece carries Boehm Studiomark Number 810, and several of the glazed, undecorated examples have been discovered with makersmark F. Thirty-one pots were produced in all, 25 glazed and 6 bisque, and none of these has appeared at auction to our knowledge.

RPC-814-01 ROSE SUGAR BOWL, 5″ high, glazed, undecorated (RP-915) 24 made
RPC-814-02 ROSE SUGAR BOWL, 5″ high, bisque, undecorated (RP-916) 5 made

RPC-815-01 ROSE CREAMER, 4½″ high, glazed, undecorated (RP-917) 24 made
RPC-815-02 ROSE CREAMER, 4½″ high, bisque, undecorated (RP-918) 4 made

Obviously meant as companion pieces to the Rose Coffee Pot, and also introduced and discontinued in the same year (1956). The numbers produced seem to be 24 each of the glazed pair and, of the bisque, five sugar bowls and four creamers. Again, examples of the two glazed pieces have been found to bear makersmark F. They carry Boehm Studiomark Numbers 811 and 812 respectively. The Rose Sugar Bowl is a four-sided square bowl and lid with a square knob. It has square scroll handles at two corners, a square base and panels which are cross-hatched and decorated with raised roses. The Rose Creamer is the same as the Rose Pitcher (RPC-812).

The Rose Sugar Bowl and Creamer should be considered as a set. It is unlikely that a set survived, especially since the bisque Sugar Bowl and the bisque Creamer were done in such small quantities.

RPC-816-01 TULIP PITCHER, 6½″ high,

glazed, decorated (RP-950) unique
RPC-816-02 TULIP PITCHER, 6½″ high, glazed, undecorated (RP-902) 185 made
RPC-816-03 TULIP PITCHER, 6½″ high, bisque, undecorated (RP-903) 40 made
RPC-817 TULIP PITCHER, LARGE, 7½″ high, glazed, undecorated (RP-954) 5 made
RPC-818-01 TULIP CUP, glazed, decorated —rare
RPC-818-02 TULIP CUP, glazed, undecorated—rare
RPC-818-03 TULIP CUP, bisque, undecorated—rare
RPC-819 TULIP NUTMEG SHAKER, glazed, decorated—extremely rare

The Tulip series was first introduced in 1956. It is a pear-shaped pitcher on a round base with an uneven mouth and a curved spout. The handle is entwined tulip stems. Raised tulips and leaves decorate the body of the pitcher. In 1956 the glazed, undecorated pitcher (6½″) with Boehm Studiomark Number 802 was listed on the Boehm Studio price list. It was discontinued late in 1957. There were approximately 185 in this decoration, 40 bisque, undecorated and

190

RPC-820-02

RPC-821-01   RPC-822-01

RPC-823

RPC-824

only one glazed and decorated. Examples of the glazed, undecorated Pitcher have been found with makersmark F.

The only other piece in this series to appear on any price list we have been able to locate is the large Pitcher (Boehm Studiomark Number 806), which is listed in 1959. Neither the Tulip Cups nor the Tulip Nutmeg Shaker have turned up on these price lists, nor have any of the series been sold at auction.

There is every possibility that this series was actually introduced in 1954 or 1955. If so, the cups may well have been marketed during that time. However, this is purely speculative. The Nutmeg Shaker, on the other hand, may not have been marketed at all, since our information indicates that only the glazed, decorated example was produced and it carries no Boehm Studiomark number.

RPC-820-01 GRAPE PITCHER, 8½″, glazed, decorated, Purple Grape (RP-907) 55 made

RPC-820-02 GRAPE PITCHER, 8½″, glazed, decorated, Natural Grape (RP-906) 178 made

RPC-820-03 GRAPE PITCHER, 8½″, glazed, decorated, Blue Grape (RP-905) 61 made

RPC-820-04 GRAPE PITCHER, 8½″, glazed, undecorated, approximately 200 made

RPC-820-05 GRAPE PITCHER, 8½″, bisque, undecorated (RP-904) approximately 200 made

This piece also first appears on the price lists (under Boehm Studiomark Number 803) in 1956. It is a pear-shaped pitcher with a high curving spout and scroll handle on a circular pedestal base. It has raised grape leaves on the handle, grape clusters on the body of the pitcher at the base of the handle and on the rim beside the handle. By 1960, the undecorated bisque was the only one still in production. It was finally discontinued during the collection revision of 1962.

The quantities of the decorated examples are fairly small: 55 purple, 178 natural and 61 blue. However, the undecorated example was obviously quite popular, with 400 having been completed by 1962.

The Grape Pitcher series is interesting

from a collector's point of view because it should be possible to put together a set of these pieces without too much difficulty. Pitchers survive better than other pieces since they are a recognizable use item and tend not to be thrown away. There was a sufficient quantity produced so that it is not unlikely that they can be found. The other interesting fact about this series is that this is one of the few series in which each piece was made in three separate colors.

Makersmark F has been discovered on all the glazed examples.

RPC-821-01 HOLLY PITCHER, 7½″ high, glazed, decorated (RP-908) 525 made

RPC-821-02 HOLLY PITCHER, 7½″ high, glazed, decorated Blue (RP-909) 6 made

RPC-822-01 HOLLY CUP, 2½″ high, glazed, decorated (RP-910) 3,768 made

RPC-822-02 HOLLY CUP, 2½″ high, glazed, decorated Blue (RP-911) 36 made

RPC-823 HOLLY NUTMEG SHAKER, 2″ high, glazed, decorated (RP-912) 372 made

191

RPC-824 HOLLY TRAY, 13″ diameter, glazed, decorated (RP-960) unique

First appearing on the price lists in 1956, the Holly series was the most popular of the dinnerware and serving pieces. There were 525 decorated pitchers and 3,768 decorated cups produced. The Holly Pitcher is a pear-shaped pitcher with a high spout and scroll handle on a circular base with raised holly leaves and berries on the handle and beside the top and the base of the handle. The Holly cups are bell-shaped mugs, without handles, with raised holly sprigs on the sides. The Holly Nutmeg Shaker is bell-shaped, rising to a narrow neck and circular top, pierced with holes. It has a scroll handle of holly branches, raised holly leaves and berries at the base of the handle. The Holly tray is a flat circular tray, with raised holly leaves and berries around the rim. The center is decorated with a bird (Trogon). In addition, there were six Blue sets, consisting of the pitcher and six cups in each set. The Blue cups and pitchers and the Nutmeg Shaker were discontinued in 1958. The pitchers bear Boehm Studiomark Number 804, and the cups Boehm Studiomark Number 805. The Nutmeg Shaker carries Boehm Studiomark Number 808. The Tray is a unique piece, there having been only one produced; the year of production is unknown.

Except for the Tray, which bears makersmark D, examples of all pieces in the Holly series have been found bearing makersmark F.

RPC-825-01 CRIMPED BOWL, 5″ diameter, glazed, ground color body Pink—12 made

RPC-825-02 CRIMPED BOWL, 5″ diameter, glazed, undecorated (RP-941) 12 made

RPC-826 FRUIT BOWL SET, glazed, decorated (RP-922) 12 made

RPC-827-01 SHELL PLATTER, 10″ diameter, glazed, undecorated (RP-952) 25 made

RPC-827-02 SHELL PLATTER, 10″ diameter, bisque, undecorated (RP-975) 25 made

RPC-827-03 SHELL PLATTER, small, glazed, undecorated—12 made

RPC-827-04 SHELL PLATTER, small, bisque, undecorated—unique

RPC-828 CRIMPED CANDY DISH, 5″ diameter, glazed, decorated white with gold trim (RP-942) 12 made

RPC-829-01 FLUTED NUT DISH, 5″ diameter, glazed, decorated white with gold trim (RP-962) 12 made

RPC-829-02 FLUTED NUT DISH, 5″ diameter, glazed, ground color body Pink —12 made

RPC-829-03 FLUTED NUT DISH, 5″ diameter, glazed, ground color body Celadon—12 made

RPC-829-04 FLUTED NUT DISH, 5″ diameter, bisque, undecorated (RP-961) 12 made

The Crimped Bowl is round on a circular base, rising to a narrow crimped mouth. The Fruit Bowl Set is comprised of one large and four small bowls. They are shallow round bowls on circular bases decorated with raised strawberry clusters.

The Shell Platter is a flat, circular platter molded in the form of a mussel shell. The Crimped Candy Dish is a round shallow bowl on a circular base rising to a flared, crimped mouth. The Fluted Nut Dish is a round dish with flared and fluted sides.

This group were all experimental, unmarketed pieces (since none carry any Boehm Studiomark Numbers) and all, with the exception of the Shell Platter, were produced in quantities of a dozen or less. The platter is believed to have been produced in a quantity of approximately 50 and may have been offered for sale either in 1954 or 1955. However, we cannot verify this.

RPC-825-02

RPC-826

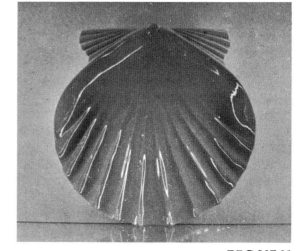

RPC-827-01

These pieces were probably all produced during those two years, although, again, we have no proof. The only thing we can say with any certainty is that none survived the collection revision of 1962, nor have they been available since.

Since this group was experimental in conception, they offer a considerable insight into what Ed Boehm decided was marketable and what was not. For this reason, an example or two of these pieces would be an interesting addition to any serious collection.

RPC-830-01 SHELL NUT DISH, glazed, decorated white inside, pink outside—rare

RPC-830-02 SHELL NUT DISH, glazed, ground color body Pink (RP-897) 98 made

RPC-830-03 SHELL NUT DISH, glazed, ground color body Celadon (RP-898) 94 made

RPC-830-04 SHELL NUT DISH, glazed, decorated (RP-899) 62 made

RPC-830-05 SHELL NUT DISH, glazed, undecorated (RP-896) 150 made

The fact that over 400 of these were produced leads us to believe that the correct year of introduction was either 1954 or 1955, since they were obviously marketed but do not appear on any of the price lists we have located. The piece is 5″ x 4¼″ and bears Boehm Studiomark Number 772. It is an oblong shell with an irregularly peaked rim and an upward curving scroll handle, on an oval base. Examples of all decorations have been discovered with makersmark F.

RPC-831 TRIPLE LOTUS BOWL, glazed, decorated (RP-953) possibly unique

In the 1964 Retrospective Exhibition Catalog, this piece was incorrectly designated as "Three Section Nut Dish." We have since discovered its proper designation and the fact that it carries Boehm Studiomark Number 776. It is composed of three irregularly circular dishes joined by a green asparagus-tip knob. It was originally believed to be a unique piece, but since it carries a Studiomark Number, I am led to the assumption that it may have been produced in larger quantities and even marketed (probably in 1954 or 1955). However, to date only one has come to light and our assumption must remain that it is unique until further information becomes available.

RPC-832-01 FLUTED SHELL, SMALL, 5″, glazed, undecorated, probably less than 100 made

RPC-832-02 FLUTED SHELL, SMALL, 5″, bisque, undecorated (RP-919) 50 made

RPC-832-03 FLUTED SHELL, LARGE, 7″, glazed, undecorated—probably less than 100 made

RPC-832-04 FLUTED SHELL, LARGE, 7″, bisque, undecorated (RP-920) 200 made

This piece enjoyed some degree of popularity, especially in bisque, with 200 large and 50 small produced between 1959, the year of its introduction, and 1961. The small size carries Boehm Studiomark Number 771 and the large, 778. It is an oval shell, fluted on the outside in four tiers, with four small feet formed from projections of the fluting. The flared and fluted handle curves up.

RPC-833 CHERUB NUT DISH, bisque, undecorated (RP-930) 10 made

This 5″ x 11″ double dish (cherub holding bird between two leaf-shaped dishes) carries Boehm Studiomark Number 780. There were only about 10 produced and it, too, if it was marketed at all, must have been introduced either in 1954 or 1955.

RPC-S34-01 "GOLDEN-CROWNED KING-LETS" SERVICE PLATE, glazed, decorated—unique*

*See page 85

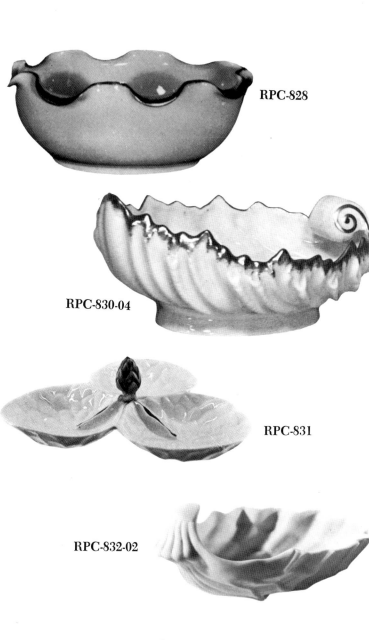

RPC-828

RPC-830-04

RPC-831

RPC-832-02

RPC-832-04

RPC-833

RPC-835   RPC-836-01

RPC-834-02 "GOLDEN-CROWNED KING-LETS" CUP, glazed, decorated—unique

These are definitely unique, being models for a dinnerware pattern that had been planned for future introduction. They are still in the possession of the Boehm Studio.

RPC-835 MUG, white, undecorated pottery—approximately 20 made

These are an example of one of the few pieces of pottery Ed Boehm ever made (as distinguished from the hard-paste porcelain body which Ed made famous). They are, in all probability, from commercial molds and were done in extremely small numbers.

It is believed that between 15 and 20 of these pieces were made, around 1951-1952.

I have seen five pieces signed on the bottom with the name "Alex." It is conceivable that this name was put on the bottom to prevent the piece from being identified as one from the Boehm Studio. Obviously even in those early days Ed felt secure about his talent and didn't want his name associated with a piece of this type.

We acquired five pieces from Mr. and Mrs. Howard Cugle (he is a brother-in-law of one of Mr. Boehm's uncles). They gave me a letter, reproduced here in full, in which they authenticate the pieces. The provenance is from Ed Boehm, directly to his uncle, Willard T. Boehm, directly to Mr. and Mrs. Cugle, directly to me. Since there is an unbroken succession involved, I am prepared to believe the authenticity.

Dear Mr. Palley:
About fifteen years ago, 5 glazed white mugs were given to Mr. and Mrs. Howard Cugle by an uncle of Edward Marshall Boehm (Willard T. Boehm).
Willard T. Boehm had had these mugs for several years before giving them to the Cugles.
At the time they were given to the Cugles, Willard T. Boehm stated that the mugs had been given to him personally by Edward Marshall Boehm. The mugs had been one of the first pieces ever done by Ed Boehm and had been done as a gag.
September 24, 1971
Howard Cugle
Mr. and Mrs. Howard Cugle
2212 Eastlake Rd.
Timonium, Md. 21093

RPC-836-01 ROOSTER CUP, glazed, decorated—extremely rare

RPC-836-02 ROOSTER CUP, glazed, undecorated—extremely rare

The records and recollections of the Boehm Studio on the Rooster Cup are vague. The Studio remembered the piece only in white, but we know of two examples that were decorated. The Studio indicates that it was not sculpted by Ed Boehm. My feeling is that since the records are vague, it is quite possible that it was an experimental piece of extreme rarity.

RPC-837 TURKEY SALT AND PEPPER SHAKERS, glazed, white—approximately 25 made

These shakers were made from a hobby mold. They are in the shape of turkeys and measure about 1¾". The pieces carry the Boehm makersmark D.

RPC-838 EAGLE DINNER BELL, bisque, undecorated rare

The Eagle Dinner Bell measures 5" and depicts an eagle perched on top of a bell-like base. It carries makersmark D. It was originally made for Mrs. Mary Roebling of Trenton to be given as gifts. The Boehms thought so highly of this attractive piece that they also gave several as gifts.

RPC-838

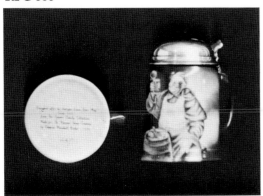

RPC-839-01 HAND-PAINTED BEER MUG WITH PEWTER TOP, varying decorations—6 made

RPC-839-02 HAND-PAINTED BEER MUG, varying decorations—44 made

A total of 50 beer mugs were made. Twenty-three were hand-painted by Franz Fenzel. They were done in 50 different decorations. The mugs are catalogued according to those with pewter tops and those without.

The 840s are RPS rather than RPC because they were actually produced after Ed Boehm died, and to conform with the rest of this catalogue they must carry an RPS designation.

RPS-840 "WOOD THRUSHES" SERVICE PLATE, glazed, decorated—unique

Designed in the latter part of 1969, this plate was originally intended as the model for the limited issue service plate to be produced by Lenox, Inc. (See RPC-835-01 below.) However, after the model was completed, changes in design were made and the original design discarded. Only the one service plate exists and it will never be produced in quantity in its original form.

RPS-840-01 "WOOD THRUSHES WITH AZALEAS" SERVICE PLATE, glazed, decorated with 24 karat gold border

This is the first in a series of Edward Marshall Boehm dinnerware designs to be produced by Lenox, Inc., on Lenox China, as an annual series of limited issue service plates. As will all the future introductions, this plate, which measures 10½″ in diameter, bears the Boehm signature on the front and additional Boehm-Lenox identifications in gold on the reverse. Also on the reverse is the new feather makersmark G. It was produced in a quantity in excess of 10,000 pieces.

RPS-840

RPS-840-01

RPS-840-02

RPS-840-02 "THE GOLDFINCH" SERVICE PLATE, glazed, decorated with 24 karat gold border

This is the second in a series of Edward

195

RPS-840-03

RPS-840-06

RPS-842

RPS-840-04

RPS-840-07

RPS-843

RPS-840-05

RPS-841

RPS-844-01

196

Marshall Boehm dinnerware designs to be produced by Lenox, Inc., on Lenox China.

RPS-840-03 "MOUNTAIN BLUE BIRD" SERVICE PLATE, glazed, decorated with 24 karat gold border

This is the third in a series of Edward Marshall Boehm dinnerware. The Mountain Blue Bird is the official State Bird of Idaho and Nevada.

RPS-840-04 "MEADOWLARK" SERVICE PLATE, glazed, decorated with 24 karat gold border

Issued in 1973, this is the fourth in a Boehm/Lenox Bird plate series. The Meadowlark is the official State Bird of Kansas, Montana, Nebraska, North Dakota, Oregon and Wyoming.

RPS-840-05 "RUFOUS HUMMINGBIRD" SERVICE PLATE, glazed, decorated with 24 karat gold border

This plate was issued in 1974. The Boehm signature appears on the front, while on the back, in gold, are the Boehm feather makersmark G and the Lenox mark.

RPS-840-06 "AMERICAN REDSTART" SERVICE PLATE, glazed, decorated with 24 karat gold border

Based on designs of Edward Marshall Boehm, American Redstart is the sixth in the series of limited edition plates. This plate was issued in 1975.

RPS-840-07 "CARDINAL" SERVICE PLATE, glazed, decorated with 24 karat gold border

Issued in 1976, the Cardinal is the seventh in the Boehm/Lenox service plate series. The Cardinal, an especially popular native American bird, has been honored by being named State Bird of seven of our fifty states.

RPS-841 "BIRD OF PEACE" PLATE (13″) limited to 5,000

Introduced in 1972, the "Bird of Peace" plate is the finest bone porcelain and of regal size. It has an intaglio border filled with hand-applied pure gold. And comes in a handsome white leatherette case. The "Bird of Peace" plate celebrates the porcelain sculpture Mute Swans.

RPS-842 "YOUNG AMERICA 1776" PLATE (13″) limited to 6,000

The "Young America 1776" plate is a companion piece to the "Bird of Peace" plate. This 1973 limited issue is adapted from the young eagle sculpture by Edward Marshall Boehm. The plate features the American Eagle, symbol of the Republic of the United States of America. Like the "Bird of Peace," this plate is of the finest bone porcelain and has an intaglio border filled with pure gold. The white leatherette case is lined with royal blue and red satin.

RPS-843 "HONOR AMERICA" PLATE (10½″) limited to 12,000

Introduced in 1974, the "Honor America" plate features Ed Boehm's famous eagle sculpture completed in 1961. The eagle, the Great Seal of the United States, and the border are of pure gold. A royalty from the net proceeds of the sale of this commemorative Boehm plate goes to the American Historic and Cultural Society, sponsor of Honor America, which supports programs to increase knowledge and appreciation of our cultural heritage, our constitutional form of government and our history.

RPS-844-01 "RACCOONS" WILDLIFE PLATE (10½″) issued only in 1973

Again, as in the Bird plates, artistic beauty and fine craftsmanship are a tribute to two of the most respected names in ceramics— Edward Marshall Boehm and Lenox China. Each plate is crafted of Lenox, enhanced by a border of deep cobalt blue and trimmed with 24 karat gold. Each plate depicts one or more of the following animals in their favorite woodland surroundings. The first in the series was the "Raccoons," issued in 1973.

RPS-844-02 "RED FOXES" WILDLIFE PLATE (10½″) issued only in 1974

The second in the Wildlife series was the "Red Foxes," issued in 1974. It is enhanced by a rich border of deep cobalt blue and trimmed with 24 karat gold.

RPS-844-03 "COTTONTAIL RABBITS" WILDLIFE PLATE (10½″) issued only in 1975

RPS-844-02

RPS-844-03

RPS-844-04

The "Cottontail Rabbits" is the third of the Wildlife plates.

RPS-844-04 "EASTERN CHIPMUNKS" WILDLIFE PLATE (10½") issued only in 1976

The fourth of the Wildlife plates is the "Eastern Chipmunks." All of these plates are well on their way to becoming collector's items.

RPS-845 MALVERN BIRD PLATES— COMPLETE SET OF 8 Individually listed below (10") white bone china, limited to 5,000 sets

This set of eight Bird plates on the purest white bone china represents the first efforts of the Malvern Studio to produce a collector's plate on their own. Introduced in 1974, the set was originally sold only in Europe. The colors are more brilliant and more true than anything that has been seen before. For the most part the plates were sold as sets of eight, but some dealers did sell them separately and we therefore give each of the plates its own unique Reese Palley Studio Number.

RPS-845-01 "SWALLOWS"
RPS-845-02 "BLUE TITS"
RPS-845-03 "KINGFISHER"
RPS-845-04 "GOLDCREST"
RPS-845-05 "CHAFFINCH"
RPS-845-06 "LINNETS"

RPS-845-07 "COAL TITS"
RPS-845-08 "TREE SPARROWS"

ASHTRAYS, BOTTLES AND BOXES
RPC-850-01 SMALL ASHTRAY, glazed, undecorated—quantity made unknown
RPC-850-02 SMALL ASHTRAY, bisque, undecorated—quantity made unknown

This simple, unfluted round ash-tray is a rather early piece and may have been made in fairly large quantity, although it does not appear on any of the price lists in our possession.

RPC-851-01 ROUND FLUTED ASHTRAY, LARGE (4") glazed, ground color body Pink—24 made

RPC-851-02 ROUND FLUTED ASHTRAY, LARGE (4") glazed, ground color body Celadon—24 made

RPC-851-03 ROUND FLUTED ASHTRAY, LARGE (4") glazed, decorated white with gold trim—36 made

RPC-851-04 ROUND FLUTED ASH-TRAY, LARGE (4") glazed, undecorated—24 made

RPC-851-05 ROUND FLUTED ASHTRAY, LARGE (4") bisque, undecorated—24 made

RPC-851-06 ROUND FLUTED ASH-TRAY, SMALL (3") glazed, ground color body Pink—24 made

RPC-851-07 ROUND FLUTED ASH-TRAY, SMALL (3") glazed, ground color body Celadon (RP-969) 24 made

RPC-851-08 ROUND FLUTED ASH-TRAY, SMALL (3") glazed, decorated white with gold trim—48 made

RPC-851-09 ROUND FLUTED ASH-TRAY, SMALL (3") glazed, undecorated (RP-852) 48 made

RPC-851-10 ROUND FLUTED ASH-TRAY, SMALL (3") bisque, undecorated (RP-958) 200 made

This piece has had many names and many numbers in various listings. However, our research, backed by the assistance of the Boehm Studio, indicates that this piece was introduced either in 1952 or earlier and was assigned, in both sizes, Boehm Studiomark Number 708. It is a round, fluted, shallow ashtray, rising to a flared mouth.

In 1952 only the large size was offered, at $2 each. They were discontinued by 1954 and we assume that in total several hundred were produced.

The smaller size does not seem to have been merchandised, unless the 1954 and 1955 price lists carried them.

Although these are extremely small objects, the fact that they were done in such limited quantities makes them valuable. Also, since they were a "throw-away" piece (at $1 apiece, they would be), it is unlikely that many of them survived.

RPC-852-01 RECTANGULAR FLUTED ASHTRAY, glazed, decorated white with gold trim—less than 5 made

RPC-852-02 RECTANGULAR FLUTED ASHTRAY, glazed, undecorated (RP-959) less than 5 made

This piece is not listed on any of the price lists we have nor has it been assigned a Boehm Studiomark Number. We must assume, therefore, that it was an early piece and was not widely merchandized. It is believed that few were produced. It is a 3" rectangular tray with fluted sides that slope up and out.

RPC-853-01 FLUTED CIGARETTE BOX, glazed, decorated, two-tone effect—4 made

RPC-853-02 FLUTED CIGARETTE BOX, glazed, ground color body Pink (RP-818) 9 made

RPC-853-03 FLUTED CIGARETTE BOX, glazed, ground color body Celadon (RP-819) 11 made

RPC-853-04 FLUTED CIGARETTE BOX, glazed, undecorated (RP-820) 49 made

In 1952 the Boehm Studio price list offers a "Fancy Fluted Cigarette Box" in all of the above decorations. The size is listed as 6" x 2½" and it is a rectangular fluted box with a flat, fluted cover. In 1953, the list shows a fluted cigarette box, size 5" x 2", with no mention of a two-toned decoration. The latest complete listing of Boehm works lists three different fluted cigarette boxes (one comprising part of the Medallion Cigarette Set) with two hexagonal fluted ash trays with nest (see RPC-863), glazed and decorated only. However, our research has ascertained, and the Boehm Studio has confirmed, that there was actually only one fluted cigarette box. The correct size is 4¼" x 3" and it carries Boehm Studiomark Number 707. It was not popular, and was discontinued in 1953. The Medallion Cigarette Set was an attempt to sell those cigarette boxes that had been left over. There were perhaps 70 to 75 boxes in all.

RPC-854-01 HEXAGONAL FLUTED ASH-TRAY, glazed, undecorated (RP-821) 250 made

RPC-854-02 HEXAGONAL FLUTED ASH-TRAY, bisque, undecorated (RP-822) 250 made

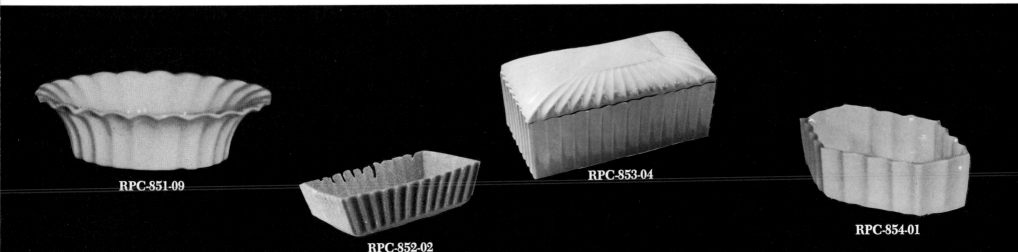

RPC-851-09

RPC-852-02

RPC-853-04

RPC-854-01

RPC-856-01

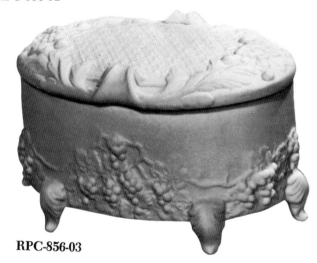

RPC-856-03

RPC-857-02

It is believed that this 3″ long piece is the one listed on the 1952 Boehm price list as "Long Fluted Ash Tray"; however, the listing might have referred to the Rectangular Fluted Ash Tray, RPC-852. The RPC-854 is a rimless fluted ashtray, generally hexagonal in shape, with two side panels, and two panels at each end forming points. The side panels are twice as long as the end panels.

The quantity produced seems to be quite high, 500 or so, and this fact leads us to believe that the merchandizing of this ash tray took place between 1954 and 1955. We have no further information on this piece.

RPC-855-01 BUNNY BOX WITH CAR-ROT, glazed, decorated (RP-869) 63 made

RPC-855-02 BUNNY BOX WITH CAR-ROT, bisque, decorated (RP-974) approximately 10 made*

RPC-855-03 BUNNY BOX WITH CAR-ROT, glazed, undecorated approximately 20 made

RPC-855-04 BUNNY BOX WITH CAR-ROT, bisque, undecorated approximately 20 made

This delightful box was introduced sometime between 1954 and 1956 under Boehm Studiomark Number 715. It first appears on the 1956 price list, decorated. The number actually produced is not known, but it is known that the number is approximately 100. It is an ovoid box and cover, the bottom half being a plain bowl, the top half being the lid. The lid is molded in the shape of a reclining rabbit with a carrot in its mouth.

The piece was discontinued in 1957, and several glazed and decorated examples have been found to bear makersmark F.

RPC-856-01 GRAPE JEWEL BOX WITH TWO CUPIDS, glazed, decorated (RP-921) 2 made

RPC-856-02 GRAPE JEWEL BOX (no

*See page 86

cupids) glazed, undecorated (RP-872) 12 made

RPC-856-03 GRAPE JEWEL BOX (no cupids) bisque, undecorated (RP-871) 124 made

The only one of this series to be merchandized was the undecorated bisque without the cupids. It was introduced between 1954 and 1956 and was discontinued in 1959. There seem to have been about 125 made and the 5″ x 2½″ piece bears the Boehm Studiomark Number 717. The Grape Jewel Box is oval on six scroll-shaped legs. It has a flat cover, and raised grapes with leaves and stems decorate the box and circle the cover. Two curled scrolls and raised crossed lines decorate the lid. The Grape Jewel Box with Cupids is the same except for two cupids on the lid: one kneels, holding a tablet to which he points with his left hand; the other is seated before another tablet, holding a crayon in his right hand.

Of the other decorations, approximately a dozen were made in the undecorated glazed finish and only two were produced of the glazed, decorated example bearing the two cupids on the lid.

There have been examples of the bisque found bearing makersmark F, but for the most part the piece carries makersmark D.

RPC-857-01 FRENCH CACHETTE, glazed, decorated white with gold trim (RP-874) 20 made

RPC-857-02 FRENCH CACHETTE, bisque, undecorated (RP-873) 1,746 made

The French Cachette was introduced between 1954 and 1956. The gold-trimmed one does not seem to have been popular and was discontinued the same year after only about 20 had been produced. The bisque example, however, continued to be available until 1960, in which year it was discontinued, there having been 1,746

RPC-859

RPC-861

made. It is a circular fluted cachette and cover on a circular base, with ring handles and a ring knob. The piece is 7″ high and bears Boehm Studiomark Number 718.

RPC-858 FLUTED PERFUME BOTTLES

(pr.) glazed, undecorated (RP-875) 31 made

These bottles were introduced sometime between 1954 and 1956 and appear on the 1956 price list as "Ribbed Perfume Bottles." They were discontinued in 1956, after only 31 pairs were made. The bottles are 6½″ high and bear Boehm Studiomark Number 720. It is a round diagonally fluted bottle on a circular base, rising to a short, narrow octagonal neck and flared mouth. The stopper is topped by a round, diagonally fluted knob. Fluted Perfume Bottles are rare and for the most part have been lost.

RPC-859 SMALL PERFUME BOTTLE,

glazed, decorated yellow (RP-963) unique

Oddly enough, this piece, of which only one was made, also carries Boehm Studiomark Number 720, even though it bears no resemblance to the Fluted Perfume Bottle

but is actually identical in design to the Bud Vase (RP-944) except for the addition of a stopper which raises its height to 5″.

It is quite possible that this bottle was, in fact, the forerunner of the Bud Vase, perhaps first designed as a bottle and later modified. Whether or not this theory is correct, the two pieces must have been produced at the same time. This would place the date of the small perfume bottle at 1954 or, at the latest, 1955, since it bears makersmark C and the Bud Vase had not appeared on a price list up to 1953.

This unique piece was donated by the Boehm Studio to Syracuse University and is, at present, in its collection.

RPC-860-01 LARGE ROUND ASH TRAY,

glazed, ground color body Celadon—approximately 200 made

RPC-860-02 LARGE ROUND ASH TRAY,

glazed, undecorated (RP-957) approximately 300 made

From the fact that a great many of these ash trays were produced (well over 500) and from the further fact that they do not appear on any of the price lists, we must assume that the piece was available in

1954 and 1955. Its size is 4″ in diameter and it carries no Boehm Studiomark Number as far as we can tell. It is a round fluted ash tray with ½″ fluted lip.

RPC-861 ROUND FLUTED CANDY BOX,

glazed, decorated white with gold trim (RP-876) 32 made

There were only about 32 made of this 6″ x 4½″ piece when it was introduced, under Boehm Studiomark Number 721, sometime between 1954 and 1956. It appears only on the 1956 price list, and was discontinued the same year.

RPC-862 BEE HIVE, glazed, decorated

(RP-825) approximately 50 made

This 5″ high piece seems to have been introduced, under Boehm Studiomark Number 743, in 1956. This also appears to be the year of its discontinuance, as it appears on no other price list. This bee-hive jar has a lid, with a bee in the center of the lid at the top. It also has a bee above and to the side of the door-shaped indentation at the bottom. It is decorated with raised crosses.

RPC-863-02

RPC-864-01

RPC-865-01

RPC-863-01 GRECIAN CANDY BOX, glazed, decorated with sprays of flower leaves and gold trim—12 made

RPC-863-02 GRECIAN CANDY BOX, glazed, decorated white with gold trim (RP-826) 24 made

RPC-863-03 GRECIAN CANDY BOX, glazed, undecorated—60 made

In the past, this piece has also been known, incorrectly, as "Empire Cachette." It is an 8″ high circular urn with ring handles; it is bowl-shaped, rising from a narrow neck on a small circular base. The lid is a squat, concave cone topped by a pyramid-shaped knob. Approximately 100 were produced, all in 1956. It bears Boehm Studiomark Number 744 and examples of the white with gold trim have been found with makersmark F.

RPC-864-01 HEXAGONAL FLUTED ASH TRAY WITH REST, glazed, decorated white with gold trim (RP-846) approximately 30 made

RPC-864-02 HEXAGONAL FLUTED ASH TRAY WITH REST, glazed, undecorated (RP-845) approximately 30 made

RPC-864-03 HEXAGONAL FLUTED ASH TRAY WITH REST, bisque, undecorated (RP-847) approximately 30 made

This is an oval-shaped hexagonal fluted ash tray, having four long panels at the sides. The two ends are half as long as each side panel. On the top rim of each short end rests a horizontal fluted square cigarette holder.

This 3″ piece was available singly only in 1957. Pairs, together with the Fluted Cigarette Box, were also intended for sale as the Medallion Cigarette Set. Our information would suggest a total number made of 395; however, we believe the quantity to be actually somewhat smaller: perhaps only about 100 in all.

This is a beautifully made small example of Ed Boehm's early work. For the serious collector the glazed, undecorated

example is the most interesting, due to the immaculate glazing which Ed Boehm was putting on inexpensive commercial items during those years.

RPC-865-01 HALF FLUTED ASH TRAY, glazed, undecorated (RP-855) 60 made

RPC-865-02 HALF FLUTED ASH TRAY, bisque, undecorated (RP-856) 215 made

Introduced in 1957 under Boehm Studiomark Number 759 and discontinued in 1958, this 3″ ash tray was made in a quantity of approximately 250 pieces. The preferred piece is the RPC-865-01, which has the beautiful glazing of early Boehm. This is a circular plain ash tray with a horizontal fluted rim of seven indentations extending around one-third of the circumference of the tray.

RPC-866-01 MAPLE LEAF ASH TRAY, bisque, decorated (RP-862) 9 made

RPC-866-02 MAPLE LEAF ASH TRAY, glazed, undecorated—rare

RPC-866-03 MAPLE LEAF ASH TRAY, bisque, undecorated (RP-861) 250 made

RPC-867-01 GRAPE LEAF ASH TRAY, bisque, decorated (RP-864) 11 made

RPC-867-02 GRAPE LEAF ASH TRAY, bisque, undecorated (RP-863) 250 made

These two ash trays were both introduced in 1958, under Boehm Studiomark Numbers 762 and 763 respectively, and we assume that both were discontinued the same year.

The undecorated bisque examples were the only ones that were merchandized, in a quantity of about 250 each. Of the decorated bisque, there were nine Maple Leaf Ash Trays and 11 Grape Leaf Ash Trays and we have no information regarding the quantity of the glazed, undecorated Maple Leaf Ash Tray.

The RPC-866-01 and RPC-867-01 are rare and beautiful examples of early bisque decoration.

RPC-866-03

RPC-867-02

RPC-869-01

RPC-868-01

RPC-868-01 CLOVER ASH TRAY, glazed, decorated (RP-887) 81 made

RPC-868-02 CLOVER ASH TRAY, glazed, undecorated (RP-886) 89 made

RPC-868-03 CLOVER ASH TRAY, bisque, undecorated 90 made

RPC-869-01 CLOVER CIGARETTE BOX, glazed, decorated (RP-848) 85 made

RPC-869-02 CLOVER CIGARETTE BOX, bisque, decorated (RP-849) 84 made

RPC-870-01 ACORN ASH TRAY, glazed, decorated (RP-889) 89 made

RPC-870-02 ACORN ASH TRAY, bisque, decorated (RP-976) 80 made

RPC-870-03 ACORN ASH TRAY, glazed, undecorated (RP-888) 80 made

RPC-871-01 ACORN CIGARETTE BOX, glazed, decorated (RP-850) 50 made

RPC-871-02 ACORN CIGARETTE BOX, bisque, decorated (RP-851) 83 made

RPC-871-03 ACORN CIGARETTE BOX, bisque, undecorated 86 made

All of these pieces were introduced in 1953 and bear, in sequence, Boehm Studiomark Numbers 768, 755, 769 and 756. Both styles

of ash trays are 4″ in diameter; the cigarette boxes are 5″ high.

The Clover Ash Tray is a shallow circular dish with three raised stems in the center, two of which bear three clover leaves, one of which bears five.

The Clover Cigarette Box is a tall bell-shaped urn on a circular base. The overhanging circular lid with raised three-leaf-clover stems rises slightly in the center to a clover-blossom knob.

The Acorn Ash Tray is a shallow circular dish with an acorn over three oak leaves in the center.

The Acorn Cigarette box is a tall bell-shaped urn on a circular base. The overhanging circular lid has raised oak leaves with a knob of two acorns.

Since there exists a fairly substantial quantity of these and since they are large pieces, their chance of survival is good. The preferred items out of this group would be the glazed, decorated pieces such as the RPC-868-01, RPC-870-01 and the RPC-871-01. However, one of each of this series would make an extremely interesting collection.

RPC-870-01

RPC-871-01

X. Decorative Accessories

RPC-901-01

RPC-901-02

RPC-900 CANDY EGG, glazed, decorated (RP-972) rare*

This strange piece bears makersmark **A** and, therefore, must have been producd between 1950 and 1951. We do know that the Candy Egg was given to Mr. Boehm, Sr., by Ed Boehm and remained in his collection for over 20 years. It is 6″ long and 4⅛″ wide. From the base to the top of the applied rose, it stands over 5″. It must have been modeled and sculpted by Ed Boehm himself. It was an extremely ambitious undertaking for a young potter.

I consider this one of the keystone pieces of the entire collection. There are a few pieces which forecast (had we but known) the kind of work of which Ed Boehm was capable, and the Candy Egg is one of them.

Its early date, complicated construction, the attempt to build a box which requires matching of top and bottom without warping, and the fact that it was undoubtedly Ed's own work put this in a category by itself.

RPC-901-01 SMALL SWAN, glazed, decorated, with gold trim—25 made
RPC-901-02 SMALL SWAN, glazed undecorated (RP-807) 150 made
RPC-901-03 SMALL SWAN, bisque undecorated (RP-806) 1,146 made
RPC-902-01 LARGE SWAN, glazed, decorated white with gold trim—25 made
RPC-902-02 LARGE SWAN, glazed, undecorated (RP-809) 25 made
RPC-902-03 LARGE SWAN, bisque, undecorated (RP-808) 568 made

*See page 86

Both sizes, the 4½″ and the 8″, appeared in the gold-trimmed decoration on the 1952 price list. The sculpture is a swan swimming, wings raised, with its neck bent and its head down.

Sometime between 1953 and 1956 the gold-trimmed examples were discontinued and replaced by the undecorated, both in glazed and bisque finishes. In 1956 these pieces were last offered in glazed finish. Both pieces were discontinued in 1961.

The swan has always played an important part in the work of potters and especially the Boehms. Perhaps the most important one the atelier ever turned out is the Mute Swan, which was commissioned by President Richard M. Nixon. The Swan series started in 1952 with a small piece, and shortly thereafter a larger example of the Swan appeared. They were made in widely varying numbers. They carry Boehm Studiomark Numbers 701 and 702 respectively.

RPC-903-01 PERCHERON STALLION BOOKENDS (pr.), glazed, decorated (RP-940) probably unique
RPC-903-02 PERCHERON STALLION BOOKENDS (pr.), glazed, undecorated (RP-982) 2 made

This piece was never merchandized and, in fact, only three have thus far come to light: one decorated and two undecorated. The decorated example is a dapple-gray horse head on a gold, black and white base, fluted at the front.

The Bookends are believed to have been produced sometime between 1953 and 1956 and, oddly enough, none of the pieces carries a signature or makersmark, although the Boehm Studio has assigned them Boehm Studiomark Number 741. Despite the lack of signature, they are definitely Boehm porcelains. The Bookends became the basis for the Boehm makersmark that can be seen by turning over any later piece of Boehm. I have never seen a pair, although I have seen single examples. They

RPC-903-02

are quite large and an ambitious undertaking for a new pottery as they stand over 9½″ high and almost 7″ in length. One pair was given as a gift to Mr. Boehm, Sr., on some occasion in the 1950's and that pair was given by Mr. Boehm, Sr., to a friend of his. I believe that one of this pair was broken and there is only one glazed piece left in perfect condition.

RPC-904 TALL EGG, glazed, decorated (RP-870) 26 made

Called variously "Tall Bunny Box" and "Tall Bunny Egg," the 8″ high piece was probably introduced around 1954, under Boehm Studiomark Number 716. It appears only on the 1956 price list.

The Tall Egg is an ovoid round-based jar, the top third of which forms the lid. On top of the lid, a rabbit perches on its hind legs. The rabbit wears a long narrow ribbon knotted at the neck.

Examples of the 26 pieces that were produced have been found to bear makersmark F.

It is quite possible that Tall Egg was done in bisque, decorated, and there might have been one or two examples left in the bisque or glazed, undecorated condition; however, we have never seen them and it can only be a matter of conjecture until one or another piece shows up.

RPC-905-01 HORN OF PLENTY, glazed, decorated (RP-924) 6 made
RPC-905-02 HORN OF PLENTY, glazed, undecorated (RP-923) 12 made

Probably introduced around 1954, this piece carries no Boehm Studiomark Number and does not seem to have been merchandized to any great extent, although it may have been offered for sale during 1954 or 1955. There were only 18 produced in all: 6 decorated and 12 undecorated. It is an upright cornucopia on a dome-shaped pedestal base. The point of the cone curls up to form a handle. It has a raised band

RPC-904   RPC-905-01

around the body just below the flared, irregularly fluted mouth.

This is one of those pieces which Ed Boehm made in imitation of other potters. It is not particularly interesting, but it is extremely scarce.

RPC-906-01 FRUIT PYRAMID AND STAND (pr.) glazed, decorated (RP-837) 2 made
RPC-906-02 FRUIT PYRAMID AND STAND (pr.) bisque, undecorated (RP-836) 32 made

The Fruit Pyramid is made in two pieces, much on the order of a lidded urn, with the mound of fruit forming the lid. It is 13½″ high and bears Boehm Studiomark Number 751. It is a cylindrical urn resting on a pedestal base, topped with a tall pyramid of fruit.

RPC-906-02

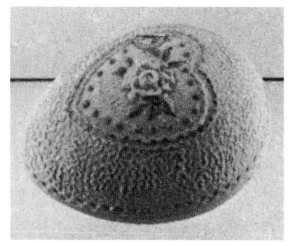

RPC-907-01

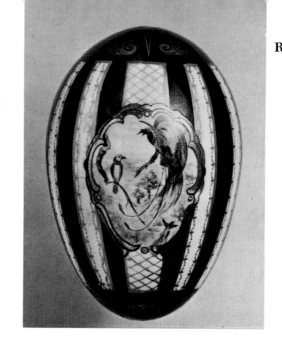

RPC-908-01

RPC-910

The only merchandizing record is in 1957, when the air, undecorated bisque only, was offered. As far as we have been able to discover, only two decorated, glazed pairs were made and these were not offered for general sale. There appear to have been approximately 32 pairs made of the undecorated. This is another piece which was done in imitation of other potters but this is somewhat more elegant than the RPC-905-01.

RPC-907-01 EASTER EGG PAPER-WEIGHT, glazed, decorated (RP-971) unique
RPC-907-02 EASTER EGG PAPER-WEIGHT, bisque, undecorated—2 made

This was designed by the sculptor's wife, Mrs. Helen Boehm, while Ed Boehm was on safari in Africa. She would not have dared to attempt it while he was around. When he returned, he had the molds broken. This piece was never intended for sale, and, in fact, only three exist: one glazed and decorated and two undecorated bisque. Were they ever to reach the market, they would prove extremely valuable.

This is the only example we know which was designed by other than Ed or one of his associated artists (except for the Ichabod Crane and the Kneeling Nude). Evidently at some point or other, Helen Boehm

decided that she too wanted to participate in the creative activity (thereby anticipating the job she would have to undertake after Ed's death). She really turned out quite a beautiful design.

RPC-908 "FABERGÉ" EGG, glazed, decorated—unique

The "Fabergé" Egg is a unique piece and its history is interesting. It was produced within a period of 10 days, at the request of Neiman-Marcus, for inclusion in a group of eggs decorated by various well-known personalities. The eggs were to be auctioned for the benefit of the 1966 Easter Seal campaign. Rather than sign his name to the plaster-of-paris egg sent him by Neiman-Marcus, Ed Boehm started from scratch and produced this magnificent seamless piece in his own hard-paste porcelain. The "Fabergé" Egg brought more than 50 percent of the proceeds of the entire auction.

RPC-909 EDWARD MARSHALL BOEHM ORCHID, bisque, decorated (RP-1179) nonlimited, still in production

This lovely 5″ x 8″ orchid, which bears the sculptor's name, was introduced by the Boehm Studio as an unlimited edition in 1970. At this writing it is available, and there are no immediate plans for its dis-

continuance. It carries Boehm Studiomark Number 400-08.

This orchid piece is derived directly from the Orchid Centerpiece which was produced as a limited edition by the Studio. This flower sculpture is a composition featuring one large orchid with a fern and a male hummingbird.

It is also interesting to recall that the Orchid Centerpiece was done only after an orchid firm on the West Coast (Rod McLellan Co. of San Francisco) bred a special species of orchid and named it after Ed Boehm. It is called the "Edward Marshall Boehm Orchid" and, for those of you who are interested in live flowers, you can obtain it if you look hard enough. We introduced the Orchid Centerpiece in our Frank Lloyd Wright Building in San Francisco in 1969. The firm that developed the "Edward Marshall Boehm Orchid" sent thousands of orchids to decorate the building. Being inside that marvelous space designed by Wright and seeing it filled with 5,000 fully bloomed orchids was an experience I am not likely to forget.

RPC-910 BABY LAZULI BUNTINGS PAPERWEIGHT, bisque, decorated (RP-981) nonlimited

Also introduced in 1970 as a nonlimited edition, the piece is 2½″ in diameter and carries Boehm Studiomark Number 400-10.

VASES, URNS, CANDLESTICKS AND CENTERPIECES

RPC-925 RING TOP VASE, glazed, undecorated (RP-977) 3 made. Description unavailable

Only three examples of this 15″ high vase were produced, the last in 1951. It has been assigned no Boehm Studiomark Number, nor has it ever been offered for sale, either by the Studio or at auction.

RPC-926-01 MINIATURE VASE, 1⅜″, glazed, decorated white with flowers—unique
RPC-926-02 MINIATURE VASE, 1⅜″, glazed, undecorated—unique
RPC-926-03 MINIATURE VASE, 1⅝″, glazed, decorated white with flowers—unique
RPC-926-04 MINIATURE VASE, 1⅝″, glazed, undecorated—unique

These lovely miniatures have never appeared on any price list of the Boehm Studio nor have they been assigned a Boehm Studiomark Number. They are believed to be unique and are all in private collections.

RPC-927-01 VASE WITH DRAPE, glazed, decorated pink—extremely rare
RPC-927-02 VASE WITH DRAPE, glazed, decorated with gold trim—rare

This is also an early piece and few were produced. There is no merchandizing record and the vase was not assigned a Boehm Studiomark Number. We have no way of determining how many of these vases were made. We can only assume that they were rare and that they were made prior to 1953.

RPC-928-01 MING BOWL CENTERPIECE, glazed, decorated on inside with flowers, possibly unique
RPC-928-02 MING BOWL CENTER-
PIECE, glazed, decorated (RP-813) 50 made
RPC-928-03 MING BOWL CENTERPIECE, glazed, undecorated (RP-811) 51 made
RPC-928-04 MING BOWL CENTERPIECE, bisque, undecorated (RP-812) 635 made

This was first offered in 1952. The finish is not specified on the 1952 list. We would be inclined to believe that only the glazed examples were available at that time.

By 1956 the bisque finish had been introduced; in 1957, the bisque, undecorated was the only one available. The piece was finally discontinued in 1961.

The Ming Bowl Centerpiece is 8½″ in diameter and 4″ high and carries Boehm Studiomark Number 704. It is a circular bowl on a porcelain base molded in the shape of crossed, gnarled branches, joining the bowl at five points, from which raised branched trees climb the bowl.

The example decorated on the inside of the bowl with flowers (RPC-928-01) is believed to be a unique piece, since only one has come to light. Of course, from experience with Boehm pieces, others may be found.

RPC-929-01 FLUTED GRECIAN VASE, glazed, decorated white with gold trim (RP-810) 205 made
RPC-929-02 FLUTED GRECIAN VASE, glazed, undecorated (RP-956) 50 made

This 10″ high vase is an early piece, first appearing (as Large Fluted Vase with Gold Trim) in 1952, but we have no information regarding 1954 and 1955. Its next appearance was in 1956, and it was discontinued that same year.

The piece bears Boehm Studiomark Number 703 and, in addition to the usual makersmark D, some of both decorations have been discovered with makersmark F. The vase, set on a square plinth, has a cir-

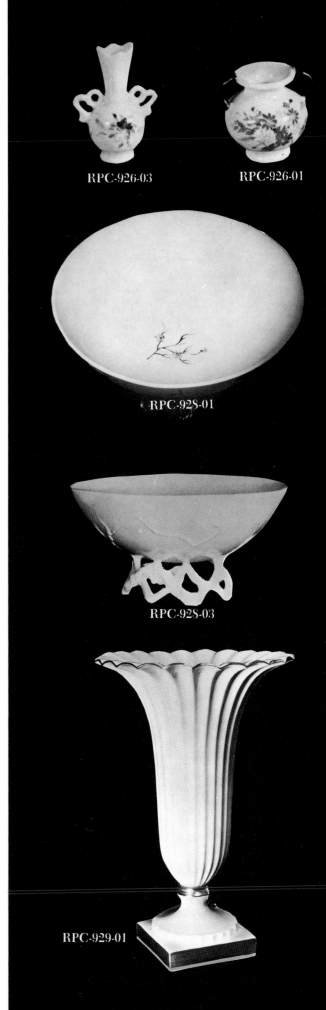

RPC-926-03   RPC-926-01

RPC-928-01

RPC-928-03

RPC-929-01

RPC-930-01

RPC-931-05

cular fluted base which narrows sharply to a round neck; above this the fluted body widens to an elongated inverted bell shape.

A fairly large quantity was produced (255 in all), but few of these vases have turned up.

RPC-930-01 PLAIN URN, 4½", glazed, decorated, white with gold trim (RP-838) 12 made

RPC-930-02 PLAIN URN, 4½", glazed, undecorated (RP-839) 17 made

RPC-930-03 PLAIN URN, 4½", bisque, undecorated (RP-840) 77 made

RPC-930-04 LARGE PLAIN URN, 6", glazed, undecorated (RP-966) unique

RPC-931-01 FLUTED URN, 4", glazed, decorated white with gold trim (RP-842) 101 made

RPC-931-02 FLUTED URN, 4", glazed, ground color body pink (RP-841) 50 made

RPC-931-03 FLUTED URN, 4", glazed, ground color body celadon (RP-844) 32 made

RPC-931-04 FLUTED URN, 4", glazed, undecorated (RP-947) 150 made

RPC-931-05 FLUTED URN, 4", bisque, undecorated (RP-843) 204 made

With the exception of the Large Plain Urn, which is believed to be a unique piece, these urns were introduced in 1952. The Plain Urn is bell-shaped with flared mouth rising from a circular base upon a square plinth. The Fluted Urn is a flared-mouth, cylindrical urn, resting on a squat thin neck and round base, upon a square plinth.

The urns were temporarily discontinued after 1952 and do not appear again until 1957. In that year, both Plain and Fluted Urns were offered only in undecorated bisque. The quantities produced of the other decorations lead us to conclude that they were merchandized during 1954 and/or 1955. There were over 100 Plain Urns (12 with gold trim, 17 glazed and 77 bisque) and well over 500 of the Fluted Urns (204 bisque, 150 glazed undecorated, 32 Celadon, 50 pink and 101 with gold trim), and neither piece was merchandized after 1957.

The Large Plain Urn is believed to have been produced around 1954 or 1955 and only one was made. It bears the same Boehm Studiomark Number as the small Plain Urn (752) even though its plinth is round, rather than square. It was never offered for sale.

All of the urns bear makersmark D; however, examples of the two glazed Plain Urns have been discovered to have makersmark F and one glazed undecorated Plain Urn has been found with makersmark C.

RPC-932-01 FRENCH FLUTED VASE, glazed, decorated white with gold trim (RP-882) 205 made

RPC-932-02 FRENCH FLUTED VASE, glazed, undecorated—rare

RPC-932-03 FRENCH FLUTED VASE, bisque, undecorated (RP-881) 10 made

This vase was introduced sometime between 1954 and 1956 and, from the quantity produced (nearly 225 in all), we would assume the former year to be more likely the correct one. The vase, bearing Boehm Studiomark Number 738, was merchandized only in the gold-trimmed decoration and it appears on the 1956 price list. There seem to have been only 10 examples left in their undecorated bisque state; the number glazed and undecorated is not known. This vase has a fluted knob rising to a narrow concave neck, gradually increasing in size to a circular plain-banded mouth. It is on a stepped circular base.

RPC-933-01 FLUTED CANDLESTICKS (pr.) glazed, undecorated (RP-894) 51 made

RPC-933-02 FLUTED CANDLESTICKS (pr.) bisque, undecorated (RP-895) 14 made

These were introduced, under Boehm Studiomark Number 709, in 1953 and were available through 1956. They were not too well received, however, as only 51 pairs of the glazed were produced and only 14 pairs left in their bisque state. The Candlesticks have a wide fluted circular base, rising to a narrow neck and fluted, flared-mouth nozzle.

The Candlesticks are 4″ high and bear makersmark D, except for a few glazed decorated pairs which bear makersmark F.

RPC-934-01 OVAL FLUTED CENTERPIECE, small (11″ x 3″), glazed, undecorated (RP-814) 85 made

RPC-934-02 OVAL FLUTED CENTERPIECE, small (11″ x 3″), bisque, undecorated (RP-815) 300 made

RPC-934-03 OVAL FLUTED CENTERPIECE, large (15½″ x 7½″), glazed, undecorated (RP-816) 68 made

RPC-934-04 OVAL FLUTED CENTERPIECE, large (15½″ x 7½″), bisque, undecorated (RP-817) 200 made

The Oval Fluted Centerpiece is a fluted bowl with the sides flaring out from an oval base.

These were extremely popular pieces and were available from 1953 through 1960, when the bisque were discontinued.

The glazed pieces were discontinued in 1958, after 85 small and 68 large were produced. The bisque, which continued to be available through 1960, reached quantities of approximately 300 small and 200 large.

The Boehm Studiomark Numbers are 705 and 706, and glazed examples of both sizes have been found to bear makersmark F.

RPC-935 OVAL FLUTED CANDLESTICK, glazed, undecorated (RP-944) 192 made

Although this piece (a fluted nozzle set in the center of an oval fluted dish) does not appear on any of the price lists we have found, its quantity (192 pieces) leads us to assume that it was merchandized in 1954 and/or 1955. However, we do not know at what price it was offered. It is 3⅓″ x 3″ and carries no Boehm Studiomark Number. Al-

though we would expect that some examples had been left in their bisque state, we have no definite evidence to support this theory and have, therefore, omitted a bisque example from the listing.

This is a beautiful example of the early glaze and as such would grace any collection. The chance of finding a pair is unlikely since, because of their small size, they are likely to have been cast aside and destroyed.

RPC-936-01 CORINTHIAN CANDLESTICKS (pr.) 11½″ high, glazed, undecorated (RP-877) 21 made

RPC-936-02 CORINTHIAN CANDLESTICKS (pr.) 11½″ high, bisque, undecorated (RP-878) 4 made

RPC-937 TULIP CANDLESTICK, 4″ high, bisque, undecorated (RP-968) 4 made

RPC-938 BELL CANDLESTICK, 5¼″ high, glazed, undecorated (RP-965) unique

None of these appear to have been merchandized. In fact, the Bell Candlestick appears to be a unique piece and there were only four Tulip Candlesticks produced. The latter is nearly identical to the small Tulip Vase (RPC-950) with the addition of a candle holder on the inside.

The Corinthian Candlesticks are tall fluted columns on three-tiered pyramidal bases rising to a Corinthian capital which forms the square-rimmed nozzle. Raised leaves, scrolls and blossoms decorate the base. (Boehm Studiomark Number 722)

The Tulip Candlestick is a tulip blossom on a square pedestal. The S-shaped handle curves down to its pedestal base with the nozzle set inside the bowl.

The Bell Candlestick has an inverted-bell base with a narrow neck and a flared nozzle. The Corinthian Candlesticks were made in a quantity of approximately 25 (21 pairs glazed, 4 pairs left bisque) and may, after all, have been merchandized for a short time. If so, it would be most likely that their sale occurred during 1954 or 1955. They were an ambitious undertaking and appear to have been copies of similar candlesticks done by other makers.

RPC-934-03

RPC-935

RPC-936-01

RPC-937

RPC-939-04

RPC-940-01   RPC-940-03   RPC-940-02

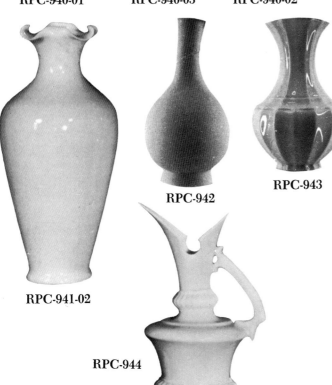

RPC-941-02   RPC-942   RPC-943

RPC-944

RPC-939-01 LARGE TULIP VASE, glazed, decorated (RP-928) unique
RPC-939-02 LARGE TULIP VASE, glazed, undecorated—3 made
RPC-939-03 LARGE TULIP VASE, bisque, decorated—unique
RPC-939-04 LARGE TULIP VASE, bisque, ground color body pink (RP-927) unique

These are extremely rare pieces, the existence of only six having been verified. Three of these 11″ vases, glazed and undecorated, are in the possession of one collector and have been converted into lamps. At least one other of the glazed, decorated is believed to exist and perhaps one each of the two bisque examples. They were, of course, not merchandized, nor is any auction record available.

The vase is cylindrical, with an indented mouth and with raised images of tulip plants decorating the body.

RPC-940-01 FLOWER VASE, 8¾″ high, glazed, decorated with branch and blossoms (RP-932) 6 made
RPC-940-02 FLOWER VASE, 8¾″ high, glazed, decorated with ferns (RP-934) 6 made
RPC-940-03 FLOWER VASE, 8¾″ high, glazed, decorated with falling leaves (RP-993) 6 made
RPC-940-04 FLOWER VASE, 8¾″ high, glazed, undecorated (RP-945) 2 made
RPC-941-01 CRIMPED VASE, 6½″ high, glazed, ground color body pink— 12 made
RPC-941-02 CRIMPED VASE, 6½″ high, glazed, undecorated (RP-943) 12 made
RPC-942 THIN-NECKED VASE, 8″ high, bisque, undecorated (RP-946) 12 made
RPC-943 RIBBED VASE, 6½″ high, glazed, undecorated (RP-955) 2 made
RPC-944 ORNATE URN, 9″ high, glazed, undecorated (RP-935) 12 made

None of this group was produced in a quantity that would indicate their having been merchandized to any extent, nor do any carry Boehm Studiomark Numbers. In fact, the Ribbed Vase is believed to be a unique piece. There seem to have been six of each decoration of the Flower Vase, and only two in the glazed, undecorated. The rest seem to number approximately a dozen each. If any merchandizing did take place, it would have to have been during 1954 or 1955. None of these vases have appeared at auction.

With the exception of the undecorated Flower Vase, which bears makersmark C, all the vases are marked with makersmark D.

These pieces were important for their size and the indication they give that Ed Boehm was experimenting in dozens of shapes and sizes. A group like this certainly indicates that we may have overlooked an enormous amount of material, examples of which have not yet come to light.

The Flower Vase is an ovoid body on a circular base, rising to a long, narrow, diagonally fluted neck ending in a flared mouth with eight scallops. It has two thin, diagonally fluted handles and the body is decorated with branches and blossoms.

The Crimped Vase is a slender ovoid body with a short neck, contracted in the middle and rising to a flared, crimped mouth.

The Thin-Necked Vase has a round body rising up to a long cylindrical neck.

The Ribbed Vase is fluted and has a bowl-shaped bottom with a narrowing thin neck with flared mouth. There are two ribs at the base of the neck.

The Ornate Urn is circular and single-handled. From a molded gadroon knob on a circular base, the body flares gently for 2″, then narrows sharply to a thin, short concave neck encircled by a thin ridge. Atop the neck is a second molded gadroon knob from which rises a tall, slender, double-peaked mouth.

RPC-945-01 BUD VASE, glazed, undecorated (RP-880) 200 made
RPC-945-02 BUD VASE, bisque, undecorated (RP-879) 2,808 made

This 3″ high vase, which bears Boehm

Studiomark Number 730, was introduced in 1956, quite possibly even earlier. It was discontinued at the end of 1961. It is an ovoid vase rising to a narrow cylindrical neck and flared mouth. Twelve scrolled lines rise from a circular base to the center of the vase, above which is a profusion of wild flowers.

How pleasant it must have been for the Boehms in these early days to discover a small piece which could be sold in large quantities. I have been told that the small amount of money which came in from this little Bud Vase was, at the time, important in keeping the Boehm operation alive.

RPC-946-01 DOLPHIN SHELL VASE, glazed, undecorated (RP-823) 101 made

RPC-946-02 DOLPHIN SHELL VASE, bisque, undecorated (RP-824) 409 made

Both decorations of this 7½″ high piece were introduced, under Boehm Studiomark Number 742, in 1956. It was discontinued in the latter part of 1958, after 101 had been produced. Several examples of this decoration had been discovered with makersmark F. The vase is modeled of two rounded upright shells joined at the base and the sides. The Dolphin head is at either side of the base with its snake-like body running up the sides. The base is molded in stylized waves.

The bisque vase was discontinued late in 1960. A total of 409 pieces were produced in the bisque finish.

RPC-947-01 BASKET CENTERPIECE, glazed, decorated, quantity unknown

RPC-947-02 BASKET CENTERPIECE, glazed, undecorated, quantity unknown

RPC-947-03 BASKET CENTERPIECE, bisque, undecorated, quantity unknown

RPC-948-01 OVAL GRAPE CENTER-PIECE, glazed, decorated (RP-829) 6 made

RPC-948-02 OVAL GRAPE CENTER-PIECE, glazed, undecorated (RP-973) 3 made

RPC-948-03 OVAL GRAPE CENTER-PIECE, bisque, undecorated (RP-830) 30 made

These two pieces offer us an excellent opportunity to make some educated guesses. Both pieces were introduced, as separate listings, on the 1956 price list. In 1957, only the Oval Grape Centerpiece found its way onto the list. Both are 14″ x 8½″.

The Oval Grape Centerpiece contains two pieces. The oval basket bowl with twisted-rope border and two handles has a lid molded in the shape of grapes in a bunch with the stem and leaves on a flat oval base with a twisted-rope border.

They carry successive Boehm Studiomark Numbers 747 and 748. We wonder if, perhaps, the Oval Grape Centerpiece has not been incorrectly identified as a two-section piece: bowl and lid. It is quite possible that the bowl section was originally intended to be sold separately as the Basket Centerpiece, while the ornate lid was to have been designed as the Oval Grape Centerpiece. This is complicated by the fact that the lower portion of the Oval Grape piece does not look like a basket and, in fact, we have yet to discover an example of the Basket Centerpiece. (Although this latter complication could well be construed as evidence in support of our supposition.) Whatever the truth of the matter, we will retain our pet theory until someone, sometime, proves us wrong.

In any event, we know that approximately 40 Oval Grape Centerpieces were produced (six decorated, three glazed undecorated and 30 or more bisque, undecorated) and they were discontinued at the end of 1957.

RPC-949-01 GRAPE CANDLESTICKS (pr.) glazed, undecorated (RP-859) 2 made

RPC-949-02 GRAPE CANDLESTICKS (pr.) bisque, undecorated (RP-860) 4 made

Although these carry Boehm Studiomark Number 761, they do not seem to have been merchandized and, in fact, it is believed that only six pair were produced in all: two glazed and four bisque. They are 7½″ high and several of the glazed ex-

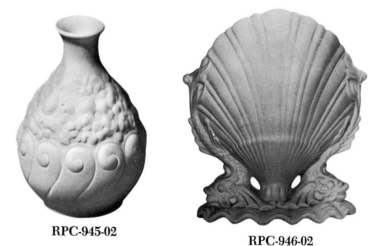

RPC-945-02   RPC-946-02

RPC-947-03

RPC-948-03

RPC-949-01

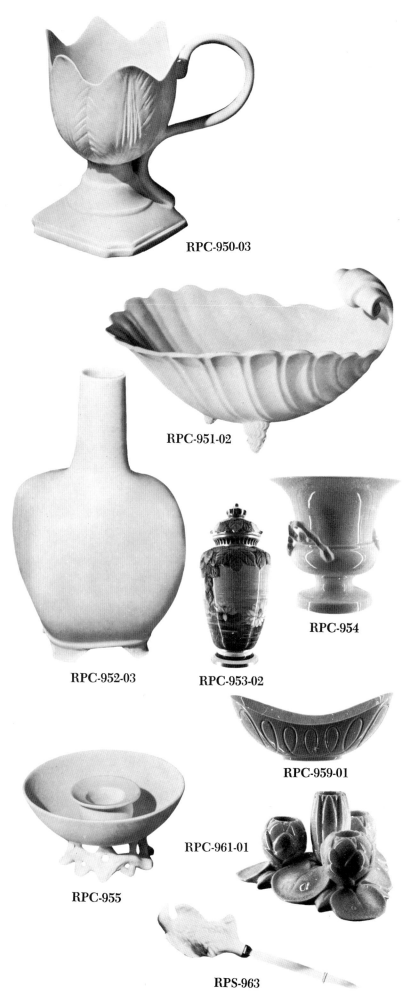

RPC-950-03

RPC-951-02

RPC-952-03

RPC-953-02

RPC-954

RPC-959-01

RPC-955

RPC-961-01

RPS-963

amples bear makersmark F. The candlesticks are on a flat circular base narrowing to a tall pear-shaped neck. The bell-shaped nozzle with ridged rim rests on the ridge above the neck.

RPC-950-01 TULIP VASE, glazed, decorated (RP-833) 5 made
RPC-950-02 TULIP VASE, glazed, undecorated (RP-834) 50 made
RPC-950-03 TULIP VASE, bisque, undecorated (RP-835) 175 made

The vase is made in the shape of a tulip blossom on a square pedestal. An S-shaped handle curves down to the pedestal base. Although our research indicated more than 50 examples of the glazed, undecorated Tulip Vase were produced, we can find no record of that decoration being merchandized. There were only five of the decorated vases produced, and these, too, never entered into trade.

The undecorated bisque, however, was included on the 1957 price list. There appear to have been approximately 175 of that decoration produced before it was discontinued late in 1959. All bear Boehm Studiomark Number 750. Of course in this group the glazed, decorated are extremely valuable. But any of the early painted decorations of these pieces are a special addition to any collection. It must be understood that after the shapes were sculpted it was a fairly simple matter with these early uncomplicated shapes to turn out large numbers of undecorated or glazed models. However, it took the master's hand to decide what to put on it and to actually do the decoration.

RPC-951-01 SHELL FLOWER HOLDER, glazed, undecorated (RP-854) 10 made
RPC-951-02 SHELL FLOWER HOLDER, bisque, undecorated (RP-853) 50 made

This piece was introduced, under Boehm Studiomark Number 758, in bisque only, in 1957. It was discontinued in 1958. There seem to have been only 10 glazed examples

made, and these do not appear to have been offered for general sale. This fairly undistinguished late addition to the collection has only scarcity value. It is a bowl-shaped fluted shell with a scalloped rim of 18 indentations. The rim rises to a curled scroll at one end, resting on three conical shell legs.

Examples of both decorations have been found with makersmark F.

RPC-952-01 CHINESE VASE, glazed, decorated (RP-858) 14 made
RPC-952-02 CHINESE VASE, glazed, undecorated
RPC-952-03 CHINESE VASE, bisque, undecorated (RP-857) 30 made

These were made in small quantities and, although they are listed in the collection as Boehm Studiomark Number 760, they were not merchandized. Only 30 were produced in the bisque and 14 glazed and decorated. The number of glazed, undecorated is not known at present. The vase is 9″ high. It is a four-footed vase, with a generally square-shaped bowl rising to a narrow cylindrical neck.

Someday, someone will go to the trouble of putting together a collection of the decorated examples of Ed Boehm's early work. In the RPC-952-01 we have decorated examples made in a relatively large number.

RPC-953-01 BIRD URN, glazed, decorated Green Parakeets (RP-936) unique
RPC-953-02 BIRD URN, glazed, decorated Water Lilies (RP-937) unique
RPC-953-03 BIRD URN, glazed, decorated Cockatoos (RP-938) unique
RPC-953-04 BIRD URN, bisque, undecorated—12 made
RPC-954 PLANTER, glazed, undecorated (RP-967) unique

None of this series was officially designated with a Boehm Studiomark Number. The Bird Urns, 11½″ high, are particularly beautiful. It is a round-based urn, with a narrow neck widening toward the top, then narrowing sharply to a flared mouth. The dates of production are difficult to ascertain, although it is believed that they are not earlier than 1956 nor later than 1960. The Planter is glazed, white, 5¾″ high. Only one was made, and it was completed prior to 1960. It has a bell-shaped body on a circular base, a short narrow neck, and two small handles.

These pieces, of course, are enormously valuable. They were made during a most creative time, around 1957 and 1958, and are as fine a work as Ed Boehm ever turned out.

RPC-955 MING CANDLESTICKS (pr.) bisque, undecorated (RP-926) 78 made

These candlesticks, 4″ in diameter, were obviously designed to complement the Ming Bowl Centerpiece (RPC-928). They were introduced in 1958, under Boehm Studiomark Number 766, and were discontinued late in 1959.

The Ming Candlesticks were done as an afterthought to the Centerpiece and as such they never really had the acceptance or the popularity of the bowl.

Each Ming Candlestick is a circular bowl on a base. The base is molded in the shape of crossed, gnarled branches, joining the bowl at five points. A round nozzle with a flared mouth is set into the center of the bowl.

RPC-956 LARGE CANDLESTICKS (pr.) bisque, undecorated (RP-926A) probably unique

These are similar in appearance to the Ming Candlesticks, but with a smooth bowl, about the size of a finger bowl. They were never made in quantity, do not bear a Boehm Studiomark Number and, in fact, may well be unique.

RPC-957-01 TRADITIONAL CENTERPIECE, glazed, undecorated—rare
RPC-957-02 TRADITIONAL CENTERPIECE, bisque, decorated white with black trim—rare

RPC-957-03 TRADITIONAL CENTERPIECE, bisque, undecorated—rare
RPC-958-01 TRADITIONAL CANDLESTICKS, glazed, decorated—rare
RPC-958-02 TRADITIONAL CANDLESTICKS, 4″ high, glazed, undecorated—rare
RPC-958-03 TRADITIONAL CANDLESTICKS, 4″ high, bisque, undecorated—rare
RPC-959-01 MODERN CENTERPIECE, 11″ x 4″, glazed, undecorated (RP-964) 12 made
RPC-959-02 MODERN CENTERPIECE, 11″ x 4″, bisque, undecorated—12 made

None of this group was made in large quantities, although all were listed on the 1958 price list and carry, in sequence, Boehm Studiomark Numbers 773, 774 and 775. We are unable to determine an accurate production quantity of the Traditional pieces but we believe that no more than a dozen of each of the Modern Centerpieces were made. This is a boat-shaped bowl on an oval base with etched loop design.

RPC-960 LARGE FLUTED CANDLESTICKS (pr.) bisque, undecorated (RP-970) 50 made

These appear only on the 1959 price list, under Boehm Studiomark Number 771. There appear to have been approximately 50 of these 5″ diameter candlesticks. Their shape is a circular flared dish on a circular base, fluted, with a tall fluted nozzle set into the dish.

RPC-961-01 LOTUS CANDELABRA, glazed, decorated—2 made
RPC-961-02 LOTUS CANDELABRA, glazed, undecorated (RP-929) 4 made

This piece, Boehm Studiomark Number 779, has been variously called "Lily Candelabra" and "Lotus Candlesticks." It rises from a triangular lily-pad base, supporting three lily-blossom nozzles at points of a triangle with an elongated lily-blossom nozzle in its center. It is rare, only six having been

produced in all, probably between 1958 and 1960.

RPC-962-01 ORCHID CENTERPIECE, bisque, decorated (RP-976) limited edition of 300
RPC-962-02 ORCHID CENTERPIECE, bisque, undecorated—unique*

This magnificent orchid grouping, with the lovely hummingbirds Stellula Calliopi, is the latest in this category. It was introduced in 1970, as a limited edition of 300 decorated pieces. The edition was reduced to 150 in 1975, probably due to its complexity. The undecorated example is a unique piece, over and above the edition number.

The RPC-962-01 carries the Boehm Studiomark Number 400-09, and as of February 1, 1976, 139 pieces had been made.

There are endless stories concerning the Orchid Centerpiece. It was obviously a labor of love for Ed Boehm and it grew out of a rather touching bit of recognition, by the Rod McLellan Co. of San Francisco, who bred a new example of orchid and named it after him. (See RPC-909.) It is a registered species of the orchid family. Ed was touched by this recognition and set to work converting it to porcelain. Characteristically, he wasn't satisfied with just rendering the piece in porcelain; instead, he created an entire rain forest. Later in his life Ed more and more tended to take great chunks of nature in all of its balance and relationship and render them in porcelain.

RPS-963 EAGLE LETTER OPENER (8″ x 2¼″) bisque, glazed white, nonlimited edition still in production

Toward the end of 1975 the Boehm Studio issued what they refer to as the Bicentennial Letter Opener. The handle depicts an Eagle perched on a branch. It is glazed and undecorated. This piece carries no Studiomark Number or makersmark. It carries an RPS rather than an RPC designation because it was actually produced after Ed Boehm's death.

XI. The Birds of Boehm

In the world of Boehm porcelains the place of honor is reserved for the birds. Were some dreadful catastrophe to destroy all of Edward Boehm's work except the birds, these would still show the full development of the man and his talent, from the relatively simple early ducks to the structural intricacies and exquisite design of the Blue Jays and the Song Sparrows and the perfection of the porcelain process necessary to produce the magnificent Ivory-Billed Woodpeckers.

The Boehm birds, of all his sculptures, are the most beautiful, the most carefully and lovingly designed and constructed. They are creatures alive and breathing in their native habitats and, as one watches, one expects to see—can almost believe one sees—the movement of a wing or the flutter of a tail.

Of all the work Ed ever did, however, the birds were certainly not his favorites. One can trace from his own interests his admiration for the dogs and, perhaps even more than that, for the horses. Ed Boehm was basically a breeder of animals. He believed in improving the intelligence and the physical stamina and the grace and beauty of animals through breeding. It is extremely difficult to breed birds. In addition birds don't have that powerful nobility that Ed Boehm was attracted to in animals such as the horse. In spite of all this, the collectors have made their own decisions, and they have voted for the birds. It is in the birds that the market is the most active...it is in the birds that the prices are the highest... and it is in the birds that, when you mention "Boehm" to people, they automatically come back with the associated word "bird."

Of course, it is obvious that Ed was fas-cinated by the variety that he was able to experience in the bird sculptures. Everything was there: structure, color and an enormous variation. Sizes were within the framework of full-scale models, and birds presented an endless demand on his ability to render detail in porcelain. Once he became involved in the bird sculptures, he found it difficult to get out. Not only were his own energies involved in the birds, but his collectors and admirers tended to reject other than bird sculptures as they appeared. The pressure from his dealers, from his collectors and from the public at large was for the bird sculptures. For 200 years the world had seen endless variations of good, bad and indifferent horses and cows and pigs and turtles and donkeys and elephants. But it had not, until this century, seen the beginnings of what a great and creative craftsman could do with birds.

One of the things that struck me most about Ed Boehm was the basis on which he chose birds. Sometimes it was obvious: the Blue Jay and the Robin for their popularity and their recognizability; the Nonpareil and the Ceruleans for their color and the Song Sparrows for their generality. But then one wonders why the strange birds. . . . why go to that enormous trouble to do an Ivory-Billed Woodpecker? Why birds like the Lesser Prairie Chickens since they are considered ugly and deformed, and why, of all things, the Mearns Quail?

I once asked him and got a character-istically straightforward answer. These were the birds which were on the verge of extinction, the endangered species. Before they died out, Ed wanted to be able to study them in life and render them in porcelain. Of all the bird sculptures, these, the ugly ones, are perhaps the most noble, both in conception and in the tragedy of their content. Boehm was acutely aware of the dangers to the animals that he loved so much. There were, from his point of view, in Ed Boehm's life too many people and too few (and in ever-decreasing numbers) animals.

All of the decorated limited edition pieces may be assumed to bear makersmark E, with the exception of those pieces produced earlier than 1959. Most of the undecorated bisque limited editions carry makersmark D. The unlimited pieces bear either makersmark D or makersmark F, depending on the date of production of a particular example. All exceptions to the above will be noted.

RPC-1000 WOODTHRUSH WITH CRAB APPLE, glazed, decorated (RP-1032) 2 made

This 8″ x 5″ piece was made in 1951 and carries Boehm Studiomark Number 400. It is one of the first bird subjects designed by Boehm and only two examples were produced.

The Woodthrush was the earliest attempt at a limited edition piece by the Studio and it was aborted because it did not sell. As a result, the Mallards are the first limited edition which succeeded in the market.

RPC-1001-01 CANVASBACK DUCKS, on Cattails (pr.) glazed, decorated (RP-1001) 74 made
RPC-1001-02 CANVASBACK DUCKS, on Cattails (pr.) glazed, undecorated (RP-1003) 10 made
RPC-1001-03 CANVASBACK DUCKS, on Cattails (pr.) bisque, decorated (RP-1002) 42 made

Our research indicates that this piece was introduced in 1951. The last year in which the glazed finish was offered was 1958; the bisque, decorated piece was discontinued late in 1959. Altogether, 126 pairs had been produced: 42 decorated bisque, 74 glazed, decorated and 10 glazed, undecorated.

The Canvasback Ducks carry Boehm Studiomark Number 401 and examples bear their makersmark D or makersmark F. The male and female are identical in structure, although the coloring varies on the decorated pieces, and each measures 4″ high. The sculpture depicts Canvasback Ducks

RPC-1000

RPC-1001-03

in flight above cattails. The wings and head are pointing down.

I would like to mention in passing that almost every piece I see is damaged at the point where the leaves of the cattails grow from the stem at the base of the piece. In picking them up, people invariably put their fingers on the cattail leaves and break them. This is one of the few examples of Boehm the value of which is not affected by the fact that it is not mint. With almost no exceptions, these small birds, including the Teals and the Wood Ducks, are damaged.

RPC-1002-01 GREEN-WINGED TEAL, on Cattails (pr.) glazed, decorated (RP-1004) 52 made

RPC-1002-02 GREEN-WINGED TEAL, on Cattails, glazed, undecorated (RP-1006) 14 made

RPC-1002-03 GREEN-WINGED TEAL, on Cattails (pr.) bisque, decorated (RP-1005) 30 made

RPC-1002-04 WOOD DUCKS, on Cattails (pr.) glazed, decorated (RP-1007) 143 made*

RPC-1002-05 WOOD DUCKS, on Cattails (pr.) bisque, decorated (RP-1008) 49 made

RPC-1002-06 WOOD DUCKS, on Cattails, bisque, undecorated (RP-1009) 18 made

Although these 5″ high ducks bear different Boehm Studiomark Numbers (the Teal, 402, and the Wood Ducks, 403) and although their decoration varies, these are actually all the same sculpture. Naturally, in view of this, it is impossible to decide which duck was made in glazed, undecorated and which in bisque, undecorated. We have, therefore, simply followed historical usage to avoid confusion.

The male and female of both are identical in structure as well. They rest on a porcelain base, above cattails, with wings outspread and heads turned one-eighth left.

Introduced in 1951, neither of these

*See page 88

Ducks appeared·on a price list until 1952. During 1956 and 1957 the pieces were listed as "decorated," finish unspecified. This leads us to believe that, if the undecorated examples were actually merchandized in 1952 and 1953, they were discontinued sometime between 1954 and 1956. However, it may well be that only the decorated examples were available throughout and the undecorated simply leftovers, since there were only 32 pieces in all (not pairs): 18 bisque pieces and 14 glazed pieces.

By 1958, the female was abandoned and we find only the male of the pair available that year, decorated of course. By late 1958, all glazed and decorated pieces had been discontinued after production of approximately 143 pairs of Wood Ducks and 52 pairs of the Teal sculpture in that finish. The last year these Ducks were offered was 1959, at which time the bisque, decorated was available. Approximately 49 pairs of Wood Ducks and 30 pairs of Teal were produced in decorated bisque.

215

All decorations bear either makersmark D or makersmark F.

RPC-1003-01 LEGHORNS (pr.) glazed, decorated (RP-1010) 10 made

RPC-1003-02 LEGHORNS (pr.) bisque, decorated (RP-1146) 4 made

RPC-1003-03 LEGHORNS (pr.) bisque, undecorated (RP-1011) 24 made

The Leghorn sculpture depicts a rooster and hen on individual bases, standing in front of tree stumps which provide support to the body of the animal. The rooster is shown with his head up and forward. The hen faces one-eighth right.

The Leghorns were introduced under Boehm Studiomark Number 404 in 1952, undecorated bisque only; they were discontinued in 1956. Sometime between 1954 and 1956 the glazed and decorated examples were introduced. No Leghorns were available after 1956.

These 8″ high pieces were done in small quantity—only 24 pairs undecorated and 10 pairs glazed and decorated. The decorated bisque are the rarest of all, there having been only four pairs made, none of which was offered for general sale. The Leghorns also bear either makersmark D or makersmark F.

Not even the most brain-washed admirer of Ed Boehm's work can call these pieces beautiful. They are, indeed, very ugly. Perhaps the live Leghorn himself is ugly, but the conception was particularly inelegant and the sculpture is quite graceless. However, there is a great strength in it and no important collection of Boehm can possibly be complete without a pair of Leghorns in one or another of the decorations. Their value is enhanced not only by their scarcity, but by the fact that they represent an extremely early example of Ed's work.

RPC-1004-01 EVENING GROSBEAKS (pr.) glazed, decorated (RP-1015) 3 made

RPC-1004-02 RED-BREASTED GROSBEAKS (pr.) glazed, decorated (RP-1012) 50 made*

RPC-1004-03 RED-BREASTED GROSBEAKS (pr.) glazed, undecorated—24 made

RPC-1004-04 RED-BREASTED GROSBEAKS (Male only) bisque, decorated

*See page 88

(RP-1014) 48 made

RPC-1004-05 RED-BREASTED GROSBEAKS, bisque, undecorated (RP-1013) 300 made

The Red-Breasted Grosbeaks were introduced in 1952 under Boehm Studiomark Number 405. In view of the subsequent price history, we must assume that only the undecorated bisque were available in 1953 and that the decorated example was glazed. The glazed, undecorated was not offered after 1956. In 1958, we find the decorated female discontinued and only the male offered (very probably glazed). The undecorated was discontinued in 1959. There is no record of any decorated bisque females being produced.

This 6″ sculpture shows a pair of Grosbeaks standing on gnarled logs. The tails are stretched back with heads and breasts forward and the heads tilted left.

The quantities in the various decorations vary from 50 glazed and decorated pairs to over 300 individual pieces in undecorated bisque, and 24 undecorated, glazed. The quantity in decorated bisque was originally believed to be nearly 300 individual pieces; however, in view of the fact that this decoration was available for only one year, we feel this estimate must be revised considerably downward to arrive at any realistic amount.

The Evening Grosbeaks are identical in structure to their Red-Breasted cousins, varying only in coloration. Three pairs are believed to have been produced, early in 1952. Mrs. Boehm recalls selling a pair in Pittsburgh through the Hough and Keenan Galleries. It is likely that this sculpture was originally intended to be decorated as Evening Grosbeaks and not Red-Breasted Grosbeaks, although we have no way of verifying this.

All of the decorations of this 6″ high piece bear the makersmark D or makersmark F.

The undecorated bisque examples of Boehm's porcelains are, unfortunately, extremely vulnerable to "alteration," and such has been the case with at least one of the undecorated bisque Grosbeaks, which has turned up with a decoration quite obviously not originating from the Boehm Studio. It is doubtful that an actual fraud was intended; more likely the original purchaser of the piece decided he preferred his grosbeak in a more colorful (if less valuable) state.

The glazed, decorated Evening Grosbeaks are close to being unique. The Red-Breasted Grosbeak in the glazed, decorated condition is one of the great examples of Ed Boehm's early work. This is most mature work, considering both its sculpture and the beautiful glaze that Boehm developed during those earlier years.

RPC-1005-01 MALLARDS (pr.) (11″ high) glazed, decorated with leaves applied—13 made*
RPC-1005-02 MALLARDS (pr.) (11″ high) glazed, decorated (RP-1089) 15 made
RPC-1005-03 MALLARDS (pr.) (11″ high) bisque, decorated (RP-1088) limited edition of 500
RPC-1005-04 MALLARDS (pr.) (11″ high) bisque, undecorated (RP-1090) extremely rare

The Mallards (Boehm Studiomark Number 406) was the first officially listed limited edition Boehm sculpture and was introduced in 1952 in an edition of 500 pairs (decoration and finished unspecified). The bisque, decorated examples were never specified and we must assume that all decorated examples were glazed, at least until 1954, or possibly 1955. That the glazed examples were still being offered even after 1955, when all new pieces were being done in bisque only, is borne out by an illustrated catalog which, though undated, is believed to have been put out in 1959. The illustration of the Mallards in that catalog is undoubtedly of a glazed pair. The sculpture is composed of a male and female on individual bases, in flight over cattails.

*See page 89

The undecorated bisque examples were not offered for sale after 1957, and by 1962 only decorated bisque examples were being produced.

The example "with leaves applied" (RPC-1005-01) is a rare and marvelous work. The only example of this that I have ever seen was in the collection of Mr. Boehm, Sr., and had been a gift from the son to the father on a family occasion sometime in the late 1950's. It is the only example of this kind of work in the entire Boehm repertoire, and, in addition to its scarcity, as a glazed piece it carries additional interest because of the application of the leaves. The example from the Mr. Boehm, Sr., collection also had numbers fired on the bottom. In the early pieces of Boehm, the Studio was still attempting to number each piece individually and this decorated, glazed example with the numbers applied dates from 1952 from the first of the Mallards Boehm made. Other examples of the early Mallards also are individually numbered.

This bird is enormously important. It ranks in importance with the Percheron Mare and Foal which was done by Ed in 1944. The Mare and Foal was the first example of Boehm sculptures and, in a like sense, the Mallards can be considered the first example of the Boehm *limited edition* Bird collection. The glazed, decorated-with-leaves-applied example is the keystone of that whole group of limited editions on which the reputation of Ed Boehm was to be subsequently built.

The glazed and decorated examples carry either makersmark D or makersmark E, the former most probably having been used during the earlier years. The undecorated bisque also carries makersmark D but the decorated bisque has been found only with makersmark E.

RPC-1006-01 BOB WHITE QUAIL (pr.) (Male 7½″ high, Female 6″ high) glazed, decorated—rare
RPC-1006-02 BOB WHITE QUAIL (pr.)

(Male 7½″ high, Female 6″ high) bisque, early decoration approximately 250 made
RPC-1006-03 BOB WHITE QUAIL (pr.) (Male 7½″ high, Female 6″ high) bisque, final decoration (RP-1091) approximately 500 made

RPC-1006-04 BOB WHITE QUAIL (pr.) (Male 7½″ high, Female 6″ high) bisque, undecorated (RP-1092) 9 made

This sculpture depicts a male and female on individual bases. The female is running and the male is perched on a log, with his wings spread.

The Bob White Quail was introduced, under Boehm Studiomark Number 407, in 1953, as a limited edition of 750 pairs, decorated only. The first pairs produced were glazed and decorated and the first indication we have of undecorated bisque is in 1956. This decoration was again offered in 1957 and seems to have been withdrawn shortly thereafter, since our research indicates only nine undecorated bisque pairs produced in all.

Sometime before 1961, the decoration of the Bob White was changed. The new decoration (a great improvement) gave the piece a more lifelike quality than the original decoration had. We have not been able to determine exactly how many were done in the old decoration; however, we are sure that at least the first 250 had been completed before the decoration was revised.

On June 7, 1969, an example of the glazed decoration was offered at Parke-Bernet Galleries. Although the pair offered consisted of a male and female, it was not an original pair, since one sculpture bore the edition number 18 and the other, number 20. This was another example of the individual numbering of some of the earlier examples. Of all the work that the Boehm Studio made over the 20 years of Ed's active involvement, I dare say that not more than 100 have ever been numbered. Any numbered pair is early and extremely valuable.

Only nine examples of the Quail were

*See page 90

217

left in their undecorated bisque state, all of them bearing makersmark D. It is impossible, at this point, to place a quantity on the glazed and decorated pairs. However, it is almost certain that all of them were examples of the original decoration. The bisque, decorated bear makersmark E, and although we suspect the existence of several with earlier makersmarks, none has yet come to light.

RPC-1007-01 CANADA GEESE (pr.) (7½" x 7½") glazed, decorated (RP-1158) rare

RPC-1007-02 CANADA GEESE (pr.) (7½" x 7½") glazed, undecorated (RP-1034A) rare

RPC-1007-03 CANADA GEESE (pr.) (7½" x 7½") bisque, decorated (RP-1034) open nonlimited

RPC-1007-04 CANADA GEESE (pr.) (7½" x 7½") bisque, undecorated (RP-1035) extremely rare

RPC-1007-05 CANADA GEESE (pr.) (7½" x 7½") bisque, decorated "error"—6 made

RPC-1007-06 CANADA GEESE (pr.) (7½" x 7½") glazed, decorated, "hefty," rare

The male and female are on separate bases. The female is protecting three goslings. The Canada Geese were introduced in 1953 as an unlimited edition under Boehm Studiomark Number 408. The Canada Geese were probably the first birds to be done in the more natural bisque finish and most of them were done this way, although several glazed and decorated pairs have been discovered. The piece is expected to remain in production for some time.

Although none of the decorated bisque examples has been found with any other than makersmark F, there must exist a number of pairs with an earlier makersmark. The undecorated bisque bears makersmark D exclusively.

I have seen a pair of glazed Canada Geese (RPC-1007-06) with "heft" unlike any Boehm I know except the large Cocker Spaniel. These were certainly early and experimental. These few "hefty" pieces which survive are, in collectors' terms, most desirable.

*See page 91

Collectors who are always on the lookout for the unique should be aware that in 1968 several pairs of the Geese, RPC-1007-05, were delivered without the white marking under the beak. The omission was called to the Studio's attention and those pairs still on dealers' shelves were recalled for correction. However, a number of the "mistakes" had already been sold and were not returned. We are certain that only a few escaped correction. Several collections, we know, are enhanced by this valuable Studio error.

The Geese have also been the victims of at least one out-and-out fraud. There has been discovered a female goose with goslings that is obviously an attempt at forgery. Whether more of these are around is unknown, but collectors would be well advised to check new acquisitions of this piece carefully, especially if they come from a questionable source.

RPC-1008-01 RING-NECKED PHEASANTS (pr.) (13" x 7½") glazed, decorated, extremely rare

RPC-1008-02 RING-NECKED PHEASANTS (pr.) (13½" x 7½") numbered bisque, early decoration—20 made

RPC-1008-03 RING-NECKED PHEASANTS (pr.) (13½" x 7½") bisque, final decoration (RP-1093) limited edition of 500*

RPC-1008-04 RING-NECKED PHEASANTS (pr.) (13" x 7½") bisque, undecorated (RP-1094) 12 made

Introduced in 1954, under Boehm Studiomark Number 409, as a limited edition of 500 pair, the Ring-Necked Pheasants were the last limited edition birds to be made in a glazed finish, and only a few were produced in this finish. The piece was intended as a limited edition of 750, but in 1962 the edition quantity was reduced to 500. The sculpture depicts a male and female on individual rectangular bases with the male running.

The undecorated birds were discontinued in 1958; the decorated continued to be pro-

*See page 92

duced until the edition was completed in 1972. Although most of those that came through decorated bear makersmark E, those pairs produced before 1959 must, we are sure, carry an earlier makersmark. The number would be fairly small, however, since we note that less than half the edition had been completed by 1965, and we assume that the greater part of these were done after 1959. The undecorated bisque carry makersmark D.

Ed Boehm was attracted to birds as models for sculptures because they could be done full scale. For some reason the Ring-Necks were made approximately half scale. As such they are the only limited bird edition to be made this way. It is too bad, since the Ring-Neck is a magnificent animal and deserved to be shown life size. I believe Ed Boehm always intended to rectify this, but, alas, he ran out of time.

The RPC-1008-02, the numbered early decoration, has not only a scarcity value with only 20 made and the added attraction of being numbered, but some examples of these were exquisitely decorated. In all probability the decoration was done either by Ed himself or by Mr. Fenzel, the German decorator who worked with Ed on some of these early pieces.

RPC-1009 GOSLING (5" x 2"), glazed, decorated (RP-1016) 124 made

The Gosling was introduced in 1954, but the piece was not a popular one. Records show that 124 were produced and the price was dropped in 1957 to close out the remainder. The piece bears Boehm Studiomark Number 410 and makersmark D. The piece shows a gosling swimming with legs out behind, its head turned one-fourth right and its pulled-in beak resting on its breast.

This obviously was sold cheaply and probably used as gifts for children and subsequently thrown away or destroyed. It is not a beautifully finished piece; that is, it is not something that a layman would look at and recognize value immediately, but it is

RPC-1014-01

RPC-1009

RPC-1011

beautifully conceived and would grace any collection. When the prices dropped in 1957, the remainders were closed out from the Studio. There is no telling to what shops and outlets they went. It is certain that of the 124 pieces originally made not more than 20 or 30 can be accounted for.

RPC-1010 GUN STOCK BOX WITH ONE MALE MALLARD, glazed, decorated (RP-1017) 2 made

This was an experimental piece and was made in 1954. There were only two examples produced and neither found its way onto the open market, nor have any auction records come to light. The piece carries Boehm Studiomark Number 411. This piece is 7″ x 5″.

RPC-1011 CHICK (3½″) glazed, decorated (RP-1018) 320 made

Also introduced in 1954, under Boehm Studiomark Number 412, the Chick was made in fairly large quantity, approximately 320.

The same thing we said for the Gosling can be said for the Chick. It is a small, undistinguished but beautifully conceived piece and one which has been dissipated and destroyed.

RPC-1012-01 WOODCOCK (10″ high) bisque, decorated (RP-1095) limited edition of 494*
RPC-1012-02 WOODCOCK (10″ high) bisque, undecorated (RP-1096) 6 made

The Woodcock, shown standing, facing one-half right, among tall leaves, was introduced in 1954 under Boehm Studiomark Number 413 as a limited edition originally intended as 1,000 (reduced in 1962 to a total of 500). This was the first bird subject to be produced entirely in the bisque finish. Only six of the edition were left undecorated. In September 1966, the edition was completed.

RPC-1013-01 GOLDEN ORIENTAL PHEASANT (21″ x 6″) bisque, decorated (RP-1020) 7 made**
RPC-1013-02 GOLDEN ORIENTAL PHEASANT (21″ x 6″) bisque, undecorated (RP-1019) 7 made

The Golden Pheasant was the most ambitious of the Boehm pieces up to 1954, the year of its introduction. It was intended originally to be a limited edition piece and carried the Boehm Studiomark Number 414. Unfortunately, the technical difficulties encountered in its production forced the re-

tirement of the piece after only seven in each decoration had been finished. Aside from the extraordinarily delicate construction of the long tail, which proved almost impossible to fire successfully, the piece was also vulnerable to breakage in shipment. Because of the enormous difficulty in firing the heavy tail, I am inclined to consider Oriental Pheasants with firing cracks as in mint and perfect condition. It must be assumed that, of the 14 pieces completed, several were broken during shipment, thus limiting the number of mint-condition Pheasants in collections today.

This sculpture shows a Golden Oriental Pheasant running, left leg leading, right wing raised, tail stretched out and head turned three-quarters right.

The last decorated piece was completed in January of 1956 and the last undecorated in April of the same year.

RPC-1014-01 TUMBLER PIGEONS (pr.) (10½″ high) bisque, decorated (RP-1036) unlimited discontinued—approximately 2170 pairs made
RPC-1014-02 TUMBLER PIGEONS (pr.) (10½″ high) bisque, undecorated (RP-1037) rare

Introduced in 1955 as an unlimited edition under Boehm Studiomark Number 416, the

*See page 93
**See page 28

RPC-1015-01

Tumblers, presented in display position, were available until the edition was discontinued in August of 1970. Apparently, not many undecorated pairs were produced, and the total must be estimated at 2,100.

RPC-1015-01 MACAWS (pr.) (9″ high), glazed, decorated (RP-1021) 6 made
RPC-1015-02 MACAWS (pr.) (9″ high), glazed, undecorated (RP-1023) 12 made
RPC-1015-03 MACAWS (pr.) (9″ high), bisque, decorated (RP-1156) probably unique
RPC-1015-04 MACAWS (pr.) (9″ high), bisque, undecorated (RP-1022) 50 made

This piece shows a pair of Macaws perched on a leaf-rimmed stump, tail sweeping down with wings crossed over back and head cocked and turned one-half right.

This unlimited edition was introduced in 1955 under Boehm Studiomark Number 417. By 1957, all decorations (save the undecorated bisque) had been discontinued and the latter remained in open edition until 1960. The rarest of all decorations of this bird is the decorated bisque, only one pair having turned up thus far. Of the glazed, approximately six were decorated and 12 undecorated, while the quantity of undecorated bisque was well over 50 pairs.

RPC-1016-01 CARDINALS (pr.) (15″ high), bisque, decorated (RP-1097) limited edition of 500*
RPC-1016-02 CARDINALS (pr.) (15″ high), bisque, undecorated (RP-1098) 4 made

The sculpture is of a male and female on individual bases. The female is perched on a grape vine with grapes. The male is in flight above a grape vine with grapes.

The Cardinals, Boehm Studiomark Number 415, were the first important songbird edition to be produced by Boehm. After their introduction in 1955 as a limited edition of 500 pairs, the glazed finish for bird subjects was discontinued and all editions after that date were done only in bisque, including those examples of earlier editions that were still in production.

The Cardinals marked yet another milestone in Boehm: the first time that importance was given to the foliage in the composition. The grape vine of this sculpture is as true to nature and as finely designed as the birds themselves.

Approximately four pairs of Cardinals were produced undecorated but these were not as popular as the decorated. The edition was completed in February 1966.

RPC-1017-01 CEDAR WAXWINGS ON WILD BLACKBERRY (pr.) (12½″ high) bisque, decorated (RP-1080) limited edition of 100*
RPC-1017-02 CEDAR WAXWINGS ON WILD BLACKBERRY (pr.) (12½″ high) bisque, undecorated (RP-1081) 7 made

This sculpture depicts a male and female on individual pedestal bases. Each bird is perched on a wild blackberry bush with the male feeding a blackberry to two fledglings.

The Cedar Waxwings were introduced in 1956 under Boehm Studiomark Number 418, and closed in November 1961. The undecorated examples were not too popular and only seven pairs were produced.

This edition raises a question. When you are in the business as long as I have been, you start sensing that there might be something wrong with a particular edition. I have been aware for a long time that the Cedar Waxwings, which closed early, are much rarer and appear much less frequently than do any of the other editions of 100. In fact, we tend to see more Song Sparrows than we do Cedar Waxwings. The only conclusion I can come to is that 100 were not completed. My guess is that the Boehm atelier decided either for technical or merchandising reasons, or for reasons that were private, to stop making Cedar Waxwings before the complete edition of 100 were sold.

RPC-1018-01 GOLDEN CROWNED KINGLETS with Oriental Poppies (13″ high) bisque, decorated (RP-1099) 494 made**
RPC-1018-02 GOLDEN CROWNED

*See page 94

*See page 95
**See page 96

KINGLETS with Oriental Poppies (13″ high) bisque, undecorated (RP-1100) 4 made

Introduced as a limited edition of 500 in 1956 under Boehm Studiomark Number 419, the Golden Crowned Kinglets closed in August of 1968. In addition, several examples of undecorated bisque were produced. The sculpture shows the male and female perched among Oriental Poppies.

The Golden Crowned Kinglets have proved themselves a favorite with the ladies. The beautiful orange of the poppies was never again used by the Boehm Studio.

RPC-1019-01 SONG SPARROWS with Tulips (17″ x 9″) bisque, decorated (RP-1078) limited edition of 50*
RPC-1019-02 SONG SPARROWS with Tulips (17″ x 9″) bisque, undecorated (RP-1079) 5 made

The piece shows the male in full song, perched on a gardener's trowel, among a cluster of tulips. The female is perched on a flowerpot, among a cluster of tulips, hungrily eyeing a butterfly on a dandelion bud.

A limited edition of 50 pairs (plus five pairs in undecorated bisque), the Song Sparrows were introduced in 1956 and are among the best of Boehm. They carry Boehm Studiomark Number 421. The edition was completed in November 1960.

Some years ago, I became curious about who bought the Song Sparrows. So, we spent a year tracing the sales from the Boehm Studio to the dealers and finally to the customers. We came up with a curious fact: we were able to trace only some 34 pieces plus indications that four others were made. But that makes a total of 38 Song Sparrows and not the 50 which the catalog says were produced. We have asked the Boehms about this and they suggest that the records were not clear in the early days and that a decision to close the edition could easily have taken place before the entire edition was completed. I believe,

therefore, that there were only 38 Song Sparrows completed.

RPC-1020-01 CAROLINA WRENS on Sugar Maple (10″ x 15″) bisque, decorated (RP-1101) limited edition of 100*
RPC-1020-02 CAROLINA WRENS on Sugar Maple (10″ x 15″) bisque, undecorated (RP-1102) 2 made

Introduced in 1957 as a limited edition of 100 under Boehm Studiomark Number 422, the sculpture is a male and female among fallen sugar maple. The female is perched in a log and the male is in flight. The edition was completed in April 1964.

The Carolina Wrens sculpture was one of two pieces that Ed did on a long flat base; the other was the Cerulean Warbler. As far as I can determine, the edition was completed and Ed Boehm never went back to this format. It is interesting to note that the experience gained by the Studio in the casting of the flat surface was called upon when the time came to cast the plaques for the porcelain paintings.

RPC-1021-01 BLACK-TAILED BANTAMS (pr.) (Male 13″ high, Female 9¾″ high) bisque, decorated (RP-1024) limited edition of 56**
RPC-1021-02 BLACK-TAILED BANTAMS (pr.) (Male 13″ high, Female 9¾″ high) bisque, undecorated (RP-1159) unique

Originally introduced in 1957 as a limited edition of 200 pairs, under Boehm Studiomark Number 423, the Bantams were discontinued after only 57 pairs had been produced, one of which (probably the last pair made) was left in the undecorated state. The date of discontinuance is March 1962, and the reason is the same as for the Golden Pheasant: the technical difficulties involved in the firing of the tail and extensive breakage during shipment.

RPC-1022-01 CERULEAN WARBLER,

SMALL (8″ x 7¼″), bisque, decorated— 3 made
RPC-1022-02 CERULEAN WARBLERS on Wild Rose (14″ x 7½″) bisque, decorated (RP-1082) limited edition of 100*
RPC-1022-03 CERULEAN WARBLERS on Wild Rose (14″ x 7½″) bisque, undecorated (RP-1083) 4 made

Practically nothing is known of the small Cerulean sculpture except that it does bear, according to studio records, the same Studiomark Number as the larger, better-known piece. It may have been the original design model for this piece, abandoned when the piece was modified to its limited edition form. It was made simultaneously with the original large Cerulean Warbler. Pope John XXIII received one of the three, Mrs. Boehm had one and the third was sold to a lady in London, Ontario, in 1959.

The sculpture depicts a male and female on a single base. The female is on an egg-filled nest among branches of Wild Rose.

The limited edition Cerulean (100 pieces plus 4 undecorated bisque) was introduced under Boehm Studiomark Number 424 in 1957; the edition was completed in October 1963.

I want to point out that the Prothonotary Warbler, an unlimited piece, is a major portion of the Cerulean Warbler sculpture. This procedure of excerpting a part of a sculpture has been repeated, most recently, with the Swan Bird of Peace in which the Cygnet is offered as a non-limited piece.

RPC-1023-01 RED-WINGED BLACK-BIRDS on Cattails (pr.) (17″ high) bisque, decorated (RP-1103) limited edition of 100**
RPC-1023-02 RED-WINGED BLACK-BIRDS on Cattails (pr.) (17″ high) bisque, undecorated (RP-1104) 2 made

This piece has a male and female on individual bases of cattails in water. The male is perched on the cattails with beak open.

*See page 46

*See page 97
**See page 50

*See page 13
**See page 98

A few pairs of Blackbirds, the early pairs, bore shadows of the birds in the blue water of the base. The collectors who have these are particularly fortunate.

This piece was another 1957 introduction. It bears Boehm Studiomark Number 426 and was limited to 100 pairs, plus two pairs in undecorated bisque. It closed in April of 1964.

The Red-Winged Blackbirds has a special problem. It is tall and thin and the heavy cattails at the top of the sculpture cause a good deal of breakage. Especially in the early days, few of the large sculptures survived without some damage and it is my guess that only a quarter of the edition remains in mint condition. Therefore, if you do get a pair that are mint when examined under black light, you are getting one of the rarer examples of the edition.

Because of the fragility of this piece, I would not completely discount the purchase of a broken pair as it may be the only example of this important bird that you will ever be offered.

RPC-1024-01 DOWNY WOODPECKERS on Trumpet Vine (13″ x 5½″) bisque, decorated (RP-1105) limited edition of 500*

RPC-1024-02 DOWNY WOODPECKERS on Trumpet Vine (13″ x 5½″) bisque, undecorated (RP-1106) 4 made

Introduced in 1957, the Downy bears Boehm Studiomark 427 and was a limited edition of 500. Only a few undecorated pieces were done and they were available only in 1957. The piece never enjoyed the popularity of most of the other Boehm birds. The edition was completed in January 1969.

This sculpture shows a male and female perched beside a hollow log bedecked with trumpet vine in which two fledglings are squalling for dinner.

For some reason, the Downy Woodpecker was an early and continuing favorite of Ed Boehm. He spent much time pointing out the complications, involvements and

grace of this piece on the one occasion when I asked him to identify his favorite sculpture from among all of his birds.

The piece was repeated conceptually in the Ivory-Billed Woodpecker: the same use of a tree stump, the same baby birds inside the nest. It is obvious that Ed's affection for the early piece led him to this later monumental one.

RPC-1025-01 AMERICAN EAGLE, LARGE (18¼″ high), bisque, decorated eyes only (RP-1026) 8 made*

RPC-1025-02 AMERICAN EAGLE, LARGE (18¼″ high), bisque, undecorated (RP-1025) 23 made

RPC-1025-03 AMERICAN EAGLE, SMALL (15½″ high), bisque, decorated eyes only (RP-1028) 12 made

RPC-1025-04 AMERICAN EAGLE, SMALL (15½″ high), bisque, undecorated (RP-1027) 64 made

Introduced in 1957 under Boehm Studiomark Number 428, both sizes were available through 1961. In all, 31 large (eight decorated) and 76 small (12 decorated) were produced. The American Eagle is shown standing upon a broken column, with wings up and half spread, head thrust forward and one-quarter left, beak open.

In 1961, the large decorated Eagle was chosen as a gift to former President Herbert Hoover from the Explorers Club of New York and as a birthday gift to President John F. Kennedy from the Democratic Committee of New Jersey. This latter gift earned for the piece the name "Kennedy Eagle" and many of the subsequent examples were offered with a replication of the ebony base and plaque that had been affixed to the presentation piece. Which of these replications was, in fact, the one which was presented to the President is impossible to say. In accordance with John Kennedy's long-standing practice of not accepting gifts worth over $25, he gave the original example of the Eagle back to the Democratic Committee of New Jersey

which then auctioned it with no record of who bought it. There is, however, an indication that subsequently it did come back onto the market. Of the three or four replicas around, therefore, there is no way of determining the piece that was actually handled by John Kennedy. But, obviously, only one was.

RPC-1026-01 INDIGO BUNTING, Male on Wild Rose (10″ high) bisque, decorated (RP-1083) nonlimited edition discontinued*

RPC-1026-2 INDIGO BUNTING, Male on Wild Rose (10″ high) bisque, decorated, black base, rare

RPC-1026-03 INDIGO BUNTING, Male on Wild Rose (10″ high) bisque, undecorated (RP-1039) approximately 6 made

The Indigo Bunting was introduced as an unlimited edition in 1957 under Boehm Studiomark Number 429 and is illustrative of the change in the character of the new introductions that began at that time. The larger, more ambitious pieces were still slow to sell, and full recognition had not yet been achieved. For this reason, Ed Boehm turned to smaller, nonlimited and less expensive subjects, and the Indigo was the first of this group which also included the early examples of the Fledgling Collection.

This piece shows a male Indigo perched on a Wild Rose on a formal pedestal base.

RPC-1027-01 WHITE-THROATED SPARROW on Cherokee Rose (9½″ high) bisque, decorated (RP-1040) nonlimited edition discontinued**

RPC-1027-02 WHITE-THROATED SPARROW on Cherokee Rose (9½″ high) bisque, undecorated (RP-1041) approximately 6 made

Another unlimited 1957 introduction, the history of this piece parallels that of the Indigo Bunting. The White-Throated Sparrow bears Boehm Studiomark Number 430,

*See page 48

*See page 48

*See page 99
**See page 100

RPC-1029-01

and was also discontinued in May, 1972.

It is on a pedestal base. The bird, a male, is perched on a Cherokee Rose, with wings half spread.

RPC-1028-01 YELLOW-THROATED WARBLER on Crimson-Eye Mallow (10″ high) bisque, decorated (RP-1042) nonlimited edition discontinued*
RPC-1028-02 YELLOW-THROATED WARBLER on Crimson-Eye Mallow (10″ high) bisque, undecorated (RP-1043) approximately 6 made

This piece was the third unlimited edition adult bird introduced in 1957, and it carries Boehm Studiomark Number 431. The sculpture, which was discontinued in June, 1975, shows a male, in song, perched on a Crimson-Eye Mallow on a formal pedestal base.

RPC-1029-01 BABY CEDAR WAXWING on Myrtle Leaves (3″ high) bisque, decorated (RP-1044) nonlimited edition discontinued
RPC-1029-02 BABY CEDAR WAXWING on Myrtle Leaves (3″ high) bisque, undecorated (RP-1045) rare

*See page 101

The Baby Cedar Waxwing is shown perched on Myrtle Leaves, wings folded, head cocked to right.

The first of the Fledgling Collection, the Baby Cedar Waxwing was introduced in 1957 carrying Boehm Studiomark Number 432. It was discontinued in 1973.

RPC-1030-01 CALIFORNIA QUAIL (pr.) (Male 8½″ high, Female 7½″ high) bisque, decorated (RP-1107) limited edition of 500*
RPC-1030-02 CALIFORNIA QUAIL (pr.) (Male 8½″ high, Female 7½″ high) bisque, undecorated (RP-1108) 12 made
RPC-1030-03 CALIFORNIA QUAIL (pr.) (large) bisque, undecorated—possibly unique

This sculpture shows a male and female on individual oval bases. The male is standing in alert position and the female is walking.

Originally intended as a limited edition of 750 pairs, the Quail were introduced in 1957, under Boehm Studiomark Number 433. During the collection revision of 1962, it was decided to lower the total edition quantity to 500. The edition closed in January 1968.

At first the California Quail was made about 13–15 percent larger than the eventual edition size. About six pairs of these "large" Quail had been made when Mr. Boehm determined that they were too large. He took a mold off a large pair which then, when cast and fired, shrank down to the present edition size.

When purchasing this piece, a collector would be well advised to inspect with great care the topknot of the male's head. Most of the damage done to this piece involved breakage at that point, and I believe relatively few of them did not sustain that damage.

RPC-1031-01 MEADOWLARK (8½″ x 7½″) bisque, decorated without mushroom (RP-1157) probably unique
RPC-1031-02 MEADOWLARK (8½″ x

*See page 102

7½″) bisque, decorated (RP-1084) limited edition of 730*
RPC-1031-03 MEADOWLARK (8½″ x 7½″) bisque, undecorated (RP-1085) 20 made

The Meadowlark was introduced in 1957, as a limited edition of 750 pieces, under Boehm Studiomark Number 435. The edition was completed in January 1964. The example without the mushroom is believed to have been produced around 1964 at the request of a dealer in Minneapolis and approved by Mrs. Boehm. When Mr. Boehm learned of this, he stopped it and put the mushroom back on the piece. Included in the total of 750 were 20 undecorated bisque pieces. The sculpture shows a male standing beside dandelion and rock, with mushroom. The bird, as befits a meadowlark, is in full-throated song.

The Meadowlark was an early favorite. It was, in fact, the first limited edition to close completely. Photographs of this piece were featured in the mid 1960's in an article in the *Saturday Evening Post* just prior to completion.

RPC-1031-01 Meadowlark which was made without the mushroom is probably unique. There were, indeed, two of these made but only one example remains intact and it is in the hands of a collector who is not likely to sell it.

RPC-1032-01 BABY BLUE JAY (4½″) bisque, decorated (RP-1046) nonlimited edition in production**
RPC-1032-02 BABY BLUE JAY (4½″) bisque, undecorated (RP-1040) approximately 12 made
RPC-1032-03 BABY BLUE JAY (4½″) "Where's Ma?" bisque, decorated—rare

This piece shows a Baby Blue Jay standing with Johnny-jump-ups. The second in the series of Fledglings, the Baby Blue Jay was also introduced in 1957, under Boehm Studiomark Number 436 and was often, in the early days, referred to by the whimsical title "Where's Ma?" (RPC-1032-03).

*See page 103
**See page 104

223

RPC-1033-01 BABY ROBIN (3½" high) bisque, decorated (RP-1048) nonlimited in production*

RPC-1033-02 BABY ROBIN (3½" high) bisque, undecorated (RP-1049) approximately 12 made

RPC-1033-03 BABY ROBIN "First Venture" bisque, decorated, rare

Another 1957 Fledgling introduction, the Baby Robin bears Boehm Studiomark Number 437. The piece shows a baby robin with wings slightly spread, in first flight from the nest.

RPC-1034-01 BLACK-CAPPED CHICKA-DEE, Male on Holly Leaves (9" high) bisque, decorated (RP-1050) nonlimited edition discontinued**

RPC-1034-02 BLACK-CAPPED CHICKA-DEE, Male on Holly Leaves (9" high) bisque, undecorated (RP-1051) approximately 15 made

In 1957 Boehm introduced the unlimited adult Black-Capped Chickadee, showing a male with Holly Leaves and berries on a pedestal base, under Studiomark Number 438. It was discontinued in March 1973.

RPC-1035-01 HUMMINGBIRD, Male on Cactus (8½" high) bisque, decorated (RP-1052) nonlimited edition discontinued***

RPC-1035-02 HUMMINGBIRD, Male on Cactus (8½" high) bisque, undecorated (RP-1053) approximately 6 made

The first introduction of 1958, the Hummingbird, under Boehm Studiomark Number 440, is an unlimited edition. The sculpture shows a male hovering over a Ladyfinger blossom. It was discontinued in June 1975.

RPC-1036-01 RUBY-CROWNED KING-LET, on Bloodroot (8" high) bisque, decorated (RP-1029) 300 made****

RPC-1036-02 RUBY-CROWNED KING-LET, on Bloodroot (8" high) bisque, undecorated—rare

*See page 104
**See page 105
***See page 106
****See page 107

This piece, though purported to have been introduced in 1957, does not appear on the price lists until 1958. We have therefore assigned it that introductory date, despite the fact that it carries a 1957 Boehm Studiomark Number 434. Approximately 300 examples of the Kinglet were produced, and thus far none has been discovered in the undecorated state.

This sculpture shows a Ruby-Crowned Kinglet perched on a large leaf of a bloodroot plant which has two blossoms. The bird faces right with wings folded, tail down, beak open, on a formal pedestal base.

The petals of the flowers of this piece are extremely fragile. They are placed exactly where you might put your thumb when you pick up the piece. As a result I have rarely seen a piece that has not been broken. Examine the petals of the flower carefully before purchasing this piece and be sure to black-light it.

RPC-1037-01 BLACKBURNIAN WARBLER WITH MOUNTAIN LAUREL (10½" x 5") bisque, decorated (RP-1033) unique

RPC-1037-02 BLACK-THROATED BLUE WARBLER, Male on Mountain Laurel (10½" x 5") bisque, decorated (RP-1109) limited edition of 500 made*

RPC-1037-03 BLACK-THROATED BLUE WARBLER, Male on Mountain Laurel (10½" x 5") bisque, undecorated (RP-1110) 2 made

With the exception of the coloration of the Warbler's plumage, these are all identical sculptures bearing Boehm Studiomark Number 441. The Blackburnian is a unique piece and may have been the original model for the edition. However, it was the decoration of the Black-Throated Blue Warbler that was introduced in 1958 as a limited edition of 750. That number includes two examples left in their undecorated state. This sculpture shows a male, perched in Mountain Laurel and holding a ladybug in his mouth.

*See page 108

The edition quantity was reduced to 500 in 1962, and the edition was completed in August of 1966.

RPC-1038-01 BABY BLUEBIRD (4½" high) bisque, decorated (RP-1054) nonlimited edition in production*

RPC-1038-02 BABY BLUEBIRD (4½" high) bisque, undecorated (RP-1055) approximately 12 made

The sculpture depicts Baby Bluebird perched on leafy twigs, wings folded, head turned one-quarter left. Also called the "Baby Bluebird of Happiness," this piece was one of only two unlimited fledglings introduced in 1958, and bears Boehm Studiomark Number 442.

RPC-1039-01 MOURNING DOVES (14" x 8") bisque, decorated (RP-1111) limited edition of 500**

RPC-1039-02 MOURNING DOVES (14" x 8") bisque, undecorated (RP-1112) rare

The Mourning Doves, male and female perched on a tree trunk, facing in opposite directions (Boehm Studiomark Number 443) was introduced in 1958 in a limited edition of 750 pieces. In 1960 it was decided to decrease the total edition, and 1962 found the number at 500 pieces. This edition was completed in June, 1973.

The Doves suffer from the fact that they are *too* lifelike. Living mourning doves have a smooth silky body which shows little feather texture. Collectors who are used to birds with deep feather texture complain of the "lack of detail." They could just as well complain to Mother Nature herself since Ed Boehm was, as usual, true to that lady.

The number produced in undecorated bisque is not known; however, it is unlikely that more than two or three in that finish exist.

RPC-1040-01 BABY WOODTHRUSH with Insect (4½" high) bisque, decorated (RP-1145) unique

RPC-1040-02 BABY WOODTHRUSH with

*See page 109
**See page 50

Butterfly (4½″ high) bisque, decorated (RP-1056) nonlimited edition in production*

RPC-1040-03 BABY WOODTHRUSH with Butterfly (4½″ high) bisque, undecorated (RP-1057) rare

This sculpture depicts a Baby Woodthrush with a butterfly in its mouth. Introduced in 1958, under Boehm Studiomark Number 444, the Baby Woodthrush with Butterfly is an unlimited piece. The example with insect is a unique piece, produced sometime before 1963 and it bears makersmark D.

The actual number of undecorated examples must be assumed to be few.

RPC-1041-01 PROTHONOTARY WARBLER, Female with Eggs and Fledgling (5½″ high) bisque, decorated (RP-1058) nonlimited edition discontinued**

RPC-1041-02 PROTHONOTARY WARBLER, Female with Eggs and Fledgling (5½″ high) bisque, undecorated (RP-1059) extremely rare

Although the Prothonotary (also called "Wild Canary Warbler") bears its own Boehm Studiomark Number 445, it is actually the same sculpture as the female on the Cerulean Warbler (female with eggs and day-old chick). It was introduced in 1958 as an unlimited edition.

RPC-1042-01 NONPAREIL BUNTINGS on Flowering Raspberry (8½″ x 5″) bisque, decorated (RP-1113) limited edition of 740***

RPC-1042-02 NONPAREIL BUNTINGS on Flowering Raspberry (8½″ x 5″) bisque, undecorated (RP-1114) 10 made

The piece is a male and female perched on a flowering raspberry plant. The male is holding a butterfly in his mouth. Originally intended as a limited edition of 1,000, the Nonpareils (Boehm Studiomark Number 446) were introduced in 1958. The 1962 collection revision, however, found the edi-

RPC-1046-01

tion quantity reduced to 740. The edition was completed in December 1967. The number of the undecorated pieces (included in the total edition quantity) is approximately 10.

RPC-1043-01 AMERICAN REDSTARTS on Flowering Dogwood (11½″ x 6½″) bisque, decorated (RP-1115) limited edition of 500*

RPC-1043-02 AMERICAN REDSTARTS on Flowering Dogwood (11½″ x 6½″) bisque, undecorated (RP-1116) rare

The Redstarts were introduced in 1958. They do not appear on a price list until 1959, when they are described as a limited edition of 750 pieces (Boehm Studiomark Number 447). By 1962, the edition quantity had been reduced to 500. It closed in January 1968.

The American Redstart is the only example of a nesting bird that Ed Boehm ever did. The male is perched above the nesting female among flowering dogwood. The manner in which Ed achieved the illusion of a lightly sitting bird is remarkable. I am fond of this piece, and except for the fact that it was done on a formal white base, it could well have been an example of his more mature work.

RPC-1044-01 BABY GOLDFINCH with Violet (4½″ high) bisque, decorated (RP-1060) nonlimited edition discontinued*

RPC-1044-02 BABY GOLDFINCH with Violet (4½″ high) bisque, undecorated (RP-1061) extremely rare

This addition to the Fledgling collection, under Boehm Studiomark Number 448, was introduced in 1959 and discontinued in 1972. It shows a Baby Goldfinch perched on a log festooned with violets, with its beak open.

RPC-1045-01 FLEDGLING KINGFISHER (6″ high) bisque, decorated (RP-1062) nonlimited edition still in production

RPC-1045-02 FLEDGLING KINGFISHER (6″ high) bisque, undecorated (RP-1063) rare*

The Kingfisher sitting on a log first appears on the 1960 price list, as an unlimited edition, Boehm Studiomark Number 449. The piece is, at this writing, still available in open, unlimited edition.

RPC-1046-01 FLEDGLING PURPLE FINCHES (4½″ high) bisque, decorated (RP-1030) 420 made

*See page 109
**See page 110
***See page 50

*See page 11

*See page 111

RPC-1047-01   RPC-1048-01

RPC-1046-02 FLEDGLING PURPLE FINCHES (4½″ high) bisque, undecorated (RP-1031) 12 made

The Fledglings were the first baby birds to be discontinued. They first appeared on the price lists in 1960 and, probably due to lack of sales appeal or to the fact that they were more expensive than the other fledglings, were discontinued in 1963, after 420 decorated and 12 undecorated had been produced. They bear Boehm Studiomark Number 450.

I never really understood why the Studio discontinued this marvelous piece. It is tender and amusing and enormously attractive. We were able to sell all we could get during the time it was available. Of all the examples of the Boehm baby birds that were produced, this was the most successful. The sculpture showed three baby birds (purple finches) on a log with the center bird asleep.

RPC-1047-01 EASTERN BLUEBIRDS on Rhododendron (pr.) (Male 14″ high, Female 12″ high), bisque, decorated (RP-1086) limited edition of 100
RPC-1047-02 EASTERN BLUEBIRDS on

Rhododendron (pr.) (Male 14″ high, Female 12″ high) bisque, undecorated (RP-1087) 2 made

The Eastern Bluebirds mark another milestone in Boehm. For the first time fine metals were used to enhance the naturalism of the sculptures. In the case of the Eastern Bluebirds, the stamens of the rhododendrons are of metal. The sculpture depicts a male and female on individual bases with Rhododendron. The wings of the male are spread.

Although this piece is said to be the only limited edition introduced in 1959 (Boehm Studiomark Number 451), it did not actually appear on a price list until 1960.

RPC-1048-01 OWLS (pr.) (9″ high) bisque, decorated eyes and beak only (RP-1064) nonlimited edition discontinued, 1,400 made
RPC-1048-02 OWLS (pr.) (9″ high) bisque, undecorated (RP-1065) 6 made
RPC-1048-03 OWLS (pr.) (9″ high) bisque, eyes, claws and ears decorated—unique

This unlimited edition (Owls, traditionally

mounted on books) was introduced in 1960 under Boehm Studiomark Number 453. The piece was discontinued in August 1970, after approximately 1,400 pairs had been produced.

RPC-1049-01 RUFFED GROUSE (pr.) (12″ high) bisque, decorated (RP-1117) limited edition of 250**
RPC-1049-02 RUFFED GROUSE (pr.) (12″ high) bisque, undecorated (RP-1118) 2 made

Introduced in 1960 as a limited edition of 250 pairs (Boehm Studiomark Number 456), the Ruffed Grouse edition closed in April 1966. In addition to the 250 decorated examples, two Ruffed Grouse were produced in undecorated bisque.*

The male is probably the best single

---

* Note: As discussed at the beginning of this volume, the introduction of the Ruffed Grouse and Eastern Bluebirds marked a change in Boehm policy in regard to undecorated examples of limited edition sculptures. From this time on it may be assumed that one undecorated bisque piece was produced over and above the registered edition quantity for each limited piece. Any variation of this policy will be noted in the text.

**See page 112

piece of bird sculpture I have ever seen. The tensions and power of the bird are immaculately portrayed. I believe it will become one of the editions most in demand. The sculpture depicts a male and female on individual oval bases. The male perches on a log, drumming the air with his wings. The female walks, wing trailing the ground.

RPC-1050-01 GOLDFINCHES with Scottish Thistle (11½″ x 5″) bisque, decorated (RP-1119) limited edition of 500[*]
RPC-1050-2 GOLDFINCHES with Scottish Thistle (11½″ x 5″) bisque, undecorated (RP-1120) unique

The sculpture presents a male and female Goldfinch with Thistle with the female reaching for a ladybug. The Goldfinches were introduced in 1961 as a limited edition of 500 pieces under Boehm Studiomark Number 457. The edition was completed in June 1968.

RPC-1051-01 BABY CRESTED FLYCATCHER (5″ high) bisque, decorated (RP-1066) nonlimited edition discontinued
RPC-1051-02 BABY CRESTED FLYCATCHER (5″ high) bisque, undecorated (RP-1067) rare
RPC-1051-03 BABY CRESTED FLYCATCHER (7″ high) bisque, decorated gray base—13 made

This unlimited addition to the Fledgling collection was introduced in 1962 under Boehm Studiomark Number 458. It appears that 13 decorated examples were produced on round (3¾″ diameter) gray bases, similar in shape to those used on the Mockingbirds (RPC-1052). The Baby Crested Flycatcher sculpture shows a baby bird standing on a twisted branch, screeching for food. The piece was discontinued in 1972.

RPC-1052-01 MOCKINGBIRDS on Blossoming Bindweed (pr.) (Male 12½″

*See page 113

high, Female 11½″ high) bisque, decorated (RP-1121) limited edition 500[*]
RPC-1052-02 MOCKINGBIRDS on Blossoming Bindweed (pr.) (Male 12½″ high, Female 11½″ high) bisque, undecorated (RP-1122) 2 made

The Mockingbird sculpture shows a male and female on individual pedestal bases. The female is holding a butterfly in her mouth; the male's beak is open.

The Mockingbirds were introduced in 1961 as a limited edition of 500 pairs, plus two examples in undecorated bisque. The edition closed in December 1966. They bear Boehm Studiomark Number 459.

In 1964, the Mockingbirds, the State Bird of Texas, was chosen by Governor Richard J. Hughes of New Jersey as a gift for President Lyndon Johnson from the Democratic Party. The presentation was made at the 1964 Democratic Convention in Atlantic City.

RPC-1053-01 SUGARBIRDS (25½″ x 11″) bisque, decorated (RP-1123) limited edition of 100^{**}
RPC-1053-02 SUGARBIRDS (25½″ x 11″) bisque, undecorated (RP-1124) unique

Also introduced in 1961, the Sugarbirds bear Boehm Studiomark Number 460. The piece was originally intended as an edition of 50 and was, at that point, the most intricate of all Boehm pieces. However, the response from dealers and collectors was so overwhelming that it was decided that an edition of 50 would never suffice and the edition, therefore, was increased to 100. The edition closed in January 1966. As with the Bindweed blossoms of the Mockingbird, the Orchid blooms' stems of the Sugarbirds are metal encased in porcelain and are removable. The piece shows two males and two females perched on the trunk of a tree.

The Sugarbirds represent an undertaking of such ambition that it is hard to imagine why a studio would involve itself in it. The only explanation is that Ed Boehm was

*See page 114
**See page 56

RPC-1051-01

RPC-1051-03

driven by impossible goals and set himself yet another problem to solve. There are about 100 cast parts to the Sugarbirds, parts that have to be put together in clay. The casting of these 100 parts, of course, requires 100 molds. Each mold averages about 4 sections; thus, 400 mold sections are required to make up the 100 molds which cast the 100 clay parts. When it was shown in 1961, it far surpassed any porcelain sculpture of its kind that had ever been done either here or in Europe.

RPC-1054-01 BABY CHICKADEE (3″ high) bisque, decorated (RP-1068) non-limited edition discontinued*
RPC-1054-02 BABY CHICKADEE (3″ high) bisque, undecorated (RP-1069) rare

This unlimited fledgling was introduced in 1962, under Boehm Studiomark Number 461. It was discontinued in 1972.

RPC-1055-01 PTARMIGAN (pr.) (Male 14″ high, Female 9½″ high) bisque, decorated (RP-1125) limited edition of 350 pair**
RPC-1055-02 PTARMIGAN (pr.) (Male 14″ high, Female 9½″ high) bisque, undecorated (RP-1126) unique

The Ptarmigans are a 1962 introduction, in a limited edition of 350 pairs, and bear Boehm Studiomark Number 463. The edition was completed in June, 1968. The sculpture shows a male and female on individual bases molded to resemble snow-covered rocks. A third piece, molded to resemble a smaller rock, is included. This can be used to connect the two Ptarmigans for use as a centerpiece.

I have known the Ptarmigan in its winter coat and summer coat, as I was stationed in Alaska during the Second World War. When Ed Boehm showed me the first example of the Ptarmigan, I questioned both his choice of the bird and especially his use of the winter coat. My argument was that no one ever sees the bird in that condition. But Ed was fascinated with the bird's ability to go from a dark brown coat in the summer to an absolutely white protective coloration in the winter. Ed Boehm wanted to work with that miracle of nature and it is for that reason he chose the winter coat of the Ptarmigan. I told him I understood his choice, but that the bird would never sell. I was wrong.

RPC-1056-01 LESSER PRAIRIE CHICKENS (pr.) (10″ high), bisque, decorated (RP-1127) limited edition of 300*
RPC-1056-02 LESSER PRAIRIE CHICKENS (pr.) (10″ high), bisque, undecorated (RP-1128) unique

The Lesser Prairie Chickens bear Boehm Studiomark Number 464 and were introduced in 1962. They were closed in June 1974. The sculpture shows a male and female on individual bases. The male, his feathers puffed and ruffled, courts the standing female.

Ed Boehm chose to do this piece (although one of the lesser-known birds) because of its threatened extinction.

Lesser Prairie Chickens were difficult to sell. In 1962 when they came out, I had no trouble getting men to agree to buy them, but women didn't seem to like the goiter-like air sac (the little puffy ball at the throat) of the Lesser Prairie Chicken. When I explained to them the puffy ball was the male's method of sexually attracting the female, my lady collectors got even more uncomfortable. Given the choice between a goiter and a sex symbol, the ladies chose to reject both.

The Prairie Chickens remains to this day one of the most difficult pieces to sell, although in concept, and in execution, it certainly approaches the Ruffed Grouse.

RPC-1057-01 BLUE JAYS on Strawberries (pr.) (Male 14″ high, Female 12″ high) bisque, decorated (RP-1129) limited edition of 250**

RPC-1057-02 BLUE JAYS on Strawberries (pr.) (Male 14″ high, Female 12″ high) bisque, undecorated (RP-1130) unique

Introduced in 1962 as a limited edition of 250 pairs under Boehm Studiomark Number 466, the Blue Jays proved extremely popular. The edition was completed in August 1966.

The Blue Jays raised the whole Boehm experience onto a new plateau. The ease and naturalness of the composition and an enormous amount of information which was included in the sculpture (the relationship of the male and female, the feeding of the young, the food the birds eat, their enemies and their natural setting) were brought together. In addition, the size is almost monumental, and the composition was done with such thought that there is no angle from which this piece can be viewed that it is not both beautiful and satisfying. Basically the sculpture shows a male and female on individual bases. The male perched on wild strawberry screams at its natural enemy, a chameleon mounted on its own separate base. The female feeds a strawberry to two fledglings.

RPC-1058-01 MEARNS QUAIL with Cactus (pr.) (Male 15″ high, Female 7″ high) bisque, decorated (RP-1131) limited edition of 350*
RPC-1058-02 MEARNS QUAIL with Cactus (pr.) (Male 15″ high, Female 7″ high) bisque, undecorated (RP-1132) unique

The Mearns were introduced in 1963 as a limited edition of 350 pair. The piece shows male and female on individual bases with cactus. The female protects two fledglings while the male reaches for an insect. They carry Boehm Studiomark Number 467. The edition was completed in October 1970.

Soon after its introduction, a pair of Mearns Quail was presented by New Jersey Congressman Charles Joelson to the Ha'aretz Museum in Tel Aviv, Israel.

*See page 114
**See page 115

*See page 45
**See page 116

*See page 47

RPC-1059-01

When Congressman Joelson decided to donate a piece of Boehm to the State of Israel, the question arose as to which piece it should be. The Congressman asked us if there was reference in the five books of the Old Testament to any particular bird which might serve as a basis for his choice. We went through the Old Testament and there were few birds mentioned, especially those which might have some direct relationship to the State of Israel. However, there is one story about the Israelites wandering in the desert. They grew tired of the manna which the Lord was giving them and complained bitterly to Moses. Moses berated them for being without gratitude for the food they were getting. However, he did agree to take their complaints to the Lord. When he did so, the Lord indicated that meat would be supplied, and on the following day a great flock of quail flew out of the desert. As the quail crossed over the Israelite camp, many of them fell dead at the feet of the People

of Israel. There was great rejoicing and those who had complained to Moses scooped up the birds, roasted them, and had a great feast. However, while the Lord promised them meat, He didn't say that it would not be without a lesson. The next day, all those who had eaten the quail died. We thought this was a particularly relevant insight; Congressman Joelson agreed, and the Mearns Quail rest today at the Museum in Israel. Another association that we found interesting was the fact that Mearns Quail is, indeed, a desert bird, and so much of the modern Israel's spiritual life revolves around the idea of the desert that this bird seems most appropriate.

RPC-1059-01 LAZULI BUNTING (8″ high) bisque, decorated (RP-1144) unique
RPC-1059-02 TREE SPARROW (8″ high) bisque, decorated (RP-1070) nonlimited edition discontinued
RPC-1059-03 TREE SPARROW (8″ high) bisque, undecorated (RP-1071) extremely rare

The Lazuli Bunting is a unique piece and may have been the forerunner of the Tree Sparrow, to which it is identical in structure. The piece shows a Lazuli Bunting, in song, perched on a limb. As far as we can determine, this Bunting has never come up for sale.

The Tree Sparrow, on the other hand, was introduced in 1963 as an unlimited edition. It bears Boehm Studiomark Number 468. It was discontinued in June 1975.

RPC-1060-01 NUTHATCH with Ivy and Moneywort (11″ high) bisque, decorated (RP-1072) nonlimited edition in production*
RPC-1060-02 NUTHATCH with Ivy and Moneywort (11″ high) bisque, undecorated (RP-1073) extremely rare

Also introduced in unlimited edition in 1963, the Nuthatch bears Boehm Studiomark Number 469. The sculpture shows a

*See page 116

Nuthatch on a dead tree trunk with Ivy and Moneywort.

RPC-1061-01 MOUNTAIN BLUEBIRDS on flowering Magnolia (12″ x 15″) bisque, decorated (RP-1133) limited edition of 300*
RPC-1061-02 MOUNTAIN BLUEBIRDS on flowering Magnolia (12″ x 15″) bisque, undecorated (RP-1134) unique

The Mountain Bluebirds, we are told, were originally designed as a centerpiece for Helen Boehm. Upon completion of the model, however, they were assigned Boehm Studiomark Number 470 and introduced in 1963, as a limited edition of 300. The edition closed in September 1968. The sculpture is a male and female on branches of flowering magnolia. The male has its beak open and its wings raised.

RPC-1062-01 TOWHEE with Fall-Fruiting Mushrooms (8″ x 8″) bisque, decorated RP-1135) limited edition of 500**
RPC-1062-02 TOWHEE with Fall-Fruiting Mushrooms (8″ x 8″) bisque, undecorated (RP-1136) unique

The Towhee was introduced, under Boehm Studiomark Number 471, in 1963 and achieved widespread popularity. It closed in January 1968. The Towhee sculpture shows the bird perched on a tree stump with fall-fruiting mushrooms.

RPC-1063-01 ROBIN with Daffodils (13″ x 8″) bisque, decorated (RP-1137) limited edition of 500***
RPC-1063-02 ROBIN with Daffodils (13″ x 8″) bisque, undecorated (RP-1138) unique

The Robin (Boehm Studiomark Number 472) was one of the most instantly successful pieces produced by Boehm. It shows a male perched on a rock with daffodils. Within six months of the announcement of

*See page 117
**See page 118
***See page 45

its planned inclusion in the 1964 limited edition collection, all the 500 pieces had been sold or assigned to dealers. The demand was so great that the production rate had to be accelerated and the edition was completed in record time—less than two years. When one considers that some editions took almost 20 years to close, this accomplishment is remarkable indeed. The official closing date was January 1966. However, for all practical purposes, the Robin had been closed much earlier, since the edition was totally sold out long before the last piece was produced.

The Robin has often been chosen for important gifts, such as the presentation by the Congressional Club to Queen Elizabeth II of England, and by President Nixon to Pope Paul VI in 1969.

RPC-1064-01 KILLDEER with Bluebells (pr.) (Male 9″ high, Female 8½″ high) bisque, decorated (RP-1139) limited edition of 300*
RPC-1064-02 KILLDEER with Bluebells (pr.) (Male 9″ high, Female 8½″ high) bisque, undecorated (RP-1140) unique

The Killdeer were also introduced in 1964, under Boehm Studiomark Number 473, as a limited edition of 300 pairs. The sculpture represents a male and female on individual bases with bluebells. The edition was completed in November 1970.

In spite of the fact that we now look on the Killdeer as one of the great pieces, it was slow selling in the beginning. It took a certain amount of understanding to convey the message it carried and most of the salespeople who presented the piece to collectors hadn't learned their lessons too well. It is really a beautiful example of defense mechanisms which animals have evolved. The Killdeer is a ground-nesting bird and is, therefore, subject to predators. If you look carefully at the sculpture, you will see the female is alarmed and is gathering her young about her on the ground while the male is in his defense stance.

*See page 119

This involves making himself obvious. He does so by whistling loudly, by lifting his tail high into the air (which a ground-nesting bird never does unless he wants to be seen) and by making a rustling sound in the grass with his wings. It will also be noticed that one of the wings looks as if it has been broken. This is an elegant defense which the male Killdeer displays in order to give the predator the impression that he is incapable of flying. A wounded bird is fair game for any predator, and the predator will naturally go to the source that is making the noise, is visible and seems unable to escape. The male Killdeer continues to whistle, shake his wings and back away from the nest until he feels he has lured the predator far enough away from the nest. Then he flies off. How the Killdeer survives is beautifully delineated.

RPC-1065-01 BOBOLINK with Corn Stubble (14½″ x 8″) bisque, decorated (RP-1141) limited edition of 500*
RPC-1065-02 BOBOLINK with Corn Stubble (14½″ x 8″) bisque, undecorated (RP-1142) unique

The Bobolink (Boehm Studiomark Number 475) was the last of the 1964 limited editions and the edition total was announced at 500. It closed in January 1971. This piece shows a Bobolink on a base with corn stubble.

RPC-1066-01 FLEDGLING MAGPIE (5½″ x 4″) bisque, decorated (RP-1074) nonlimited edition discontinued
RPC-1066-02 FLEDGLING MAGPIE (5½″x 4″) bisque, undec. (RP-1075) –rare

With the introduction of this addition to the Fledgling Collection in 1964, the Studio discontinued the production of undecorated examples of nonlimited birds. The Magpie (Boehm Studiomark Number 476) sitting on a log, was discontinued in 1972.

RPC-1067-01 FLEDGLING BLACKBURN-

*See page 120

RPC-1066-01

IAN WARBLER (4″ x 2½″) bisque, decorated (RP-1076) Nonlimited edition discontinued
RPC-1067-02 FLEDGLING BLACKBURN-IAN WARBLER (4″ x 2½″) bisque, undecorated (RP-1077)—rare

This sculpture, along with the Fledgling Magpie, was the last in which an undecorated example of nonlimited birds was produced. The Blackburnian (Boehm Studiomark Number 478) depicts the bird sitting on a rock.

RPC-1068-01 FLEDGLING RED-TAILED OWL (7″ x 5″) bisque, decorated—unique
RPC-1068-02 FLEDGLING GREAT HORNED OWL (7″ x 5″) bisque, decorated (RP-1151) limited edition of 750*
RPC-1068-03 FLEDGLING GREAT HORNED OWL (7″ x 5″) bisque, undecorated (RP-1152) unique

The Fledgling Red-Tailed Owl is a unique piece and is believed to have been the original model for the decoration of this edition. However, prior to introduction, the

*See page 121

Red-Tailed decoration was abandoned and the piece emerged as a Great Horned Owl.

The edition, introduced in 1965 under Boehm Studiomark Number 479 and limited to 750 pieces, represents the first fledgling subject as a limited edition. The edition closed in June 1970.

The sculpture depicts a six- to eight-week-old fledgling, beginning to acquire its adult coloring and conspicuous hornlike tufts of feathers. The coloring of this species varies from gray to brownish gray to rufous cinnamon or ocher.

Owls, like elephants, attract an enormous number of collectors. (I know one lady who has, by actual count, 100,000 different owls of every material conceivable.) Therefore, when the Boehms made a Fledgling Great Horned Owl, its popularity was ensured and, in fact, it was sought not only by the Boehm collector but by owl collectors, who quickly wiped out the edition.

RPC-1069 IVORY-BILLED WOOD-PECKERS (54″ high) bisque, decorated (RP-1143) 4 made*

Undoubtedly the most magnificent, the most intricate and the most technically difficult of all the Boehm subjects up to its introduction, and still the most exciting, the Ivory-Billed Woodpeckers (Boehm Studiomark Number 480) were never merchandized. Only four were produced in all between 1964 and March 1966. The first of these was sold to a collector in England. Two examples were donated to public collections, the Bellingrath Gardens in Mobile, Ala., and the Syracuse University collection. The fourth example of the Ivory-Billed Woodpeckers was kept as the Studio example and was fitted up in an elegant box and taken around for lectures and exhibitions. It was broken on the way to Shreveport, La., for a lecture program there. The sculpture was being driven over a highway under construction; the crate was in the rear of the vehicle and was not tied down.

*See page 31

Every time the car hit a pothole, the sculpture jumped a foot. When it was unpacked, the large bird and branch had snapped at the base. The Boehms were advised by their insurance company that they were covered for the piece and an undisclosed figure was paid to the Studio by the insurance company. The insurance people had the piece repaired and offered it at auction by mail. They wrote to everyone who might be interested, indicating that they would accept sealed bids and that these bids would be opened on a certain day and the highest bidder would get the piece. An astute and subtle collector from Chicago put in a bid for $17,000 and the piece came to him.

The Ivory-Billed Woodpecker was an enormous undertaking. It tied up Ed Boehm, the Studio, the sculptors, and the decorators for over six months and it cost no one knows how much. It cost months of lost production at a time when the demand for Boehm was strong and growing. But Ed Boehm was in one of his moods and in spite of the enormous size (almost 5′ high *without* the base) and its incredible complexity, he insisted that the piece would be produced and would be finished. It is interesting that the Ivory-Billed was also one of those birds which was nearing extinction and this probably was one of the factors driving Ed to do this piece.

Everything about the Ivory-Billed is on a monumental scale, from the conception of the piece to the problems of the enormous number and size of the molds required, of firing a piece this big, of moving the finished piece. It remains today as a monument to Ed Boehm's skill and to his enormous drive and compulsion to finish a job once started.

RPC-1070-01 VARIED BUNTINGS (18″ x 14″) bisque, decorated (RP-1149) limited edition of 300*
RPC-1070-02 VARIED BUNTINGS (18″ x 14″) bisque, undecorated, unique

*See page 122

Introduced in 1965 as a limited edition of 300 under Boehm Studiomark Number 481, the Varied Bunting edition was completed in November 1974. The piece presents a male in wine-red and wine-lavender coat attempting to draw the attention of his more modestly colored mate. It is set in a floral setting of crown imperial, a member of the lily family, having at the top of the single stalk a cluster of pendant, bell-shaped flowers surrounded by a whorl of leaves. The stalk and stems are fashioned of metal and the entire piece can be grasped and lifted by the stalk alone.

RPC-1071-01 TUFTED TITMICE with Sumac (13″ x 6″) bisque, decorated (RP-1147) limited edition of 500
RPC-1071-02 TUFTED TITMICE with Sumac (13″ x 6″) bisque, undecorated, unique

Another 1965 introduction, the Tufted Titmice bear Boehm Studiomark Number 482 and are a limited edition of 500 pieces. The edition closed in September 1972.

This sculpture depicts a male and female frolicking about snow-laden sumac panicles. In the Tufted Titmice, Ed Boehm returned to the use of snow, which also appears in the Ptarmigan sculpture and then later in the Junco (1970 release).

RPC-1072-01 CATBIRD with Hyacinth (14½″ x 7½″) bisque, decorated (RP-1150) limited edition of 500**
RPC-1072-02 CATBIRD with Hyacinth (14½″ x 7½″) bisque, undecorated—unique

One of the 1965 limited edition pieces, under Boehm Studiomark Number 483, the Catbird closed in January 1973. The sculpture is an adult bird in song perched among shoots and blossoms of hyacinth.

I am constantly asked what my favorite

*See page 122
**See page 123

piece is among the Boehm productions. It is really difficult for me to decide as I have so many favorites. However, the Catbird is one of the pieces of which I am *least* fond. There is a stiffness about the hyacinth and a coldness about the bird which turns me away from it.

RPC-1073-01 CHESTNUT-SIDED WARBLER with Morning Glories, bisque, decorated—unique
RPC-1073-02 PARULA WARBLERS with Morning Glories (14½″ x 9″) bisque, decorated (RP-1148) limited edition of 400*
RPC-1073-03 PARULA WARBLERS with Morning Glories (14½″ x 9″) bisque, undecorated—unique

The Chestnut-sided Warbler is a unique piece and was originally intended for introduction as a limited edition. However, the piece was later redesigned as the Parula Warblers, and the original retired.

The Parulas were introduced in 1965 as a limited edition of 400 pieces (Boehm Studiomark Number 484). The sculpture depicts a male and female in pursuit of a butterfly and beetle. They are set on a weathered fence post wound about with wild morning glories of the variety Ipomoea digitata. The edition was completed in June of 1973.

RPC-1074-01 WOOD THRUSHES with Azaleas (pr.) (Male 16″ high, Female 15″ high) bisque, decorated (RP-1155) limited edition of 400**
RPC-1074-02 WOOD THRUSHES with Azaleas (pr.) (Male 16″ high, Female 15″ high) bisque, undecorated—unique

Introduced in 1966, under Boehm Studiomark Number 485, as a limited edition of 400 pair, the Wood Thrushes were well received. The female is perched on a nest among azaleas, feeding berries to three fledglings. The male in full song perches on a branch of flowering azalea. On the

original dozen pairs of the Wood Thrushes there were only two buds and one flower under the nest of the female. Mr. Boehm determined they were a little sparse in that area. He proceeded to add two flowers.

The Wood Thrushes created a good many problems due to the size and complexity of the piece. The seemingly endless number of blossoms and stamens and petals, I am sure, caused the Studio troubles which they care not to remember. One of the thorniest problems was due to the frailty of the azalea blossoms. Normal packing in shredded polyethylene foam was not satisfactory. Ed Boehm actually designed the Wood Thrush container. Making molds for the container was so complicated that no molded container company wanted to do it. Ed spent considerable time with the producers of the container. Eventually Boehm wound up making the molds himself from which the container producer cast his metal molds. This fitted plastic container allows the Wood Thrushes to be delivered and handled with ease. They should not be moved without their special holder. The edition was completed in June 1975.

RPC-1075-01 GREEN JAYS with Black Persimmon (pr.) (Male 18″ high, Female 14″ high) bisque, decorated (RP-1153) limited edition of 400*
RPC-1075-02 GREEN JAYS with Black Persimmon (pr.) (Male 18″ high, Female 14″ high) bisque, undecorated—unique

The Green Jays were introduced in 1966 as a limited edition of 400 pairs. A male and female are perched on individual branches of black persimmon. The male, wings and tail spread, reaches for a persimmon while his mate, having secured a berry, settles onto her branch.

The Green Jays live in semi-tropical areas. They are a bird of the American Southwest and enjoy hot climates. Like other tropical and semi-tropical birds, their colors

tend to be harsh, as if bright and garish colors were painted on the bird. The Nonpareil Bunting has a similar aspect, and, as a result, another name for the Nonpareil is the "Painted Bunting." Like the Bunting, the Jays appear painted, and to the Northeast American (where most Boehm collectors live), the bird has an unpleasant, harsh, almost artificial quality. But to those who know the bird, it is remarkably true-to-nature.

The Green Jays were obviously conceived as a matching pair to the Blue Jays, but they never had the same acceptance as the Blue Jays because of their coloring and because they are unfamiliar. They will eventually become recognized and will reach the popularity enjoyed by the Blue Jays. The edition was completed in December 1974.

RPC-1076-01 RUFOUS HUMMINGBIRDS on Icelandic Poppy (14″ x 9″) bisque, decorated (RP-1154) limited edition of 500*
RPC-1076-02 RUFOUS HUMMINGBIRDS on Icelandic Poppy (14″ x 9″) bisque, undecorated—unique

This is the last introduction of 1966, and the edition was completed in November, 1973. The Rufous Hummingbirds are a male and female on buds and flower of yellow Icelandic poppy, with the male, in flight, distinguished by his metallic scarlet chin and throat.

RPC-1077-01 CRESTED FLYCATCHER on Sweet Gum (18½″ high) bisque, decorated (RP-1162) limited edition of 500**
RPC-1077-02 CRESTED FLYCATCHER on Sweet Gum (18½″ high) bisque, undecorated—unique

First of the 1967 editions, the Flycatcher is shown as a single bird perched on a branch of sweet gum. It bears Boehm Studiomark Number 488. The edition was completed in June, 1974.

*See page 44
**See page 124

*See page 49

*See page 125
**See page 126

RPC-1078-01 BLUE GROSBEAK with Fall Foliage (11″ high) bisque, decorated, 3 made*
RPC-1078-02 BLUE GROSBEAK with Green Oak Leaves and Acorns (11″ high) bisque, decorated (RP-1163) limited edition of 747
RPC-1078-03 BLUE GROSBEAK with Oak Leaves and Acorns (11″ high) bisque, undecorated—unique

Only three examples of this piece were decorated in fall foliage colors and these have been included in the limited edition number of 750 pieces. The edition was introduced in 1967. This piece contains a single bird perched on a branch with oak leaves and acorns. As of February 1, 1976, 656 pieces had been completed.

RPC-1079-01 NORTHERN WATER THRUSH with Ferns and Cladonia (10½″ high) bisque, decorated (RP-1161) limited edition of 500**
RPC-1079-02 NORTHERN WATER THRUSH with Ferns and Cladonia (10½″ high) bisque, undecorated—unique

The Northern Water Thrush, shown as a single bird standing among ferns and cladonia with two mushrooms, was introduced in 1967 as a limited edition of 500 pieces, which was completed in April 1973. It bears Boehm Studiomark Number 490. The original Water Thrush was shown standing. Before the Studio started producing replicas, Boehm decided the piece needed more action and changed it to a running bird.

RPC-1080-01 FLEDGLING CANADA WARBLER with Monarch Butterfly (8½″ high) bisque, decorated (RPC-1160) limited edition of 750**
RPC-1080-02 FLEDGLING CANADA WARBLER with Monarch Butterfly (8½″ high) bisque, undecorated—unique

This is the second in the limited Fledgling

°See page 127
°°See page 128

series and was introduced in 1967 as an edition of 750. It is a single bird perched on a twig, chirping angrily at the Monarch Butterfly on the branch above. The piece bears Boehm Studiomark Number 491.

Of all the birds, there are two which achieved instant and overwhelming popularity: one was the Robin and the second was this Fledgling Canada Warbler. Whether it is popular because it is a fledgling, or because of the quarrelsome nature of the warbler in chattering up at the beautiful Monarch Butterfly, or because of the Butterfly itself, or the interestingly braided base, or a combination of all these, the fact remains that the piece has become one of the most in demand among Boehm Bird collectors.

RPC-1081-01 KESTRELS (pr.) (Male 14″ high, Female 16½″ high) bisque, decorated (RP-1168) limited edition of 500*
RPC-1081-02 KESTRELS (pr.) (Male 14″ high, Female 16½″ high) bisque, undecorated—unique

This formal sculpture was introduced in 1968, under Boehm Studiomark Number 492, as a limited edition of 500 pair. The Kestrels are something of a departure for Boehm. Instead of being shown in their natural habitat, as are the other bird subjects, the Kestrels are shown surrounded by the trappings of falconry, an ancient sport for which this species was often trained.

This is one of the few bird sculptures, almost the only one, other than the Song Sparrows, in which Ed Boehm incorporated man-made objects. You will remember that in the Song Sparrow one of the birds is sitting on a trowel and the other is sitting on a clay pot. The Kestrels include those trappings connected with falconry. They are the leather hood with the beautiful feather crest which is kept on the bird's head to keep him quiet before being launched after his prey. This sculpture was never well received, as most people tend

°See page 129

to shy away from situations with which they are unfamiliar. Also, the idea of falconry is repugnant to many people and the trappings are strange.

As of February 1, 1976, 340 pairs of Kestrels had been completed.

RPC-1082-01 ROAD RUNNER with Horned Toad (14″ x 20½″) bisque, decorated (RP-1169) limited edition of 500*
RPC-1082-02 ROAD RUNNER with Horned Toad (14″ x 20″) bisque, undecorated—unique

Another 1968 limited edition of 500, the Road Runner was introduced, under Boehm Studiomark Number 493. As of February 1, 1976, 442 pairs had been completed.

The Road Runner has become one of the most popular of all of the birds of Ed Boehm. It is a no-nonsense piece. No flowers, no flora, no additions of any kind, just the bird in the configuration in which it is most likely to be seen: running full out in pursuit of its dinner in the form of a horned toad.

Stories about this bird are endless. It is a Texas bird, and Texans being what they are, the Boehm Studio was beseiged by Texas dealers offering to buy out the entire edition. These dealers knew that there would be no trouble selling the entire 500 in the State of Texas alone, and they felt a proprietary interest in the piece. It is, however, really the State Bird of New Mexico.

The story about this sculpture that I like best is the one about the full-color advertisement which appeared in a national magazine. It was prepared by Helen Boehm and Frank Cosentino. Ed Boehm usually stayed out of these matters. However, he was never bashful about letting his displeasure be known. At the time the Road Runner ad was put together, there was an automobile called the "Road Runner" on the market. This car was advertised with a "beep, beep" tagline. In a moment of

°See page 130

lightness and levity, Frank and Helen, in tiny print, added "beep, beep" to the elegant ad that went out on the Road Runner. The upshot of the story is that Ed Boehm was furious and pulled back all the ads. It was difficult to tell just what would upset Ed, but the "beep, beep" really got him. None of us could ever figure out why this and not a dozen other more important things disturbed him.

RPC-1083-01 FLEDGLING WESTERN BLUEBIRDS (5½″ high) bisque, decorated (RP-1165) nonlimited edition discontinued*
RPC-1083-02 FLEDGLING WESTERN BLUEBIRDS (5½″ high) bisque, undecorated—rare

Introduced as an unlimited edition in 1968, the piece was discontinued in 1973. This appealing sculpture shows two fledglings, one with his beak open and the other with his head down.

RPC-1084-01 FLEDGLING RED POLL (4″ high) bisque, decorated (RP-1164) nonlimited edition discontinued
RPC-1084-02 FLEDGLING RED POLL (4″ high) bisque, undecorated—rare

This is an addition to the unlimited fledgling collection and was introduced in 1968 under Boehm Studiomark Number 495. It depicts a sleeping fledgling with its head raised.

RPC-1085-01 HOODED MERGANSERS (pr.) (10½″ high) bisque, decorated (RP-1166) limited edition of 500**
RPC-1085-02 HOODED MERGANSERS (pr.) (10½″ high) bisque, undecorated —unique

The Hooded Mergansers were introduced in 1968 as a limited edition of 500 pairs. The sculpture shows the male catching a small fish while the female looks on. They bear Boehm Studiomark Number 496. As of February 1, 1976, 333 pairs had been completed.

*See page 131
**See page 132

RPC-1084-01

RPC-1086-01 COMMON TERN (16″ x 12″) bisque, decorated (RP-1167) limited edition of 500*
RPC-1086-02 COMMON TERN (16″ x 12″) bisque, undecorated, unique

The last limited edition introduction of 1968, the Common Tern was completed in November 1974 in an edition of 500. The Boehm Studiomark is 497.

As a dealer, no commercial experience has quite overwhelmed me as much as the Common Tern's. No bird ever seen, in fact, no piece of fine art or object of art that I have ever dealt with, has enjoyed an intensity of demand as has this beautiful piece of sculpture. The Tern was described as "being caught in a moment of grace." It is handsome from any position. The appeal of the cracked egg and the emerging young, I am sure, contributes to the demand for this piece. The Common Tern edition closed out within a few days of its first showing.

RPC-1087-01 YOUNG AMERICAN BALD EAGLE (9½″ x 6″) bisque, decorated (RP-1173) limited edition of 850**
RPC-1087-02 YOUNG AMERICAN BALD EAGLE (9½″ x 6″) bisque, undecorated —unique

*See page 69
**See page 66

RPC 1087-03 YOUNG AMERICAN BALD EAGLE, INAUGURAL (9½″ x 6″) bisque, decorated, limited edition of 100

The year of introduction of this new addition to the limited fledglings was 1969. The young American Bald Eagle, named "Young America" by Ed Boehm, was designed for our incoming President in January 1969 as a symbol of vigor, determination and faith in our youth. As shown, the few-weeks-old eagle is immature in its plumage and charmingly awkward in its oversized extremities. The piece bears Boehm Studiomark Number 498 and is limited to 850 pieces. The edition was completed in June 1974.

In 1973 the special edition of 100 was released to commemorate the second inauguration of President Richard M. Nixon and Vice-President Spiro Agnew. In addition to Boehm Studiomark Number 498A and markersmark I, these eaglets bear a second mark, in gold, of the Great Seal of the United States, with a special inscription.

RPC-1088-01 WESTERN BLUEBIRDS with Wild Azaleas (12½″ x 20″), bisque, decorated (RP-1170) limited edition of 400*
RPC-1088-02 WESTERN BLUEBIRDS with Wild Azaleas (12½″ x 20″), bisque, undecorated—unique

The Western Bluebirds were announced as a 1969 limited edition of 400 pieces. As of February 1, 1976, 226 were completed. The male (in deeper blue and with his wings parted) and female are depicted on a single porcelain base among six delicate clusters of wild flowering yellow azaleas.

The Western Bluebirds are one of those compositions which command more interest than others because of the beauty of the piece itself. All of Ed Boehm's work in the birds is interesting due to his strict conformity to nature, but some of them go beyond that, into the area of pure decorative beauty.

RPC-1089-01 VERDINS, on Thorn (8¾″ x

*See page 133

6″) bisque, decorated (RP-1171) limited edition of 750*

RPC-1089-02 VERDINS, on Thorn (8¾″ x 6″) bisque, undecorated—unique

This Yellow-Headed Bush Tit (as it is also known) was introduced in 1969 as a limited edition of 750 pieces. It bears Boehm Studiomark Number 400-02. The Verdins are presented in a setting of Stewart Crucifixion Thorn, one of their favorite building materials. The male, high in the sculpture, has more yellow and chestnut on the head and epaulets. In the center of the composition is a bee whose detail is emphasized by its life-thin wings. An intricate pierced-work base reveals an underlayer of earth and older foliage.

Of the total number announced for the edition, 474 had been completed as of February 1, 1976.

RPC-1090-01 BLACK-HEADED GROS-BEAK, Male on Vine Maple (10″ x 14½″) bisque, decorated (RP-1172) limited edition of 750**

RPC-1090-02 BLACK-HEADED GROS-BEAK, Male on Vine Maple (10″ x 14½″) bisque, undecorated—unique

The Black-Headed Grosbeak was the last edition introduced in 1969 and was designated as a limited edition of 750. It is a companion piece to the Blue-Headed Grosbeak. They make a beautiful pair. The male only is shown in the sculpture. He is in his best finery, partially cloaked by vine maple foliage. The airiness and freedom of the composition are aided by the incorporation into the porcelain of hand-fashioned metal stems supporting the hanging leaves and seed pods. The piece bears Boehm Studiomark Number 400-03 and, as of February 1, 1976, 535 had been completed.

RPC-1091-01 OVEN BIRD, with Indian Pipe (11″ x 7″) bisque, decorated (RP-1176) limited edition of 750***

*See page 134
**See page 135
***See page 136

RPC-1091-02 OVEN BIRD, with Indian Pipe (11″ x 7″) bisque, undecorated—unique

The Oven Bird was introduced in 1970 as a limited edition of 750 pieces. The bird of the sculpture represents both male and female, as the sexes are identically colored. Its posture captures the perky, bobbing attitude of the Oven Bird amid its surroundings of Indian pipe, ferns and bracket fungus. In its structure and design, the composition harmonizes with that of the Northern Water Thrush sculpture.

It bears Boehm Studiomark Number 400-04 and by August 1, 1975, 310 had been completed.

RPC-1092-01 ORCHARD ORIOLE on Blossoming Tulip (11″ x 14″) bisque, decorated (RP-1174) limited edition of 750*

RPC-1092-02 ORCHARD ORIOLE on Blossoming Tulip (11″ x 14″) bisque, undecorated—unique

Another 1970 limited edition of 750 pieces, the Orchard Oriole bears Boehm Studiomark Number 400-11. The sculpture emphasizes the togetherness of these Orioles, perching on a tulip tree branch with blooms. The male has reached full plumage, a maturity requiring three years, and offers a pleasing contrast with its softly colored mate.

The number of pieces produced as of August 1, 1975, was 366.

The Orchard Oriole is another of the pieces which because of its inherent decorative beauty is in substantial demand.

RPC-1093 FONDO MARINO (26″ x 26″) bisque, decorated (RP-4001) limited edition of 50**

With the creation of the Fondo Marino, an era of Boehm comes to a close. This was the last sculpture to be done by Ed Boehm

*See page 137
**See page 35

and is a fitting climax to a lifetime devoted to the perfection of the hard-paste porcelain process. The piece is the most intricate ever created in this medium. It was introduced as a limited edition in 1970.

The stories about the Fondo Marino are endless, interesting, exciting and some, perhaps, apocryphal. A mythology grows around monumental undertakings and the Fondo Marino is, if nothing else, monumental.

The Fondo Marino gives additional insight into the working of Ed Boehm's mind. From his involvement in this piece, it can be seen that he was not satisfied with his extraordinary accomplishments in the field of bird and animal sculptures. He was already looking to other and more ambitious directions. When he did turn to fish, an ordinary mortal might have been satisfied with a small experimental first attempt, but not Ed Boehm. His first attempt had to be something more than had ever been done. The Fondo Marino is the product of that kind of driving compulsion.

The technical problems in making the piece are probably as complicated as anything the Studio (or any studio) has ever undertaken. The number of molds, which must be in the thousands, the master molds and other jigsaw pieces of plaster which had to be kept and sorted and used, filled a special room at the plant. The problem of assembling the wet modeled pieces into a unified finished piece, ready for the kiln, is a job requiring patience that goes beyond imagination. I can't conceive of anyone else ever undertaking anything like the Fondo Marino, and with Boehm's death I think we can accept the proposition that nothing else like this will ever be done again.

The name "Fondo Marino" is simply Italian for the "bottom of the sea." That is what the piece is. A living chunk of the sea. Those of you who have had the good fortune to snorkel or scuba know what a startling piece of reality it is. It has always been my feeling that this piece would look best seen from above, since that's the way a diver sees these structures.

The most exciting element of the piece, as far as I am concerned, is that it is a lesson in symbiosis, in the close and intimate relationships in which the creatures of the sea live. It is indeed a beautiful work and it is a fitting final gift from the great creative personality of Ed Boehm.

In an attempt to control the ultimate distribution of the Fondo Marino, the Studio has insisted that orders for this piece be submitted with the names of the purchasers. The names are then fired into the piece. This serves to discourage the inclination to speculate in this important sculpture.

Although not a bird subject, it is so definitely a progression of the technical and artistic efforts that have gone into the development of the bird sculptures, that it must be listed with them.

The piece bears Boehm Studiomark Number 499 and is the last new edition to bear makersmark E. It had been planned as an edition of only 50, but because of the expense involved in production, the limited edition goal was cut to 25 in March of 1976. As of February 1, 1976, 23 had been completed.

XII. Miscellaneous Works

RPC-2001 FARM GIRL bisque, undecorated—extremely rare

This unusual bas relief plaque shows us a side of Ed Boehm's personality that is full of humor, earthy and spirited. This little plaque was done with considerable imagination. The surprise in the piece involves the obverse and the reverse.

It may have been done from a commercial mold as we can find little similarity between this work and any other from Ed Boehm's hand.

It is 5⅝" x 3⅜" wide in bisque white. The plaque probably was intended to be painted.

It is so unlike anything else Ed ever did that it could only have been done in the early stages of his career. Its charm lies in its mild impropriety and its unique good humor.

The obverse of this piece shows in bas relief what is obviously a farm girl on a ladder picking apples. Standing next to her is a typical "rube" type with his hand disappearing behind the derriere of the lady on the ladder.

What could have been dismissed as an affectionate pat is dispelled when one turns the piece over and finds the farmer's hand disappearing up the girl's dress. The naughtiness of the obverse is compounded by the surprise of the reverse.

For such a tiny piece, it represents a substantial amount of work and obviously it was something which Ed simply had to do. This one single little piece shows a side of his personality that remains well hidden in his more formal work.

The records concerning the number of these pieces made are obscure. Mr. Boehm Sr., told me that the piece is unique and

RPC-2001

that only one was done. The Studio indicates that a number of them were done with no definite record of the number.

To determine how many plaques there are as distinguished from how many were made is the problem that comes up time and time again with Boehm, especially in connection with those pieces that were cheap when they were made. The destruction rate on the cheap pieces was high. The destruction rate on this piece, which never carried the Boehm signature, must have been almost total.

It was done in the early bisque body which to an untutored eye gives the first impression of inexpensive pottery. This, I am sure, added to the rate at which these pieces were either broken or thrown away. But some must still lie in attics somewhere, and because they are slightly naughty, they may be deeply buried away from prying eyes.

RPC-2002 GOLDFINCHES—unique

This is a unique plaque, designed by Ed Boehm and his artisans during the early years of the Studio. It was, unfortunately, never completed.

RPC-2003 PURPLE FINCHES—unique

This painting, too, was designed by Boehm and his artisans. It is complete and it is unique.

RPC-2004 ORIENTAL PHEASANT bas relief—2 made

The Oriental Pheasant plaque was designed and executed by Boehm in 1962. Only two were produced. It measures 24″ x 12″.

RPC-2005 MAKERSMARK PLAQUE bas relief—3,500 made

The Makersmark Plaque is a replica in porcelain of the familiar Percheron Stallion makersmark used for so many years by the Studio. It is attached to the cover of the limited edition of Frank Cosentino's book "Edward Marshall Boehm," and 3,500 were made. They are 3½″ x 2″ and all are affixed to the volumes.

Strictly speaking, of course, this is not a painting on porcelain since it is totally undecorated. However, it fits into this category better than into any other. It was a beautiful tribute to include the makersmark plaque on the limited edition of the Cosentino book, but the piece was cast with such delicacy that a good number of them were broken. It was designed and sculptured by Ed Boehm many years ago when he first started considering the kind of image that should appear as the makersmark on his work. It is also an interesting insight into the man's deepest interests to note that although by that time he had become successfully associated with the making of the birds, his first love remained with the larger animals, in this case, the horse.

RPC-2002

RPC-2003

RPC-2005

237

RPC-2006 TERRAZZO FLOOR

As early as 1949 Ed Boehm's need to make his vision permanent appeared in different ways. Long before he was a serious porcelain sculptor and while he was still working in animal husbandry, Ed Boehm was thinking in visual terms.

The two photographs here are of a terrazzo floor which he designed in the office of a former employer.

The outline sketches of the four dogs are more than decoration. They are really what those dogs are all about. Terrazzo is a crude and difficult process and for Ed Boehm to get so much truth out of so difficult a material foreshadows some of the great things he was to do later on.

Works by The Boehm Studios

I. Birds

This is the beginning of the listing of the sculptures that were created after Ed Boehm died. They are designated by the letters RPS, meaning Reese Palley–Studio. Also, the term "limited edition" is now replaced by "Limited Issue Goal," abbreviated as "L.I.G." This term allows the Studio to make fewer than the number announced, but not more.

RPS-1094-01 SLATE-COLORED JUNCO on Pyracantha (11½" x 10½") bisque, decorated (RP-1175), L.I.G. 750*
RPS-1094-02 SLATE-COLORED JUNCO on Pyracantha (11½" x 10½") bisque, undecorated, unique

The last introduction of 1970, the Junco is the first Boehm sculpture not created entirely by the artist. It is designated as Boehm Studiomark Number 400-12 and was introduced in a limited edition of 750. The male and his mate are shown in a winter scene among Pyracantha, a favorite plant of the Junco.

As of February 1, 1976, production had progressed to 364 pieces. The Junco bears the new feathered makersmark for limited editions, makersmark I. This is the first bird that was not completed by Ed Boehm. The Junco was conceived by Boehm but completed by his close associates. As a result the piece does not bear the makersmark F, which would have indicated that it was Ed Boehm's work. Instead, it carries the makersmark I and includes the "fallen feather." It is interesting to note that the drawing of the feather was done by Ed himself many years earlier.

RPS-1095-01 MUTE SWANS (Bird of Peace), LARGE—no more than 3 made**
RPS-1095-02 MUTE SWANS (Bird of Peace) (17" x 17") bisque, decorated, L.I.G. 400

*See page 137
**See page 52

RPS-1095-03 MUTE SWANS (Bird of Peace) (17" x 17") bisque, undecorated, unique

The Mute Swans are a part of history. The gift of the Mute Swans to China by President Nixon in February 1972 represented the first tangible object to change hands between the United States and China in a peaceful manner for over 20 years. As such, the Mute Swans become important in the history of State gifts.

Gifts of State have their origin in the tributes which were paid to kings and princes by neighboring and less powerful principalities. Of course, modern gifts of State do not carry these overtones—indeed, they are always matched by reciprocal gifts in order to avoid the implication of tribute.

Both President Nixon and Chairman Mao went to the animal kingdom in choosing their gifts: the porcelain Mute Swans were matched by a living pair of Giant Pandas, rare animals seldom seen outside of China.

The designation of the mute swan as the American symbol of peace was no arbitrary one. The drama behind its choice began in 1969 when President Nixon invited Helen Boehm to decorate the Oval Room of the White House with a collection of her late husband's works. Mrs. Boehm took 18 porcelain birds to Washington. At a press conference a newsman asked her if there were any hawks or doves in the group. Mr. Nixon said he wished he had never heard of doves or hawks and that he hoped someone would develop a new bird which would speak of peace in less political terms.

Helen Boehm accepted the President's wish as a command, and began in a careful and exhaustive manner to investigate the problem. She followed a method Ed Boehm would have used, asking the best ornithological experts in the world what bird best exemplified the idea of peace. The majority agreed on the mute swan with its quiet and reserved elegance.

Perhaps an even deeper, more unconscious symbolism is at work here. In the Book of Genesis, when men tried to build a tower to reach heaven, the Lord caused the builders to quarrel among themselves, thus preventing the tower's completion. The Lord further confounded the plan by causing many different languages to appear among the builders of the Tower of Babel. Because they could not understand one another, the builders were forced to abandon their ambitions.

In a world of many languages and their consequent danger of misunderstandings and hatred, what better symbol of peace than an animal that is mute? If we cannot or will not speak the same language, perhaps it is better that we do not speak at all.

Thus the Mute Swans, while not specifically created for the President's gift to China, became the ideal State gift for that occasion. It is beautiful, it is important, it is expensive—but most of all it speaks quietly of peace.

The large Mute Swans is among the most ambitious works ever successfully completed in true porcelain. The present head sculptor of the Boehm studios and Boehm's assistant for 12 years states that there are more than 60,000 individually carved barbs in the featherwork alone. He and ten other head artists and craftsmen of the Edward Marshall Boehm "school"—those who were most closely associated with Boehm—devoted a full year and one-half to its creation.

On its base the composition stands 5½ foot tall, 4½ foot wide, 2½ foot deep. The wingspan of the cob is 7½ feet. Together the base and the sculpture weigh 350 pounds. There were 509 mold sections required to cast the 126 model parts. Mold work consumed approximately eight tons of plaster. Three examples of this size were made: one was presented to the White House; another will remain in the Boehm Studio collection, never to be sold; the third, purchased anonymously at an auction for the World Wildlife Fund, brought $150,000. The successful bid was announced at the reception held in London on September 11, 1975, and attended by Prince Bernhard of the Netherlands, President of the World Wildlife Fund. Mrs. Boehm plans to exhibit the Mute Swans in all the member nations of NATO.

To enable more people to enjoy this magnificent sculpture, it was decided to resculpture it in a limited edition of 400 pairs, in a smaller version about one-third the size of the large one. In 1971 this edition, RPS-1095-02, was introduced; it bears the new makersmark I, with Boehm Studiomark Number 400-14. As of February 1, 1976, 262 sculptures had been completed.

The Mute Swans, completely the work of the Boehm Studio, give some insight into the future of Boehm of Trenton. There is not another porcelain studio in the world which could undertake a work of this size, intricacy and quality. While there is certainly little market for anything as large as the Mute Swans, it is a tribute to the Studio, and the people working in it, that such a piece could be accomplished after Ed Boehm died.

RPS-1096-01 FLICKER with Chipmunk and Mushrooms (11″ x 13″) bisque, decorated, L.I.G. 400*
RPS-1096-02 FLICKER with Chipmunk and Mushrooms (11″ x 13″) bisque, undecorated, unique

Another 1971 introduction, the Flicker bears makersmark I and carries Boehm Studiomark Number 400-16.

The sculpture reveals the full beauty of the Flicker's form and color. He is landing to pluck away the unsuspecting predaceous beetle below him. Hidden from his view is an Eastern Chipmunk. As of February 1, 1976, 176 sculptures had been completed.

RPS-1097-01 WESTERN MEADOWLARK (9″ x 13″) bisque, decorated, L.I.G. 400

*See page 138

RPS-1097-02 WESTERN MEADOWLARK (9″ x 13″) bisque, undecorated, unique

The Western Meadowlark, seen throwing his song skyward, was introduced in 1971. Like all future limited editions, it bears makersmark I. The Boehm Studiomark Number is 400-15. As of February 1, 1976, 264 sculptures had been completed.

RPS-1098-01 CYGNET (Baby Bird of Peace) on Lily Pad (3″ x 6″) bisque, decorated, nonlimited edition still in production*
RPS-1098-02 CYGNET (Baby Bird of Peace), Presidential Cygnet, bisque, decorated, approximately 100 made

The Cygnet, introduced in an unlimited edition in 1971, is the same sculpture as that of the sleeping cygnet on the Mute Swans sculpture. It carries Boehm Studiomark Number 400-13.

RPS-1098-02 is called the Presidential Cygnet. From time to time the Studio has been called upon to do special things for important people. The chief user of these pieces has been the American Presidency, which long ago recognized the value of Boehm figures as State gifts.

Those familiar with the regular Cygnet will remember that it is shown snoozing with its eyes closed. Symbolizing the idea that the Presidency never sleeps, the Presidential Cygnet is shown wide awake. There is no telling how many Presidential Cygnets are being made, but I expect that the number will remain well under 100 pieces.

A new makersmark was added in 1971 for nonlimited pieces made in Trenton; this piece carries the makersmark J.

RPS-1099-01 BROWN PELICAN (25″ x 18″) bisque, decorated, L.I.G. 100**
RPS-1099-02 BROWN PELICAN (25″ x 18″) bisque, undecorated, unique

This sculpture was announced in 1972; it

*See page 139
**See page 140

RSP-1097-01

carries Boehm Studiomark Number 400-22 and makersmark I.

The Brown Pelican is a bird of great bulk; it is about 4½ feet in length and has a wingspread of some 6½ feet. It is powerful in flight and a mighty fisher. Pelicans are now on the list of endangered species and are being protected on government reservations.

This sculpture was the first in a series of endangered species that the Studio started in 1972. As of February 1, 1976, 53 pieces had been completed. The sculpture shows a male in his typical habitat of red mangrove; hammer oysters and a variety of tree snails are included on the base.

RPS-1100-01

RPS-1101-01

RPS-1100-01 CACTUS WREN (13″ x 7½″)
bisque, decorated, L.I.G. 400
RPS-1100-02 CACTUS WREN (13″ x 7½″)
bisque, undecorated, unique

The Cactus Wren was introduced in 1972. A large bird, it is recognized by its white throat and breast, which are heavily marked with round black spots. The sculpture is characteristic of the Cactus Wren and its environment: a male, alert, rests momentarily on a beaver-tail cactus abloom with rose-colored flowers; a collared lizard slithers along the cactus, eyeing a long-haired beetle. As of February 1, 1976, 152 sculptures had been completed. The Boehm Studiomark Number is 400-17 and the makersmark I.

RPS-1101-01 YELLOW-BELLIED SAP-SUCKER (14¼″ x 11″), bisque, decorated, L.I.G. 400, cut to 300
RPS-1101-02 YELLOW-BELLIED SAP-SUCKER (14¼″ x 11″) bisque, undecorated, unique

The Yellow-Bellied Sapsucker is also known as the Yellow-Bellied Woodpecker or the Red-Throated Sapsucker. A native of eastern North America, it is the most migratory of the woodpecker family. The artist has portrayed a pair of Sapsuckers on a branch of wild apple blossom, the female resting at the top and the male, wings outspread, just alighting. The piece, introduced in 1972, carries Boehm Studiomark Number 400-18 and makersmark I.

In March 1976 the Studio decided to reduce the edition size of a number of the more expensive and more complicated pieces. The Yellow-Bellied Sapsucker was one of the sculptures that fell into this category; the edition size was cut to 300. At that time the Studio had completed 161 pieces.

RPS-1102-01 SNOW BUNTINGS (12½″ x 7¼″) bisque, decorated, L.I.G. 400

RPS-1102-02 SNOW BUNTINGS (12½″ x 7¼″) bisque, undecorated, unique

Announced in 1972, the Snow Bunting bears Boehm Studiomark Number 400-21 and makersmark I. The sculpture depicts the male and female Snow Bunting in summer finery (in winter, the upper parts of both male and female are stained with a rusty color) amid vivid blue gentian. As of February 1, 1976, 225 sculptures had been completed.

RPS-1103-01 LAZULI BUNTINGS (13½″ x 9″) bisque, decorated, L.I.G. 500
RPS-1103-02 LAZULI BUNTINGS (13½″ x 9″) bisque, undecorated, unique

The Lazuli Buntings was introduced in 1973. The female, who sits on a rock formation, is plain brown with a touch of blue on her wings and tail; the male perches atop an attractive clump of wild daisies.

As of February 1, 1976, 177 sculptures had been completed.

RPS-1104-01 EVERGLADE KITES (20½″ x 14½″) bisque, decorated, L.I.G. 300, cut to 50
RPS-1104-02 EVERGLADE KITES (20½″ x 14½″) bisque, undecorated, unique

Everglade Kites with freshwater snails was announced in 1973 as a limited issue goal of 300, carrying Boehm Studiomark Number 400-24 and makersmark I. In March of 1976 a major reduction in edition sizes of a number of important sculptures was announced. As costs rise, the more expensive and more complicated pieces are affected the most. Boehm rarely raises prices and instead they opted to shorten editions when necessary. This was one of those pieces, and the edition size was reduced to only 50. As of February 1, 1976, 47 sculptures had been made, and this edition should be completed shortly. This

RPS-1102-01

will put the Everglade Kites in the category of the rarest Boehms.

The Everglade Kite is native in the United States only to the Florida Everglades, though it is also found in Cuba, eastern Mexico and throughout Central and South America. This large bird is particularly distinguished by its long and slender sickle-shaped beak, which enables it to extract the freshwater snail from its shell.

The sculpture depicts the female perched atop a rock formation and the male clutching a snail and about to extract it.

RPS-1105-01 HORNED LARKS WITH WILD GRAPE (18½″ x 13¼″) bisque, decorated, L.I.G. 400, cut to 300

RPS-1105-02 HORNED LARKS WITH WILD GRAPE (18½″ x 13¼″) bisque, undecorated, unique

RPS-1103-01

RPS-1105-01

RPS-1104-01

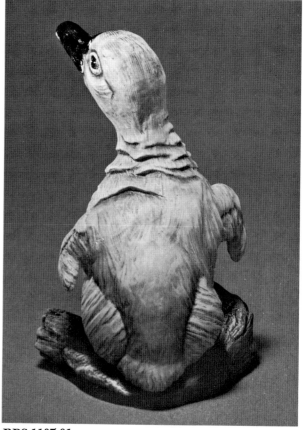

RPS-1106-01   RPS-1107-01

The Horned Larks with Wild Grape was issued in 1973; the piece carries Boehm Studiomark Number 400-25 and makersmark I. The edition goal was cut to 300 in 1975.

Horned Larks are about the size of bluebirds, with white or yellow throats and a conspicuous black mark across the breast. Just above and behind the eyes are small pointed tufts of dark feathers which give rise to the birds' common name.

The sculpture depicts both the male and female with wings outspread on a wild grape bush. The composition is completed by a cricket which the male appears to be eyeing.

As of February 1, 1976, 133 sculptures had been completed.

RPS-1106-01 BROWN THRASHER (7½″ x 10″), bisque, decorated, L.I.G. 500
RPS-1106-02 BROWN THRASHER (7½″ x 10″) bisque, undecorated, unique

The Brown Thrasher with crocus was issued in 1973, carrying Boehm Studiomark Number 400-26 and makersmark I. It depicts the state bird of Georgia, which is found throughout eastern North America. The thrasher is sedentary in the warmer parts of its range and migratory elsewhere.

The sculpture depicts the Brown Thrasher amidst yellow crocuses. As of February 1, 1976, 187 sculptures had been completed.

RPS-1107-01 CYGNET, STANDING (6¼″ x 4½″) bisque, decorated, nonlimited edition still in production
RPS-1107-02 CYGNET, STANDING (6¼″ x 4½″) bisque, undecorated, unique

The Cygnet, Standing was the second of the very popular Cygnets. It was issued in 1973 with Boehm Studiomark Number 400-27 and makersmark J.

RPS-1108-01 MYRTLE WARBLERS WITH TRAILING ARBUTUS FLOWERING VINES (12″ x 8¾″) bisque, decorated, L.I.G. 400

RPS-1108-02 MYRTLE WARBLERS WITH TRAILING ARBUTUS FLOWERING VINES (12″ x 8¾″) bisque, undecorated, unique

Announced in 1974 with Boehm Studiomark Number 400-28 and makersmark I, the sculpture features both male and female Myrtle Warblers amidst trailing arbutus. These birds can be quickly recognized by the conspicuous patches of bright yellow just above their tails.

As of February 1, 1976, 68 sculptures had been completed.

RPS-1109-01 VARIED THRUSH WITH PARROT TULIPS (18″ x 10″) bisque, decorated, L.I.G. 400

RPS-1109-02 VARIED THRUSH WITH PARROT TULIPS (18″ x 10″) bisque, undecorated, unique

The Varied Thrush with Parrot Tulips was introduced in 1974 with Boehm Studiomark Number 400-29 and makersmark I. The parrot tulips are yellow. As of February 1,

RPS-1108-01

1976, 129 sculptures had been completed.

RPS-1110-01 HOODED WARBLER WITH IRIS (15½″ x 8″) bisque, decorated, L.I.G. 400

RPS-1110-02 HOODED WARBLER WITH IRIS (15½″ x 8″) bisque, undecorated, unique

Hooded Warbler with Iris was announced in 1974. It carries the Boehm Studiomark Number 400-30 and makersmark I.

The sculpture depicts the male Hooded Warbler—readily identifiable by its conspicuous markings, a broad yellow mask extending over the forehead to the crown and set off by a solid black framework—amid common wild irises.

As of February 1, 1976, 36 sculptures had been completed.

RPS-1111-01 YELLOW-BILLED CUCKOO WITH HONEYSUCKLE (14½″ x 11¾″) bisque, decorated, L.I.G. 400, cut to 300

RPS-1111-02 YELLOW-BILLED CUCKOO WITH HONEYSUCKLE (14½″ x 11¾″) bisque, undecorated, unique

The Yellow-Billed Cuckoo sculpture features the subject perched on a tree stump entwined with honeysuckle. It carries Boehm Studiomark Number 400-31 and makersmark I. In February 1976 the Studio reduced the goal to 300. As of February 1, 1976, 74 sculptures had been completed.

RPS-1112-01 PURPLE MARTINS WITH GRANDIFLORA MAGNOLIA (17″ x 28″) bisque, decorated, L.I.G. 200, cut to 50

RPS-1112-02 PURPLE MARTINS WITH GRANDIFLORA MAGNOLIA (17″ x 28″) bisque, undecorated, unique

The Purple Martins were announced in 1974. The piece carries Boehm Studiomark Number 400-32 and makersmark I. The sculpture depicts a family of Purple Martins, both male and female with wings outspread over a grandiflora magnolia plant.

The edition size was cut to 50 in 1976. As of February 1, 1976, 41 sculptures had been completed. This piece will close in 1976 and is certain to become one of the more valuable Boehm editions.

RPS-1113-01 INDIGO BUNTING (10″ x 5″) bisque, decorated, nonlimited edition still in production

RPS-1113-02 INDIGO BUNTING (10″ x 5″) bisque, undecorated, unique

The Indigo Bunting was introduced in

RPS-1110-01

RPS-1111-01

RPS-1112-01

RPS-1113-01

RPS-1114-01

RPS-1115-01

RPS-1116-01

1974; it carries Boehm Studiomark Number 400-33 and makersmark J. The sculpture depicts the Indigo Bunting quietly resting among the lovely blooms of morning glory.

RPS-1114-01 YELLOW-HEADED BLACK-BIRD WITH ARROWHEAD (14¼″ x 14½″) bisque, decorated, L.I.G. 300, cut to 200

RPS-1114-02 YELLOW-HEADED BLACK-BIRD WITH ARROWHEAD (14¼″ x 14½″) bisque, undecorated, unique

Issued in 1974, the Yellow-Headed Blackbird carries Boehm Studiomark Number 400-34 and makersmark I. The sculpture depicts a male with open mouth perched atop an arrowhead plant. This is another of the sculptures that suffered a reduction in edition goals. In early 1976 the goal was cut to 200; as of February 1, 1976, 37 sculptures had been completed.

RPS-1115-01 LARK SPARROW (12¾″ x 8″) bisque, decorated, L.I.G. 400

RPS-1115-02 LARK SPARROW (12¾″ x 8″) bisque, undecorated, unique

The Lark Sparrow was announced in 1974; it carries Boehm Studiomark Number 400-35 and makersmark I. The Lark Sparrow is depicted at the top of the sculpture, surrounded by buttercups and poised for flight.

As of February 1, 1976, 73 sculptures had been completed.

RPS-1116-01 PEKIN ROBINS WITH DOUBLE RHODODENDRON (16″ x 19″) bisque, decorated, L.I.G. 100

247

RPS-1117-01

RPS-1118-01

RPS-1119-01

RPS-1116-02 PEKIN ROBINS WITH DOUBLE RHODODENDRON (16″ x 19″) bisque, undecorated, unique

Announced in 1975, the Pekin Robins sculpture was designed for an important historical purpose. In 1974 Mrs. Boehm was honored by an invitation from the People's Republic of China to visit their ancient porcelain centers. During her visit in December of that year she presented the Pekin Robins with Double Rhododendron to her host organization, The Chinese People's Association for Friendship with Foreign Countries. The inscription on the presentation piece reads:

> To the people of the People's Republic of China from the Edward Marshall Boehm Artists and Craftsmen of the United States of America, December 1974. In friendship, gratitude, and respect for the enormous contributions of the Chinese people to the honored art of porcelain.

The sculpture depicts a pair of Pekin Robins perched on a lavender double rhododendron plant. It was announced as a limited issue goal of 100 and carries Boehm Studiomark Number 400-37 and makersmark I. As of February 1, 1976, 34 sculptures had been completed.

RPS-1117-01 PAINTED BUNTING (10″ x 4½″) bisque, decorated, nonlimited edition still in production
RPS-1117-02 PAINTED BUNTING (10″ x 4½″) bisque, undecorated, unique

The Painted Bunting was announced by Trenton in 1975; it carries Boehm Studiomark Number 400-35 and makersmark J. The sculpture depicts a male with wild calla lilies.

RPS-1118-01 GOLDFINCH (5¾″ x 6½″)

bisque, decorated, nonlimited edition still in production
RPS-1118-02 GOLDFINCH (5¾″ x 6½″) bisque, undecorated, unique

Announced in 1975, the Goldfinch carries Boehm Studiomark Number 400-39 and makersmark J. The Goldfinch is the state bird of New Jersey, Minnesota, Iowa and Washington. The sculpture depicts it among violets.

RPS-1119-01 SCARLET TANAGER WITH BURR OAK (13½″ x 10″) bisque, decorated, unique
RPS-1119-02 SCARLET TANAGER WITH BURR OAK (13½″ x 10″) bisque, undecorated, unique

The Trenton Studio announced the Scarlet Tanager as a 1975 issue limited edition, but it was withdrawn from the 1975 introductions for technical reasons. It is unlikely that more than one or two were ever produced. The sculpture presents the male of the species in full splendor in a setting of burr oak.

RPS-1120-01 EASTERN KINGBIRD (18″ x 16″) bisque, decorated, L.I.G. 300
RPS-1120-02 EASTERN KINGBIRD (18″ x 16″) bisque, undecorated, unique

Introduced by the Trenton Studio in 1975, the Eastern Kingbird carries Boehm Studiomark Number 400-42 and makersmark I. The sculpture depicts the Eastern Kingbird alighting among colorful turk's cap lilies. As of February 1, 1976, 30 sculptures had been completed.

RPS-1121-01 RED-BILLED BLUE MAG-PIE WITH PLUM BLOSSOMS AND DRAGON'S-CLAW TREE (12½″ x 19″) bisque, decorated, L.I.G. 300
RPS-1121-02 RED-BILLED BLUE MAG-PIE WITH PLUM BLOSSOMS AND DRAGON'S-CLAW TREE (12½″ x 19″) bisque, undecorated, unique

The inspiration to create the Red-Billed Blue Magpie in porcelain came from the December 1974 trip taken by Mrs. Boehm to the People's Republic of China. The Red-Billed Blue Magpie is seen everywhere in northern China, and especially around the thirteen ancient Ming tombs outside Peking. This Trenton sculpture, announced in 1975, therefore commemorates the journey to China. The branch design in the sculpture is taken from the dragon's-claw tree seen in the Imperial Palace Gardens, and the piece is also adorned with the symbolically important plum blossoms. It carries Boehm Studiomark Number 400-44 and makersmark I. As of February 1, 1976, 26 sculptures had been completed.

RPS-1122-01 CYGNET, SITTING (6¼″ x 4½″) bisque, decorated, nonlimited edition still in production
RPS-1122-02 CYGNET, SITTING (6¼″ x 4½″) bisque, undecorated, unique

Issued in 1975, Cygnet, Sitting is the third of the Baby Birds of Peace, the other two being the Sleeping and the Standing Cygnet. This

RPS-1120-01

RPS-1121-01

RPS-1122-01

piece carries Boehm Studiomark Number 400-46 and makersmark J.

RPS-1123-01 YOUNG AND SPIRITED 1976
(10½″ x 9½″) bisque, decorated, available on subscription basis only until July 4, 1976

RPS-1123-02 YOUNG AND SPIRITED 1976
(10½″ x 9½″) bisque, undecorated, unique

In honor of our Nation's 200th birthday, the Trenton Studio announced the Young and Spirited 1976. This piece was available only until July 4, 1976, at which time it was closed and the molds destroyed. The sculpture shows two fledgling American Bald Eagles, which the Studio feels represents the youthful spirit of our democracy. The piece carries Boehm Studiomark Number 400-49 and makersmark I. As of February 1, 1976, 182 sculptures had been completed.

RPS-1124-01 BLACK-THROATED BLUE WARBLER (6″ x 9″) bisque, decorated, L.I.G. 500

RPS-1124-02 BLACK-THROATED BLUE WARBLER (6″ x 9″) bisque, undecorated, unique

Only the persistent birdlover with unlimited patience will enjoy a close-up view of the Black-throated Blue Warbler, for he is an extremely modest fellow and nests in the undergrowth of mountainous areas. However, Boehm has forced this bird to show himself and captured him in porcelain so that you may view his exquisite colors. The sculpture depicts a single bird amid spotted wintergreen. Produced with a limited issue goal of 500 in 1976, it carries Boehm Studiomark Number 400-43 and makersmark I.

RPS-1125 THE EAGLE OF FREEDOM I
(28″ x 32″) bisque, decorated, L.I.G. 15

Issued in 1976, the life-size Eagle of Freedom measures 32 inches from beak to tail, 24 inches across the wings, 28 inches in

°See page 141

RPS-1123-01

RPS-1124-01

height. The Studio announced it would be offering only thirteen for sale in honor of our thirteen original American colonies. A fourteenth model will be made for the President of the United States and a fifteenth for the Boehm Studio to exhibit around the world. This piece carries Boehm Studiomark Number 400-50 and makersmark I. The piece was cast from 31 molds of 178 mold parts. As of February 1, 1976, two sculptures had been completed.

RPS-1126-01 MOCKINGBIRD (5¾″ x 3½″) bisque, decorated, nonlimited edition still in production

RPS-1126-02 MOCKINGBIRD (5¾″ x 3½″) bisque, undecorated, unique

Issued in 1976, this fledgling Mockingbird became part of the open collection. It carries Boehm Studiomark Number 400-56 and makersmark J.

RPS-1127-01 CARDINAL (4¼″ x 4¼″) bisque, decorated, nonlimited edition still in production

RPS-1127-02 CARDINAL (4¼″ x 4¼″) bisque, undecorated, unique

The second baby bird announced in 1976 was the Cardinal. It carries Boehm Studiomark Number 400-57 and makersmark J.

RPS-1128-01 THE BLUE-MASKED LOVE-BIRDS (6″ x 5½″) bisque, decorated in blue, nonlimited edition still in production

RPS-1128-02 THE PEACH-FACED LOVE-BIRDS (6″ x 5½″) bisque, decorated in green, nonlimited edition still in production

RPS-1128-03 THE LOBELL LOVEBIRDS (6″ x 5½″) bisque, decorated in yellow, nonlimited edition still in production

RPS-1128-04 THE LOVEBIRDS (6″ x 5½″) bisque, undecorated, unique

Introduced in 1976 as part of the open collection, this sculpture features two delicately colored lovebirds perched on a tree limb.

RPS-1126-01

RPS-1127-01

RPS-1128-01   RPS-1128-02   RPS-1128-03

There are three variations (regarding color only)—one is done in blue, one in green and the last in yellow. Each carries Boehm Studiomark Number 400-58 and makersmark J.

RPS-1129-01 THE EAGLE OF FREEDOM II (16″ x 20″) bisque, decorated, L.I.G. 300

RPS-1129-02 THE EAGLE OF FREEDOM II (16″ x 20″) bisque, undecorated, unique

This sculpture, created to celebrate our Nation's Bicentennial, was modeled separately but is almost identical to the Eagle of Freedom I. It is not, however, life-size. The piece carries Boehm Studiomark Number 400-70 and makersmark I.

II. Paintings On Porcelain

Ed Boehm had long planned the introduction of paintings on porcelain. During the early years of the Studio, he constantly experimented in the extremely difficult art of producing these thin, fragile sheets of porcelain.

It was not, however, until after his death in 1969 that the decision was made to carry out his plans for these difficult works. Ed Boehm constantly pitted himself against the entire history of European porcelain making; the Beau Brummells were an example. With the porcelain plaques, Ed Boehm was again measuring himself against the European experience. Painted porcelain plaques had always been European and although there were not many done, even in Europe, the great ones had been done there. Thus, when Ed Boehm first started planning porcelain plaques, it was just another way of looking back over his shoulder at the entire history of European porcelain-making to see if, so to speak, history was catching up with him.

The making of the plaques seems quite straightforward. One produces a flat piece of porcelain and then paints an image on it. The problems are not that simple. In the first place, the production of a perfectly flat piece of porcelain without stains or marks of any kind (which would interfere with the decoration) is enormously difficult. The most difficult thing to do in firing ceramics is to produce a flat, even, smooth piece of porcelain, since thin sheets of porcelain have the aggravating tendency to emerge from the kiln rippled, twisted, curved, corrugated, bubbled, convexed and any shape but flat. After this job is accomplished, the painting itself requires a good deal of time and effort. If only one

piece is being done, the complications would be of one magnitude. Since a whole edition of some hundreds are being painted, and each must relate closely to all the others, the problems of control in the decoration itself become complex to the point of desperation. It would have certainly been much easier for the Boehm Studio to produce hundreds of unique plaques than to attempt the enormous challenge of duplicating the images by hand many times.

Among sophisticated collectors of porcelain (as differentiated from sophisticated collectors of Boehm), paintings on porcelain remain the rarest prize of all and it is quite possible that, at some future time, when the Boehm experience is looked at from some distance, the porcelain plaques will assume an importance beyond even the Birds themselves. In fact, among some collectors in the future, the plaques may be considered the most important work that the Boehm Studio ever did.

All of the limited edition paintings listed here and to be introduced in the future will bear makersmark H.

The Porcelain Paintings in the Round bear makersmark P. The one-of-a-kind Porcelain Paintings carry makersmark O.

RPS-2007 MOCKINGBIRDS, pr. (12″ x 15″), framed, L.I.G. 250, cut to 150 pairs

The first of the limited edition paintings, the Mockingbirds was introduced in 1970 and bears Boehm Studiomark A. Each painting is framed and wired for hanging. The works may also be displayed on holders or standards for use on mantels, sideboards or other furniture. In 1972 the edition size was cut to 150 pairs; it was completed in April 1974.

RPS-2008 EASTERN BLUEBIRDS, pr. (12″ x 13″), framed, L.I.G. 250, cut to 150 pairs

Also introduced in 1970, the Eastern Bluebirds bears Boehm Studiomark B. In 1972

the edition size was cut to 150 pairs. The frames of these paintings are hand-carved of aged Appalachian virgin yellow poplar. The corners are joined with flat wooden dowels. The surface is gessoed with several applications of paint in preparation for the 23-karat gold leafing. Following the ancient process of "water gilding," rubbing with polished agates melds and antiques the finish. These methods and materials produce a frame that will stay in perfect condition for centuries. The edition was discontinued in January 1975 after 125 pairs were completed.

RPS-2009 MEADOWLARKS, pr. (12″ x 15″), framed, L.I.G. 250, cut to 150 pairs

This 1970 introduction bears Boehm Studiomark C and is framed like the two previous listings. In 1972 the edition size was cut to 150 pairs; it was discontinued in January 1975 with 110 completed.

RPS-2010 SONG SPARROWS (12″ x 15″), framed, L.I.G. 350, cut to 150

The last of the 1970 paintings, the Song Sparrows, is a single piece bearing Boehm Studiomark D. The edition was cut in 1972 to 150; it was discontinued in January 1975 with 130 completed.

RPS-2011 DRUMMER (15½″ x 18½″), L.I.G. 50, cut to 12

Issued in 1971 by the Malvern Studio with a limited issue goal of 50, the edition was closed in August 1972 after only 12 were made. The sculpture carried Malvern Studiomark Number 6001 and was one of the first paintings executed in the Malvern Studio. It depicts the Drummer of the Royal Regimental Household Guard. The piece was discontinued not because it was not popular, but because the crest of the Queen of England appeared on the painting without her permission and the Boehm Studios were told that they could not continue painting this subject.

RPS-2010   RPS-2011

RPS-2012 COACH AND FOUR (15½" x 18½") L.I.G. 50

Issued by the Malvern Studio in 1971, and carrying Malvern Studiomark Number 6002, the edition was completed in January 1976. The 19th-century motif depicts a Coach and Four which has stopped to take on more passengers at the Inn of the Swan—which is one of the oldest pubs in England.

RPS-2013 COCKATOO AND FLOWERS (15½" x 18½") L.I.G. 50

Issued in 1971 with Malvern Studiomark Number 6003, the edition was completed in January 1973. This painting was taken from a well-known oil by the 18th-century painter Gerardus Spaendonck. However, with all due respect to the original, it is much easier to execute this piece on canvas.

RPS-2014   TWENTIETH-CENTURY FLORAL (19½" x 16½") L.I.G. 50

Issued in 1972 and carrying Malvern Studiomark Number 6004, Twentieth-Century Floral is exactly what the name implies, a still life with old world character and new world technique. The composition shows an exquisite floral arrangement in a vase placed on a marble table. As of February 1, 1976, 44 paintings had been completed.

RPS-2015 NATURE'S BOUNTY (13½" x 16½") L.I.G. 50

Issued in 1973 carrying Malvern Studiomark Number 6005, the edition was completed in December 1974. Like Twentieth-Century Floral, this is a modern painting with an old world touch. While using a floral arrangement it also shows a quantity of fruit on a marble table.

RPS-2016 THE GLORIES OF SPRING (13½" x 16½") L.I.G. 100

Issued in 1973 with Malvern Studiomark Number 6006, 82 pieces had been completed as of February 1, 1976.

The art of painting on porcelain had its beginnings 2,000 years ago in a remote section of China called Ching-Tse-Chen. This painting is most important because it symbolizes the rebirth of that ancient Chinese technique. The original artwork for these paintings was executed by Ming Hsien Hsiao, who is an expert in the oriental technique. He works at the Trenton Studio and is considered by me personally to be one of the finest artists now living and doing this work. I wish to emphasize the fact that this is authentic Chinese art. This painting represents the great Mute Swans which were given as a Gift of State from the American people to the People's Republic of China during President Nixon's visit in 1972. It is interesting to note that the frame is also executed by the same artisans. The technique used on the frame is to lacquer the wood many times. After the coats of lacquer are applied and well-dried, using gold leaf as a base, overlying color is applied in the painting of symbolic subjects.

RPS-2017 NIGHTINGALES (13½" x 19") L.I.G. 50, cut to 25

This painting was issued in 1973. The limited issue goal was reduced to 25 in 1975, and as of February 1, 1976, 22 pieces had been completed. The painting carries Malvern Studiomark Number 6007. It is yet another still life, but a pair of nightingales are included in an attempt to combine still life with a feeling of movement. The use of butterflies in this painting is another such attempt.

RPS-2018 FLORAL ENAMELED CRANE (22" x 16½") L.I.G. 30, cut to 25

Issued in 1974 with Malvern Studiomark Number 6008. The February 1, 1975, price list shows the limited issue goal at 25. As of February 1, 1976, 18 paintings had been completed.

This painting is an attempt to combine two totally different arts in the same picture. This is the first time to my knowledge this has been attempted in the twentieth century. All subject matter in this painting with the exception of the crane is painted using normal paints and techniques. However, the painting of the crane in enamel must be done as the final step. Those who are familiar with enameling know that this technique requires a much lower firing temperature and that the use of enamel on porcelain is one of the most difficult techniques. The bas-relief effect of the crane also gives it a three-dimensional quality. More than 200 hours of painting and as many as 15 days for individual color firings are involved in this porcelain.

RPS-2019 MELANGE DE FRUITS, PAIR (16½" x 22") L.I.G. 10 pair

Issued in 1974 and carrying Malvern Studiomark Number E. As of February 1, 1976, six pair had been completed.

Using all available knowledge of the technical aspects of painting on porcelain, the Boehm Studios execute this impressive pair of paintings employing almost a watercolor technique and using the style of the 18th-century Dutch Masters. The use of as many as a dozen hues of one color requires the artist to know the effects of high temperatures on colors caused by the subsequent decorating firings.

These are perhaps the largest works of their kind ever attempted; they are an especially great achievement because one of the most difficult things to do in porcelain is to fire a flat piece.

RPS-2020 FINCHES IN HARMONY (16½" x 13¼") L.I.G. 25

This painting carries Malvern Studiomark Number 6009 and was issued in 1975.

RPS-2012

RPS-2013

RPS-2014

RPS-2016

RPS-2015

RPS-2017

RPS-2018

RPS-2019

RPS-2023

RPS-2020   RPS-2021   RPS-2022

The inspiration for Finches in Harmony grew out of the Boehm Studio's association with the People's Republic of China and an appreciation of China's delicate and evocative art forms. The painting portrays a group of fantastically colored finches amid clematis and bamboo leaves. The Chinese inscription in the upper right corner reads:

The Finches, resting, are embraced by the "Metal Spring" while shadows of bamboo leaves softly dance in the wind.

The hardwood frame is made by hand. It is lacquered and goldleafed in the Chinese manner. In the cut-out window on the back appear the makersmark, title, artist's name, number and year. The edition was completed in January 1976.

RPS-2021 VENUS (18½″ x 15½″) L.I.G. 25

Issued in 1975 with Malvern Studiomark

Number 600-10. This porcelain painting was adapted from a painting by the French artist François Boucher titled "Venus Consoling Love" and dated 1751. This painting is believed originally to have been owned by Mme. de Pompadour. The frame of the porcelain is hand-carved of aged wood, doweled, gessoed and goldleafed in the style of 18th-century antiques. In the cut-out window on the back appear the makersmark, title, artist's name, number and year. As of February 1, 1976, five pieces had been completed.

As a footnote, it is interesting that this particular painting will be executed by both Trenton and Malvern artists. However, for cataloging by the Boehm Studios, a Malvern Studiomark has been used. Nevertheless, the first few were executed in Trenton.

RPS-2022 ROYAL HORSE GUARDS (22¾″ x 19¾″) L.I.G. 25

Issued in 1975, this painting carries Malvern Studiomark Number 600-11. As of February 1, 1976, three pieces had been completed.

The painting depicts the Royal Horse Guards in their vivid scarlet plumes, bearskin saddle covers and rich blue tunics or cloaks. The frame is hand-carved of aged wood, doweled, gessoed and goldleafed in the style of 18th-century antiques. In the cut-out window on the back appear the Studiomark number, title, artist's name, number and year. This painting will be executed by both Trenton and Malvern artists. However, for cataloging by the Boehm Studios a Malvern Studiomark has been used. Like Venus (RPS-2021), the first few of these paintings were executed in Trenton.

RPS-2023 SUMMER'S BEAUTY (25″ x 15″) L.I.G. 25

Issued in 1976, Summer's Beauty carries Malvern Studiomark Number 600-12. As of February 1, 1976, one painting had been completed.

The theme of this painting expresses the Chinese love for the daylily (Hemerocallis, the flower symbolic of summer). Attracted to the daylily are a sunbird, a frog, an antlion, a butterfly and honeybees. The title appears in oriental characters at top right, with the oriental signature for Boehm on the left. As in the previous two oriental paintings which were done in edition size, the frame is an integral part of the total composition. There is a mat of imported silk brocade; the insert immediately around the plaque is mahogany which has been goldleafed and lacquered. Like the other two paintings, this is authentic Chinese art, employing a technique more than 2,000 years old.

RPS-2024 FREEDOM (18¼″ x 21¼″) **L.I.G. 13**

Issued in 1976, this painting carries Malvern Studiomark Number 600-13. The inspiration for this painting is clearly the American Bicentennial. It depicts a large Bald Eagle descending with wings outspread.

RPS-2025 THE LEOPARD (18¼″ x 21¼″) L.I.G. 10

Issued in 1976, this is the first of a new series of animal portraits featuring head and shoulder studies of the great animals of our world. The artist has captured the strength and pride of the leopard. The painting carries Malvern Studiomark Number 600-14.

RPS-2026 THE RAM (18¼″ x 21¼″) L.I.G. 10

Issued in 1976, this painting carries Malvern Studiomark Number 600-15. It is one in the series of animals, the first of which was the Leopard (see above). The Ram is depicted with great spiraling horns, peering out from the canvas with enormous pride and a fearless expression.

RPS-2024

RPS-2025

RPS-2026

RPS-2027

RPS-2028

RPS-2029

RPS-2027 GEORGE WASHINGTON (21¼″ x 18¼″) L.I.G. 13

Issued in 1976, the George Washington painting carries Malvern Studiomark Number 600-16. It is based on the famous study of Washington by Gilbert Stuart which presently hangs in the White House.

Portraiture in porcelain painting is one of the most challenging and difficult to achieve —skin tones, shadowing and facial character are at the mercy of the high heat of the kiln, and additional firings are always necessary. Only the most highly skilled and experienced porcelain artists can achieve the necessary effects in this area of porcelain painting.

RPS-2028 WASHINGTON CROSSING THE DELAWARE (17¾″ x 23¾″) L.I.G. 13

Adapted from Emanuel Leutze's famous painting, this is one of the most important works for art lovers and students of American history. This painting on porcelain was issued in 1976 and carries Malvern Studiomark Number 600-17. It required an inordinate amount of time and creative energy, not only because of the number of figures in the boats and their positions, but because of the difficulty involved in achieving the brilliant shades of red which are necessary for the proper execution of the painting.

RPS-2029 BAY LYNX #1 (18¼″ x 21¼″) L.I.G. 10

Issued in 1976, this is another in the series of animal portraits. This painting depicts the beautiful Bay Lynx, ever alert, with eyes wide in a fearless expression. The small edition size reflects the difficulty which the artist encountered in executing the animal portraits. These paintings all have a three-dimensional quality which almost makes you feel like reaching out and petting the animal. The piece bears Malvern Studiomark Number 600-18.

III. One-of-a-Kind Paintings

In 1975 the Boehm Studios exhibited a collection of one-of-a-kind original paintings on porcelain. Painting on flat, glazed porcelain requires a highly skilled artist. Color control and a knowledge of the mineral pigments used are highly critical. Thousands of brush strokes and as many as 200 hours are demanded by each painting. Extremely fine portions are done under a magnifying glass with needle-like brushes. To be completed a painting must survive a total period of about 15 days in and out of the decorating kilns. Repeated heating and cooling often causes them to crack, sometimes on the very last firing. There is no reclamation.

All the paintings are less than one-quarter inch thick.

Each painting is presented in a handsome, individually selected frame. Some are hand carved of aged wood, doweled, gessoed and goldleafed in the style of 18th-century English antiques. Others are framed by hardwood assembled by hand and lacquered in the oriental manner with many applications of enamels and goldleaf to create design relief. On the reverse side of each frame is a cut-out window revealing the back, where appear the makersmark O, title, artist's name and year painted.

RPS-3000 CORRIDORS OF CORAL (18½″ x 21″)
Tony Wiggett

The artist is especially interested in sea shells, coral and all marine life. Here he has attempted an extremely difficult treatment, actually showing an underwater scene. The most incredible thing about this painting is the portrayal of the proverbial "murky depths," a very difficult thing indeed to execute in porcelain.

RPS-3001 LE BOMBARDEMENT (19″ x 21½″)
Malcolm Johnson

Based on the well-known painting titled "Bombardment of Algiers" by George Chambers (1803–1840), this is typical history painting. Before the advent of photography this was the only way of portraying important events.

The excitement of this scene is successfully conveyed by means of meticulously painted detail. There is much to see and our interest is held by these details—the tiny figures, the choppy sea, the guns, the fire and smoke. The contrast between the somber sea and the orange flames provides dramatic impact.

Our interest is held also by the tremendous action in the painting. Malcolm Johnson is one of today's deans of the art of painting on porcelain, capable of going beyond the original canvas in capturing the drama and the realism of the subject.

RPS-3002 RUNNING HOME (18½″ x 21″)
Kevan Bettison

While the important part of the painting is obviously the ship, it should be noted that the caps of the waves were painted with enamel, which imparts an almost three-dimensional quality.

RPS-3003 MARE AND FOAL (17″ x 20″)
Leighton Maybury

I have some very definite views concerning this painting. In order to accomplish what Leighton Maybury has, you must have a vast knowledge of the animals. There is no question that Maybury possesses such knowledge. The hint of a castle and the fields beyond creates an illusion of depth, something not easily accomplished, and superbly done here.

RPS-3004 DAPPLED MARE AND FOAL (16″ x 22″)
Leighton Maybury

RPS-3000

RPS-3002

RPS-3001

RPS-3003

RPS-3004

RPS-3005

Leaves, grasses and water provide a suitable setting for the mare to watch the playful antics of her foal. The artist shows his skill in capturing the landscape with many hues of colors used for shrubbery, water and sky.

RPS-3005 AT BOEHM'S DUNCRAVIN FARM (16½" x 19½")
Anthony Fritchey

The rolling countryside of Hopewell Township, New Jersey, is the location Edward Marshall Boehm selected for his animals. Here, at his beloved Duncravin Farm, he spent his most pleasant hours. Among his prized animals were many finely bred horses.

RPS-3006 MARE AT WATER'S EDGE (22" x 16")
Leighton Maybury

In this painting Maybury departed from his norm and gave this work an oriental overtone. Interestingly, he encountered difficulty in painting the reflection of the sky in the water and the grasses and reeds whose images are diffused in the water.

RPS-3007 FEBRUARY FOX (17" x 20")
Kevan Bettison

The amazing realism achieved by Kevan Bettison in this painting did not come easy;

as we have stated before, the demands made on an artist painting in porcelain are extreme. Here the painstaking application of the most minute brush strokes give one the feeling that one can reach out and touch the animal's head. Another interesting point is the treatment of the sun; it is very difficult technically to paint white on white.

RPS-3008 INSTANT INNOCENCE (17" x 20")
Simon Joyner

Very few artists are capable of capturing the innocence of young animals, but Simon Joyner has certainly done so in depicting this young leopard cub and mongoose. This painting is so well executed and of such superb quality that it has an almost photographic perfection. To date I would venture to say that it is one of the finest paintings on porcelain I have seen.

RPS-3009 AUTUMN PASTORAL (17½" x 21")
Joan Ross

This painting has an almost pastel quality, which the artist has achieved by using something close to a "water color" technique. The painting depicts a gypsy camping at a riverside. The colors are warm and soft and become softer as they fade into the distant hills, giving the painting the quality of depth.

RPS-3010 EARDISLAND (17" x 20")
Christopher Burns

Eardisland is a small village in Herefordshire, England. It was early summer when the artist captured the peaceful start of a new day. The neat, well-kept Tudor-style houses, stately old trees and green grasses reflect pride of ownership. Against this background a dog keeps watch over his master's livestock.

RPS-3011 OLD ENGLAND (17" x 20")
Freda Griffiths

Inspired by her childhood memories of rural life, Freda Griffiths has given this painting a charm which gives one a very warm feeling of the meaning of home.

RPS-3012 TRANQUILLITY (20" x 17")
Margaret Powell

There are oriental influences in this painting, particularly in the mountains and the waterfall. The artist has endeavoured to form a design from natural forms, using clear, strong colors. This shows a great knowledge of "color build" in porcelain painting.

RPS-3013 MAYTIME—HEREFORDSHIRE (19" x 21½")
Joan Ross

This painting shows the peaceful charm of the English countryside with a hint of nostalgia. The herdsman stands by the gate tending his sheep; the old wagon was at one time used for carrying grain or hay.

RPS-3014 AWAKENING (22" x 16")
Margaret Powell

What we said of the work titled "Tranquillity" is true also of this painting. However, the attention given to detail here is far greater. Here we have a contrast between the close detail of the buildings and figures and the impression of mist and water in the craggy background. There is a definite sense of movement in this second of three oriental paintings by Margaret Powell.

RPS-3015 MEDITATION (22" x 16")
Margaret Powell

The third of Margaret Powell's oriental paintings. The Chinese influence is seen immediately. The figure, sitting beneath the windswept pines, is at one with nature and landscape. In contrast to the indefinite background we have the minute detail of the old

RPS-3006

RPS-3007

RPS-3008

RPS-3009

RPS-3010

RPS-3011

RPS-3013

RPS-3012

RPS-3014

RPS-3015

RPS-3016

RPS-3017

RPS-3018

RPS-3019

RPS-3020

RPS-3021

gnarled tree trunk and grasses in the foreground. As in the two other paintings the artist has paid a great deal of attention to detail.

RPS-3016 La Moisson (The Harvest) (20″ x 17″)
Malcolm Johnson

Inspired by the Dutch still-life tradition, the artist has taken a famous painting by Jan van Os (1744–1808) and reworked the elements into his own composition. The mellow tones of the fruit and flowers are so thoughtfully portrayed that one recognizes instantly the artist's desire to match his skill against that of the Dutch Masters. And, indeed, Malcolm Johnson's work has a three-dimensional quality that makes the still life come alive before one's eyes. His extraordinary knowledge of color and command of detail help make this one of the finest pieces in the group.

RPS-3017 EVENING (16″ x 22″)
Leighton Maybury

Not every artist in the field of porcelain painting has total command of the art. In fact, many artists do much finer work on one subject matter than they would on another. However, there are exceptions, and one of these is Leighton Maybury. Earlier we saw three paintings which involved portraits of horses. Here is a painting on an entirely different subject. As we look into this picture we can imagine ourselves there. The scene takes place in the fall. Dusk is falling, and one can almost feel the cold night to come. To add an illusion of depth, the artist has added a woman by the roadside doing her chores before dark.

RPS-3018 DESERTED CASTLE (20″ x 17″)
Joan Ross

Tall trees, dramatic cliffs and crystal clear water make this a powerful landscape. It is extremely interesting in that it is almost a pastel on porcelain. Soft yellows, blues, ·

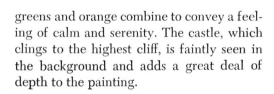

RPS-3022

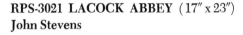

RPS-3023

RPS-3024

greens and orange combine to convey a feeling of calm and serenity. The castle, which clings to the highest cliff, is faintly seen in the background and adds a great deal of depth to the painting.

RPS-3019 LAKESIDE (18″ x 21″)
Susan Morgan

Here is a place of retreat—empty but not lifeless. Lakeside is the somewhere that everyone imagines would be the perfect escape. Its realism, combined with a touch of impressionistic style, gives it an almost hypnotic quality.

RPS-3020 HIGHLAND BURN (17½″ x 20½″)
Alan Telford

The interesting aspect of this painting is the achievement of great depth. In porcelain paintings of this type and with the use of this technique the artist must create his own depth.

RPS-3021 LACOCK ABBEY (17″ x 23″)
John Stevens

The original Lacock Abbey is owned by the National Trust and still retains its 13th-century cloisters, sacristy and nun's chapter house. It was the last religious house in England to be dissolved after the Reformation, and its conversion to a dwelling was undertaken by Sir William Sharington, who, in 1540, built the curious octagonal tower overlooking the Avon.

John Stevens has accomplished a great deal technically with this painting. Note the reflection of the abbey in the water, a technique requiring extensive knowledge of the reactions of various glazes to firing temperatures.

RPS-3022 WINTER'S GOLD (16″ x 22″)
Joan Ross

This scene successfully conveys the cold beauty of winter. The watery sun lights the small pearls of snow hanging on roofs and scattered on the frozen ground. The small

figure, warmly clad, crunches over the frosty soil.

RPS-3023 THE ODD COUPLE (20″ x 17″)
Derek Jones

This work, whose subject matter is quite unusual for porcelain painting, shows again the artist's rare understanding of the animal he has so beautifully depicted. Not only is it technically skillful, but it succeeds remarkably in conveying the character of the pair of owls. The bodies of the birds are shown in detail, and therefore they do not lose themselves in the dark background.

RPS-3024 BARN OWL WITH YOUNG (16″ x 19½″)
Ray Poole

This is a sensitive portrayal of a moment which is rarely directly observed. The artist has captured the soft, downy feathers of the fledglings, and has painted them so delicately that one can almost hear their cries.

263

RPS-3025

RPS-3026

RPS-3027

RPS-3028

RPS-3029

RPS-3030

RPS-3025 MAGPIE (14½″ x 21″)
John Smith

John Smith has painted a masterpiece. The Magpie, seen against sensitively painted apples and leaves, looks so real that one might think that this was not a painting at all but a sculpture. This three-dimensional effect is one of the most difficult to achieve in porcelain painting.

RPS-3026 SONG THRUSHES (20½″ x 17½″)
David Fuller

Another painting in which the artist's intimate knowledge of the animal he was re-creating made it possible for him to render it with absolute fidelity.

RPS-3027 PARADISE GARDEN (19½″ x 16½″)
Rita Daniel

Rita Daniel's delightful study of a peacock,

macaw, bee-eater and an urn of flowers in the garden of a stately home was, technically speaking, also a very difficult painting to execute, because it involved firing different families of colors. As we have noted, each time a painting goes into the kiln represents a new hazard, and this one required at least eight firings. From both a technical and an artistic standpoint this work is a masterpiece.

RPS-3028 KESTRELS (24" x 18½")
David Fuller

David Fuller has achieved great depth in this painting with the use of the sky and valley below and the positioning of the companion bird hovering in open air.

RPS-3029 BLUE BIRD OF PARADISE (19½" x 16½")
Val Gerischer

Among all the extraordinary birds which inhabit the earth, this is one of the most striking. The fantastic coloration of the Blue Bird of Paradise, with long flowing plumes and long blue streamers, is nature at her most inventive.

This work is based on Gould's studies of the birds of paradise of New Guinea.

RPS-3030 SPECTACLED OWLS (20" x 17")
Peter Yardley

The Spectacled Owl is a widespread species, breeding from southern Mexico, south throughout Central and South America, as far as northwest Argentina. The broad brown band through the eyes is in sharp contrast to the white streaks above and below, giving the effect of spectacles. The artist has scrupulously researched his subject, and his detailed study is a fine example of bird painting on porcelain and an equally fine example of a competent realist at work.

RPS-3031 FLOWER PIECE (19" x 21½")
Rita Daniel

This is a study of geraniums, lilies, clivias, orchids, catalpas, camellias and other flowers in a formal composition. The artist faithfully captures the vibrant fuchsias, delicate yellows and shades of blue and red of these flowers. Not only Rita Daniel's vast knowledge of the flowers themselves but her knowledge of color in porcelain painting are evident in this work.

RPS-3032 SEEDS OF TIME (24" x 17½")
Sandra Griffiths

The title refers to the use of colors and foliage from all the seasons, which contribute to the sense of completeness of the work. This is a strong painting, with positive, almost dramatic composition. The pastel-like quality of the background lends increased strength to the bright colors of the floral. Sandra Griffiths' understanding of the botanical subject and her quest for perfect form are apparent in this painting.

RPS-3033 BLUE BOW (22½" x 16½")
Susan Morgan

The warm tones in the background are a foil for the silvery-green leaves and delicate pinks and blues of the tiny flowers. Each petal is painted so carefully that we are able to see the specific character of each flower.

RPS-3034 FLORAL GARLAND (19" x 21½")
Rita Daniel

A subdued yet warm background cradles the group of varied flowers and grasses. We see the exotic and the simple, yet all blend together in a skillful interpretation of their nature. Here again we must admire Rita Daniel's obvious knowledge of the subject and its reproduction on porcelain.

RPS-3031

RPS-3032

RPS-3033

RPS-3034

RPS-3035

RPS-3036

RPS-3037

RPS-3035 SPRING (15½″ x 18½″)
Val Gerischer

The beauty and variety of flowers in this arrangement are executed with an almost pastel-like quality.

RPS-3036 AUTUMN (15½″ x 18½″)
Val Gerischer

Viburnum and chrysanthemums are interspersed among a variety of autumn flowers. The many shades of yellow and orange and the crisp detail of each flower combine to make this a pleasant floral scene.

RPS-3037 GIRL WITH WATERING CAN (23″ x 19½″)
Val Gerischer

This composition shows the skill of the painter and his knowledge of ceramic colors in capturing the style of Renoir. Employing a difficult raised enameling technique on the lace, the artist has created a successful picture. Technically speaking this would have to be considered one of the highlights of this series of one-of-a-kind paintings.

RPS-3038 STILL LIFE WITH DECANTER (19½″ x 16½″)
Alan Telford

Still life is among the most difficult subjects for porcelain painting, requiring a high degree of control and skill, discipline and talent. This painting required extra firings to mature the difficult combinations of strong and subtle colors. The crystal wine glass and decanter are the final and ultimate test. These colors do not exist in ceramic pigments. Therefore, they must be formed by the careful removal of color from the porcelain canvas by the most exquisitely controlled application of heat. This was unquestionably one of the finest porcelain paintings executed in the Boehm Studios.

RPS-3038

RPS-3039

RPS-3040

RPS-3041

RPS-3042

RPS-3043

RPS-3039 APRIL MORNING (21″ x 18″)
Rita Daniel

This painting epitomizes an English morning. The sun streaming through the trees lights up the fresh foliage. The young stag is alert to his surroundings at break of day. Although the stag is the major subject of the work, the great attention paid to detail in the painting of the foliage should not be overlooked.

RPS-3040 HUNTING BUFFALO (19″ x 22″)
Leighton Maybury

Against the characteristic Western background, the artist has depicted a typical scene of the mid-nineteenth century. The painting is reminiscent of work by Frederick Remington and Charles Russell. The Buffalo, which is the primary subject of this painting, is shown in painstaking detail.

RPS-3041 THE PEWTER BOWL (18″ x 21″)
Joan Ross

This is a traditional still-life painting. It is easy to see that the artist is a student of nature. The combination of flowers and fruit and their placement makes this an exquisite composition.

RPS-3042 THE INFANT (21½″ x 18½″)
Margaret Powell

The infant of the title is a baby hare. Tangles of thorny bushes and daisies form a frame around it. The subtle use of numerous shades of green help give the picture freshness and clarity.

RPS-3043 IN A SUMMER GARDEN (21″ x 18″)
Rita Daniel

This work depicts a formal patio graced by a magnificent peacock and other exotically colored birds. In the background stands a house surrounded by great trees, which cre-

RPS-3044

RPS-3045

ate a powerful illusion of depth. The combination of many colors makes this a technical masterpiece as well as a splendid painting.

RPS-3044 ELEPHANTINE (18⅜″ x 21¼″)
Tony Wiggett

This animal portrait is of the African forest elephant. Although a common subject for an artist working on canvas, it is a very difficult work to attempt on porcelain.

RPS-3045 EWER AND FRUIT (18″ x 21″)
R. Lewis

This work almost appears to be on canvas rather than on porcelain.

267

RPS-3046

RPS-3047

RPS-3048

RPS-3046 MELLOW SEASON (22″ x 19″)
Susan Morgan

This beautiful floral still-life combines sharp colors and those of almost pastel quality. A painted bird's nest rests upon the sandstone plinth. The use of brocade draperies gives this painting its three-dimensional effect.

RPS-3047 VICTORIAN FANTASY (20¾″ x 18″)
W. Randall Van Hise

The lush background of green brings out the color of the flora. The eggs are bright blue. The artist shows tremendous knowledge of the use of colors in his medium.

RPS-3048 MULTNOMAN FALLS (21″ x 18″)
Leighton Maybury

Another fine work by Leighton Maybury. The difficult element in executing this painting is the waterfall.

RPS-3049 SUNSET (17¾″ x 23½″)
Leighton Maybury

The dramatic colors of the evening sky dominate this scene, with the water only a mirror of the beauty of the sunset.

RPS-3050 PATIENCE (21½″ x 18½″)
Margaret Powell

Three hounds stretch out in the doorway of a battered old barn after a hard day's work. There is almost an Andrew Wyeth expression and feeling in the painting.

RPS-3051 VENETIAN SCENE (21½″ x 18½″)
Joan Ross

A great deal of activity is shown in this busy scene, yet there is also a quality of serenity.

RPS-3049

RPS-3050

RPS-3051

RPS-3052

RPS-3053

RPS-3054

RPS-3052 THE CANAL BRIDGE (17½″ x 23¼″)
Joan Ross

This charming old-fashioned scene at a bridge over a very narrow canal is most pleasing to the eye.

RPS-3053 NEVADA MORNING (18¾″ x 21¾″)
Leighton Maybury

A great deal of attention was given to creating the perception of depth in this excellent painting.

RPS-3054 RED SQUIRRELS IN WINTER COAT (18″ x 24″)
Mary Weaver

This particular Red Squirrel is now tragically extinct. It is therefore of particular interest that Mary Weaver has chosen to record this subject, and she can be very proud of her exquisite execution of a very difficult subject.

RPS-3055 THE LOGE (21″ x 18″)
Val Gerischer

This painting is in the early style of Mary Cassatt, whose original painting of the same title was created in 1882. The use of extremely delicate colors and the very subtle differences in the double portrait is an astonishing accomplishment in the medium of porcelain.

RPS-3056 THE FORGOTTEN ABBEY (18¼″ x 21″)
Susan Morgan

This work shows the ruins of an ancient building, yet one gets an idea of the majestic quality of the building that once stood. A solitary figure gazes out over the lake, perhaps reflecting on days gone by.

RPS-3057 TRANQUILLITY (18¼″ x 21¼″)
Freda Griffiths

RPS-3055

RPS-3056

RPS-3057

RPS-3058

RPS-3059

RPS-3060

RPS-3061

RPS-3062

RPS-3063

Not to be confused with an oriental painting by the same name done by the Boehm Studios. This work depicts a typical Herefordshire landscape reminiscent of years gone by. A meticulous attention characteristic only of the most skilled porcelain painters is paid to detail.

RPS-3058 BLUE COMPORT (21″ x 18″)
Alan Telford

The very difficult family of colors chosen for this painting and the great attention paid to the minutest detail make this a most exquisite work, one of the finest done to date.

RPS-3059 MORNING MIST ON LAKE SUPERIOR (19″ x 22″)
Leighton Maybury

This unusual painting features a group of

American Indians on the water at daybreak; the early morning fog settling on the lake makes the lead canoes just barely visible. There is an effect here of watching a picture in motion.

RPS-3060 LESSER BIRD OF PARADISE (19½″ x 16½″)
Val Gerischer

This is after Gould's studies of the birds of

270

paradise of New Guinea. A male is displaying the colors of his plumage. The white, brown, yellow and green make him a fantastically beautiful subject.

RPS-3061 PAIR OF OTTERS (21″ x 18″)
Derek Jones

One of the most beloved creatures of the wild is the river otter. Its playful attitude and social behavior are to be envied. Derek Jones has captured a male and a female otter at river's edge remarkably well. This painting has a photographic quality.

RPS-3062 FULMAR (21″ x 18″)
Alan Telford

This is a portrait of one of the most beautiful white sea birds of the northern region. The artist has captured with startling realism the simple yet complex beauty of nature. Fulmar is one of the finest animal portraits done to date.

RPS-3063 DAISY (21½″ x 18¼″)
Margaret Powell

Margaret Powell, who executed three of the original oriental paintings we saw earlier, has such complete command of her medium that she can accept any challenge it presents. The subject of this work is a little girl and her dog in a field of daisies. An interesting footnote is the technique of using enameling on the hem of the gown, sleeves, collar and the trim of the hat. While the subject matter may not appeal to everyone, that does not minimize the fact that this piece is exquisitely done.

RPS-3064 ICY AFFECTION (18½″ x 21½″)
Simon Joyner

We have mentioned photographic quality with regard to other paintings in this collection. None shows that quality more than this painting of two polar bears toying with one

another playfully in the water. No artist could have given more attention to the minutest detail.

RPS-3065 MORNING DEPARTURE (18″ x 24″)
Bill Scott

This painting of fishing boats departing for the day's catch includes one of the most difficult things to accomplish in porcelain painting—the sky at dawn. The artist obviously has a tremendous knowledge of color and how it changes in the intense heat of the kiln.

RPS-3066 OLD VENICE (18¾″ x 21½″)
Joan Ross

This painting could be categorized as pastel on porcelain, so soft are the colors used. The artist has created a great illusion of depth.

RPS-3067 GREEN WOODPECKERS WITH CRABAPPLE (21¼″ x 18¼″)
John Smith

With the near extinction of the ivory-billed woodpecker, this bird may be considered the largest woodpecker in existence. Every feather and every detail has been painted in,

RPS-3068

RPS-3069

RPS-3070

RPS-3071

RPS-3072

RPS-3073

reflecting the artist's knowledge of his subject.

RPS-3068 THE KING (18¼″ x 21¼″)
Margaret Powell

Reflected in this painting of a lion lying in the African grassland is the animal's great strength.

RPS-3069 HUNTER'S RETURNING (18″ x 21″)
Leighton Maybury

This painting shows an American Indian returning with his catch. The color scale is broad, and to execute this painting successfully the artist had to have great control of his colors.

RPS-3070 FAIR WIND AND SAILS (18¾″ x 21⅜″)
Kevan Bettison

This painting is reminiscent of Running Home (RPS-3002), another work by Bettison which we saw earlier.

RPS-3071 GRAY SQUIRRELS (18⅜″ x 21⅜″)
Peter Yardley

Gray Squirrels is quite different from any painting previously done by the Boehm Studios. It has almost a lithographic quality, so fine is the brush work.

RPS-3072 ARIZONA HEIGHTS (21½″ x 18¼″)
Susan Morgan

Arizona Heights shows the mountainous area in northern Arizona. It is beautifully executed and has a very peaceful quality.

RPS-3073 THE HAVEN (18¼″ x 21¼″)
Joan Ross

This painting is very similar in subject mat-

RPS-3074

RPS-3075

RPS-3076

ter and content to Old Venice (RPS-3066), with the painting being almost a pastel on porcelain.

RPS-3074 AFTER THE STORM (19″ x 22″)
Alan Telford

There are certain artists in the Studio who can paint almost any subject with equal interest and equal quality. Alan Telford's After the Storm shows the turbulence moving off into the distance, the water becoming calm, the fishermen pulling their nets out of the water and the men on shore resuming their chores. The artist has created a symphony out of many normally incompatible colors.

RPS-3075 IMAGINARY LANDSCAPE (17½″ x 23¼″)
Christopher Burns

Imaginary Landscape is a painting that demands a great deal of study. The landscape actually involves many types of terrain, and there are varying types of cloud formations. It took much imagination and a great deal of skill to combine the realism of the various landscapes with the almost fantastic appearance of the sky.

RPS-3076 THE LEDGER (22″ x 19″)
Alan Telford

The quality and richness of color of this still life show a vast understanding of the technical and artistic aspects of porcelain painting. The flora, the unlit candle, the scrolls lying in their receptacle and the open ledger with quill make you feel that you are sitting behind a desk sometime in the 18th century. One can almost smell the flowers in the vase. Note the decorative table covering painted deep purple—one of the most difficult of all porcelain colors to achieve. The green tone of the background lends itself exquisitely to the colors of the subject matter.

RPS-3077 THE CUSTOM HOUSE QUAY (18″ x 21″)
Malcolm Johnson

RPS-3077

RPS-3078

This is another of Malcolm Johnson's masterworks. Here he has captured the realism and bustling activity of ships being loaded and unloaded during our country's colonial period.

RPS-3078 REFLECTIONS OF BEAUTY (21″ x 18″)
Rita Daniel

A simple bud vase on a wall console contains freshly picked flowers. Vase and flow-

RPS-3079

RPS-3080

RPS-3081

ers are reflected in an oval gold-leaf mirror hanging on the wall. This painting exemplifies beauty in simplicity.

RPS-3079 THE FRIGATE CONSTITUTION (18″ x 21″)
Leighton Maybury

The frigate Constitution is here shown in battle. The bombardment of the vessel and its return fire are indicated by puffs of smoke and cannon balls falling into the water and causing the relatively calm sea to erupt. Like a number of other Boehm artists, Leighton Maybury can handle almost any subject and do it well.

RPS-3080 MAY MORNING (21″ x 18¼″)
Leighton Maybury

A group of mares and their foals feed on the early spring grass of the English countryside.

RPS-3081 EVENING IN VENICE (21″ x 18″)
Joan Ross

Another painting that looks like pastel on porcelain, it yet has a portrait-like quality. A woman and child sit on a balcony overlooking a canal in Venice. The gondolas in the canal add life to the scene.

RPS-3082 OLD PHILADELPHIA (18¼″ x 21¼″)
Joan Ross

One of the paintings done in honor of the Bicentennial, it includes a glimpse of Carpenters' Hall, and the old Independence Hall. Quite a bit of activity is shown going on in the town. The sense of depth of this painting is excellent.

RPS-3083 DARING ESCAPADE (21″ x 18″)
Leighton Maybury

Knowledge of firing various colors on porcelain and the extraordinary changes that take

RPS-3082

RPS-3083

RPS-3084

RPS-3085

RPS-3086

place in the high temperatures was an absolute necessity in executing this beautiful work. It depicts a frigate which has burst into flames. Flaming parts dropping into the sea and illuminating it, and the men escaping in the long boat make this a very exciting painting.

RPS-3084 HARMONY (21″ x 19″)
Susan Morgan

A fine composition showing a lyre with fruits and flowers on a marble table.

RPS-3085 THE FRIGATE ALFRED (18″ x 21″)
Leighton Maybury

The colonial frigate Alfred is seen along with its companion ship. The use of the companion ship in the background creates a beautifully executed illusion of depth.

RPS-3086 MONTICELLO (18¼″ x 21¼″)
Joan Ross

The home of Thomas Jefferson is seen with a small family group in the foreground dressed in turn-of-the-century clothing.

RPS-3087 HAYMAKING IN MATHON (21″ x 18¼″)
Jean Oram

This is what I consider a flat painting on porcelain. It is in the realm of English folk art and a most interesting study of the English countryside.

RPS-3088 ON THE BANKS OF THE AVON (19″ x 22″)
Susan Morgan

Another painting of old England, this landscape has great serenity.

RPS-3089 ON THE LIFFEY (19″ x 21¾″)
Susan Morgan

RPS-3087

RPS-3088

RPS-3089

RPS-3090

RPS-3091

RPS-3092

RPS-3093

RPS-3094

A herdsman stands on the shore with one of his herd while a small craft sails down the relatively calm river Liffey.

RPS-3090 SUMMER CHAPTER (18″ x 21″)
Susan Morgan

This beautifully executed still life shows freshly picked flowers laid gently upon two volumes which rest on a wooden table. In the right corner there is a painting framed in gold leaf which has the beginnings of a sylvan scene. The artist has an extraordinary feeling for flowers.

RPS-3091 MISSISSIPPI PADDLE STEAMERS (21″ x 18″)
Leighton Maybury

This painting has a very nostalgic quality about it. Brilliantly done, it shows one of the most recognizable symbols of a very productive era in American history.

RPS-3092 HENRY KNOX (21⅜″ x 18⅜″)
Alan Telford

This exquisite portrait on a Bicentennial theme achieves realistic flesh tones while firing very difficult colors such as reds, blues and greens.

RPS-3093 VALLEY FORGE (21¼″ x 18⅜″)
Joan Ross

This Bicentennial tribute represents troops of Washington's army in the bitter winter of '76 at Valley Forge. The treatment of the snow in this painting is fascinating. It seems to be hiding the trees in the background, thus creating the feeling of great depth. The soldiers marching through the snow reflect the pain and purpose of the times.

RPS-3094 DAY OF FREEDOM (21⅜″ x 18⅜″)
Joan Ross

This painting shows the signing of the Declaration of Independence. Again, as in previous portrait paintings, the difficulty is in capturing the flesh tones. Because there are eighteen figures in the painting, and the flesh tones of each had to vary as they do in life, this was technically an extraordinary achievement.

RPS-3095 WASHINGTON'S FAMILY (23″ x 18½″)
Leighton Maybury

Like Day of Freedom, the difficulty in this work is due to the number of figures and

RPS-3096

RPS-3095

RPS-3098

RPS-3097

RPS-3099

the flesh tones involved. The painting depicts Washington and his immediate family at home.

RPS-3096 BENJAMIN FRANKLIN (18¼″ x 22¼″)
D. R. Whitmore

This is a portrait of Benjamin Franklin during his middle years. Like the other portraits and paintings involving flesh tones, this is where the problems occur. Obviously

this painting is another piece done in honor of the Bicentennial.

RPS-3097 AMERIGO VESPUCCI (18⅜″ x 21½″)
Joan Ross

This shows a large ship under full sail. To create an illusion of depth the artist has used smaller boats in the background.

RPS-3098 KINGFISHER (22″ x 19″)

Christine Bennett

This work shows a belted kingfisher perched on a branch which juts out from a tree growing on a river bank.

RPS-3099 REGAL PRIMROSES (14¾″ x 20¾″)
W. Randall Van Hise

This painting depicts in beautiful detail a bird's nest (with eggs in and out of it) among primroses.

IV. Porcelain Paintings in the Round

Porcelain Paintings in the Round

In 1975 the Boehm Studios announced they were producing six series of handmade art plates. They are the Butterfly Series, Flower Series, Hard Fruit Series, Soft Fruit Series, Seashell Series and Oriental Bird Series.

Each series will be strictly limited to issues of 150; two plates of each series will be introduced annually. Each plate is authenticated with the makersmark P, artist's name, number and year.

These porcelain paintings in the round are handmade, hand-painted and hand-gilded. The making of fine porcelain plates by hand was almost a lost art, but Boehm, ignoring the difficulties, is creating plates of 12-inch diameter rather than the customary 10½ inches.

RPS-4000 JEZABELS, bone porcelain, decorated, full shoulder in Foshan yellow, gold border, L.I.G. 150

The first decorative art plate in the Butterfly Series is the Jezabels. Depicted on the plate is the golden-orange male with black-tipped wings and the darker female with bright red touches on her lower wings. The plate carries Malvern Studiomark Number M-100. As of February 1, 1976, 26 plates had been completed.

RPS-4001 BLUE MOUNTAIN SWALLOW-TAILS, bone porcelain, decorated, full shoulder in Foshan yellow, gold border, L.I.G. 150

The second decorative art plate in the Butterfly Series is the Blue Mountain Swallowtails, which are blue with black and brown markings on the wing edges. Accompanying the Blue Mountain Swallowtail is the Catopsilia scylla, a golden-colored butterfly with brown markings. The plate carries Malvern Studiomark Number M-101. As of February 1, 1976, 27 plates had been completed.

RPS-4100 PASSION FLOWERS, bone porcelain, decorated, full shoulder in Ching-te-Chen celadon, gold border, L.I.G. 150

The first decorative art plate in the Flower Series is the Passion Flowers. It carries Malvern Studiomark Number M-200. The flowers are comprised of a short tube which opens to a saucer shape composed of many ovate petals. A graceful corona of slender filaments surrounds the ovary and short stamens. As of February 1, 1976, 30 plates had been completed.

RPS-4101 LILIES, bone porcelain, decorated, full shoulder in Ching-te-Chen celadon, gold border, L.I.G. 150

The second plate in the Flower Series depicts the Empress of India lily, whose crimson blooms may reach a size of ten inches across. The plate bears Malvern Studiomark Number M-201. As of February 1, 1976, 29 plates had been completed.

RPS-4200 PLUMS, bone porcelain, decorated, full shoulder in Ching-te-Chen celadon, gold border, L.I.G. 150

The first decorative art plate in the Hard Fruit Series is the Plums. Victoria, the variety depicted, ripens in late August. It is red with dark speckling and often flushed with yellow. The plate bears Malvern Studiomark

Number M-300. As of February 1, 1976, 24 plates had been completed.

RPS-4201 PEARS, bone porcelain, decorated, full shoulder in Ching-te-Chen celadon, gold border, L.I.G. 150

The second plate in the Hard Fruit Series is the Pears, which bears Malvern Studiomark

278

Number M-301. It shows a plentiful crop of dull yellow pears tinged with russet. As of February 1, 1976, 27 plates had been completed.

RPS-4300 LOGANBERRIES, bone porcelain, decorated, full shoulder in Ching-te-Chen celadon, gold border, L.I.G. 150

The first decorative art plate in the Soft Fruit Series is the Loganberries. The plate depicts the dull claret-colored fruits on their spiny stems. The Malvern Studiomark Number is M-400. As of February 1, 1976, 20 plates had been completed.

RPS-4301 CHERRIES, bone porcelain, dec-

orated, full shoulder in Ching-te-Chen celadon, gold border, L.I.G. 150

The second plate in the Soft Fruit Series is the Cherries. The fruits are pale, flushed with red. The plate bears Malvern Studiomark Number M-401. As of February 1, 1976, 22 plates had been completed.

RPS-4400

RPS-4401

RPS-4500

RPS-4501

RPS-4400 ROOSTER-TAIL CONCHS, bone porcelain, decorated, full shoulder in Tangshan blue with gold border, L.I.G. 150

The first decorative art plate in the Seashell Series is the Rooster-Tail Conchs. It bears Malvern Studiomark Number 500. As of February 1, 1976, 28 plates had been completed.

RPS-4401 VIOLET SPIDER CONCHS, bone porcelain, decorated, full shoulder in Tangshan blue with gold border, L.I.G. 150

The Violet Spider Conchs, the second in the Seashell Series, bears Malvern Studiomark Number M-501. As of February 1, 1976, 27 plates had been completed.

RPS-4500 BLUE-BACKED FAIRY BLUE-BIRDS, bone porcelain, decorated, decorative floral border, L.I.G. 150

The first plate in the Oriental Bird Series, the Blue-backed Fairy Bluebirds depicts the male, mostly black below with a bright blue mantle with lilac reflections; the female is much duller. The plates bear Malvern

Studiomark Number M-600. As of February 1, 1976, 23 plates have been completed.

RPS-4501 AZURE-WINGED MAGPIES, bone porcelain, decorated, decorative floral border, L.I.G. 150

This plate is the second in the Oriental Bird Series. The Azure-winged Magpie is a beautifully colored bird with a long graduated tail. This plate bears Malvern Studiomark Number M-601. As of February 1, 1976, 23 plates had been completed.

Note on The Malvern Studio Porcelains

Early in 1971, Edward Marshall Boehm Incorporated, in concert with a group of English artists and craftsmen who had been operating "Cranleigh Art Ceramics," set up a bone porcelain studio in Malvern, England, under the name Boehm of Malvern, England, Ltd. Ed Boehm had long admired English quality and craftsmanship and had often expressed a desire to form an association—the Malvern Studio is really an extension of his planning.

The artists and craftsmen of Boehm of Malvern work in the fragile medium of bone porcelain. There are similarities but also distinct differences between the methods of working with hard porcelain and bone porcelain. Basically the two processes are the same: plasteline model, plaster model, waste molds, block molds, case molds, working molds, propping, casting, use of mineral pigments, and so on. The differences are in degree.

Because of the high percentage of bone in the formula, which melts in the high heat of the kiln, shrinkage in bone porcelain is greater—about 17 per cent as opposed to about 13 per cent in hard porcelain. Bone clay is more plastic, more malleable. It can be manipulated and shaped more than the hard clay, and with it one can obtain extreme delicacy and thinness, as is evident in the florals. The softness of the clay forces more emphasis on hand-tooling and hand-making in the shapes and fine details of each piece. This is the unique charm of the bone body.

V. Malvern Animals

It became evident when the Malvern Studio was organized that new talents and new discoveries were opening up new directions for the Boehm Studios. One of these directions was the animals. The Malvern Studio called this series "Moments of Nature."

The pieces were technically very well done but unfortunately suffered from the problem of scale. Each piece was done as a grouping of the animals and necessarily had to be very small. One of the original reasons for Boehm's success with the birds is the fact that they were done life-size. The viewer did not have to make a mental adjustment—the scale was there for him.

In the "Moments of Nature" series the very small scale gave the pieces a toylike and somewhat unpleasing quality. However, as a precursor to some of the great animals that were to come later—such as the Nyala and Panda—it was an important training ground.

RPS-8500 BOBCATS (8″ x 15″) English bone porcelain, decorated, L.I.G. 300, cut to 200

The first in the Moments of Nature series was the Bobcats, which depicts the female carrying one cub in her mouth while the other looks on. Introduced in 1971, it carries Malvern Studiomark Number 4001 and makersmark K. The edition goal was reduced to 200 in 1974 and completed in that year.

RPS-8500

RPS-8501 RACCOONS (11″ x 11″) English bone porcelain, decorated, L.I.G. 350, cut to 200

The Raccoons were the second in the Moments of Nature series done by the Malvern Studio. The sculpture depicts three raccoons on a tree trunk; the one on the top grasps a bunch of berries. The sculpture, announced in 1971, carries Malvern Studiomark Number 4002 and makersmark K. The edition was cut to 200 in 1974 and was completed in that year.

RPS-8502 FOXES (12″ x 14″) English bone porcelain, decorated, L.I.G. 350, cut to 200

The Foxes, another 1971 introduction by the Malvern Studio for their Moments of Nature series, shows the male and female guarding two cubs. The sculpture carries Malvern Studiomark Number 4003 and makersmark K. The edition size was reduced to 200 in 1974

and it was completed in July of that year.

RPS-8503 RED SQUIRRELS (13½″ x 13″) English bone porcelain, decorated, L.I.G. 350, cut to 100

This piece was announced in 1972 with a limited issue goal of 350; however, only 100 were made and the piece was closed in January 1974. The Malvern Studiomark Number is 4004 and the makersmark is K. It is the last of the animal group (Foxes, Raccoons, Bobcats) first offered by the Malvern Studio in 1971. The sculpture contains three Red Squirrels, two males and one female; also shown is a small rodent.

RPS-8504 THE NYALA (20″ x 16½″) English bone porcelain, decorated, L.I.G. 100*

The Nyala is among the rarest and most beautiful of the African antelopes. It has a long fringe under its stomach, a mane on its

*See page 55

neck, and prominent round ears. The Nyala was introduced by the Malvern Studio in 1973 and was the first of an important endangered species series by the Boehm Studios. The stimuli for this series were two. First, Mrs. Boehm was appointed by H.R.H. Prince Bernhard to "The 1001: A Nature Trust." This is an organization which the Dutch prince, as president of the World Wildlife Fund, launched in 1971. He personally invited 1,000 men and women throughout the world to join him in (1) contributing to an endowment fund for animals; (2) influencing others by their example to support the aims of the World Wildlife Fund and its sister organization, the International Union for Conservation of Nature. The second stimulus was the desire to call attention to the endangered fauna of our earth.

The sculpture carries Malvern Studiomark Number 5001 and makersmark K. As of February 1, 1976, 88 sculptures had been completed.

RPS-8505-02

RPS-8506

RPS-8507

RPS-8505-01 BENGAL CUB (6″ x 9″) Trenton hard porcelain, decorated, nonlimited edition discontinued with only a few made

RPS-8505-02 BENGAL CUB WITH BUTTERFLY (6″ x 9″) Trenton hard porcelain, decorated, nonlimited edition discontinued with only a few made

There were two Bengal Cub sculptures produced. Basically they are quite similar, the only differences being that in one, the Cub has its mouth open and a butterfly is included, while in the other the mouth is closed and the head is positioned differently. Only a few of each were executed, and the Studio has stopped making them for an indefinite period. Both were issued by the Malvern Studio in 1975 and carry the Malvern Studiomark Number 200-24 and makersmark N.

The Malvern Studio tried working with the Trenton hard body and liked working it. Some of the 1975 sculptures—specifically the animals and figurines—and most of the open issue pieces, fledglings and intermediates, are made with the Trenton formula.

RPS-8506 PUMA (13″ x 21½″) Trenton hard porcelain, decorated, L.I.G. 100

A 1975 introduction by the Malvern Studio with Malvern Studiomark Number 5002 and makersmark M. The sculpture shows a startled female who has assumed a defensive posture and keeps her curious young behind her. The animals' coats are particularly difficult to accomplish in porcelain, requiring extensive handtooling and carving. Teeth, tongue, and other details are of hand-rolled clay.

The Puma sculpture is the second introduction in a series of endangered animals, the first having been the Nyala Antelope. As of February 1, 1976, 23 sculptures had been completed.

RPS-8507 GIANT PANDA (13½″ x 9½″) Trenton hard porcelain, decorated, L.I.G. 100

RPS-8508

In 1975 the Giant Panda was introduced by the Malvern Studio. It is a remarkably life-like sculpture, showing the Panda in a characteristic sitting pose with the ever-present bamboo shoots, its favorite nourishment. President Nixon was given a pair of live Giant Pandas (Ling-Ling and Hsing-Hsing) during his visit to the People's Republic of China in February of 1972. They are now in the zoo in Washington, D.C.

The sculpture carries Malvern Studiomark Number 5003 and makersmark M. As of February 1, 1976, 53 sculptures had been completed.

RPS-8508 HARVEST MICE WITH QUINCE (9¼″ x 6½″) English bone porcelain, limited edition, no figure announced

283

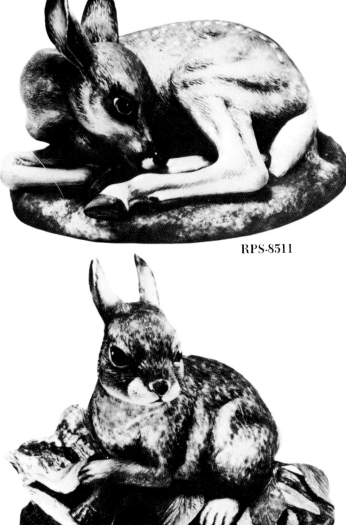

RPS-8510

RPS-8511

RPS-8509

RPS-8512

Announced as a 1975 edition from the Malvern Studio, this porcelain sculpture depicts a pair of Harvest Mice with several Quince. This sculpture was never released for sale.

RPS-8509 OTTER (13″ x 18¼″) Trenton hard paste, decorated, L.I.G. 350

Caught in pursuit of a small group of fish, this underwater acrobat has been captured by the skilled artisans of the Malvern Studio. The sculpture carries Malvern Studiomark Number 5004 and makersmark M. As of February 1, 1976, one had been completed.

RPS-8510 PAINTED TURTLE (5½″ x 4¼″) Trenton hard paste, decorated, nonlimited edition still in production

Remember the story of the tortoise and the hare? Well, like the fable, this turtle is determined to creep into your collection. Featured on a solid base amid a small grouping of flowers, the sculpture carries Malvern Studiomark Number 200-32 and makersmark N.

RPS-8511 FAWN (5¼″ x 7½″) Trenton hard paste, decorated, nonlimited edition still in production

Featured in a lying pose with one eye opened, this newborn white-tailed fawn seems frightened by his new surroundings. The sculpture bears Malvern Studiomark Number 200-33 and makersmark N.

RPS-8512 RABBIT (6″ x 7″) Trenton hard paste, decorated, nonlimited edition still in production

Another addition to the Young Wildlife of the World Series, this cottontail seems well protected, for his soft brown coloring against the newly fallen leaves of russet and gold serves as camouflage. The sculpture bears

284

Malvern Studiomark Number 200-36 and makersmark N.

RPS-8513 AMERICAN MUSTANGS (approximately 20″ x 19″ x 10½″ on base) English bone porcelain, bisque, L.I.G. 100

A masterpiece in porcelain interpretation— two Mustangs, wild, free and natural. The expressive medium of porcelain captures, in every muscle and sinew, the taut energy and unleashed spirit of these beautiful animals. The piece, which stands on an ebony walnut base, carries Malvern Studiomark Number 5005 and makersmark N.

RPS-8513

VI. Malvern Figures

This series was a new departure for the Boehm Studios. The only previous figures of this kind were done by Ed Boehm from 1961 to 1969 and ended with the Gay Nineties Set. Had Ed Boehm lived he certainly would have been involved in the human figure. Helen Boehm is, in this case, carrying forward a start by Ed Boehm.

RPS-8700 MELON BOY (12″ x 6″) Trenton hard porcelain, decorated, nonlimited edition still in production

In 1975 the Malvern Studio introduced their Growing Up Series. The first in the series is Melon Boy. It carries Malvern Studiomark Number 7001 and makersmark N. It shows a youth, reminiscent of Tom Sawyer, in worn jeans and an old straw hat, sitting on a tree stump eating watermelon.

RPS-8701 THE TRUANT (9″ x 14″) Trenton hard porcelain, decorated, nonlimited edition still in production

The second in the Growing Up Series is called The Truant. This sculpture depicts a youth with a faraway look in his eyes; his apple and slingshot are lying on a log. The piece was introduced in 1975 and carries Malvern Studiomark Number 7003 and makersmark N.

RPS-8702 TRUE LOVE (12½″ x 6½″) Trenton hard porcelain, decorated, nonlimited edition still in production

True Love is another in the Growing Up Series issued in 1975 by the Malvern Studio. The sculpture depicts a young, barefoot girl with long braids holding the flowers she has

RPS-8700

RPS-8701

285

RPS-8702

gathered. The piece carries Malvern Studio-mark Number 7003 and makersmark N.

RPS-8703 THE PAINTRESS (10″ x 9″) Trenton hard porcelain, decorated, non-limited edition still in production

Announced in 1975, this nonlimited sculpture carries Malvern Studiomark Number 7004 and makersmark N. It shows an artist, a young woman, among her paints and brushes. Her dress is beautifully bordered with forget-me-nots and one can see the composition of her painting, which is barn swallows and flowers. It has been claimed that there is a certain likeness between the artist and a young Helen Boehm.

RPS-8704 DREAMAWAY (10½″ x 8″) Trenton hard porcelain, decorated, nonlimited edition still in production

Dreamaway is another in the Growing Up Series issued by the Malvern Studio in 1975. It depicts a freckle-faced child and a new-found friend by the side of a rocky stream with wild irises. It carries Malvern Studio-mark Number 7005 and makersmark N.

RPS-8705 WAITING PATIENTLY (10″ x 11″) Trenton hard porcelain, decorated, nonlimited edition still in production

The last of the Growing Up Series to be announced in 1975 is Waiting Patiently. It is also a nonlimited sculpture and carries Malvern Studiomark Number 7006 with makersmark N. This sculpture was announced in 1975 but as of June 1976 none had been issued. It is another Tom Sawyerish image, the youth resting on a tree stump with his hat, his dog and his grapes.

RPS-8704

RPS-8703

RPS-8705

286

RPS-8800

RPS-8801

RPS-8802

RPS-8803

VII. Malvern Flowers

More than any others, the English have developed an extraordinary ability to replicate flowers in porcelain. Helen Boehm recognized this talent when the Malvern Studio was organized, and after some early floral sculptures that were nice but not really superb, in 1975 and 1976 the Malvern floral talent has really matured. The stems and stamens are hand-formed. The petals are hand-cut and shaped and then joined together by hand. This builds the first-generation group of petals. After a considerable drying period, the second generation of petals is formed and applied the same way. This process can continue for a buildup of as many as eight layers of delicate petal groups. Props must be used to fire the flowers successfully while retaining the natural curls and spacings. Each prop must be carefully placed and later carefully removed when the firings are completed. Then the flowers must survive the glazing, second firing, hand coloring and the multiple firings of the decorating kilns.

RPS-8800 BETTY SHEFFIELD SUPREME CAMELLIA (6″ x 4½″) English bone porcelain, decorated, nonlimited edition still in production

The Betty Sheffield Supreme Camellia was issued in 1971 as a nonlimited sculpture carrying Malvern Studiomark Number 2002 and makersmark L. The piece depicts a single pink camellia and is one of the first flowers of the flower program offered by the Malvern Studio. It touched a nerve not only among porcelain collectors but also among camellia fans. The camellia lends itself very well to this kind of sculpture, for its full bloom is unhampered by a long, awkward stem.

RPS-8801 MALVERN ROSE (7″ x 3½″) English bone porcelain, decorated, nonlimited edition closed in 1972

The Malvern Rose was one of the very first sculptures from the Malvern Studio. It was announced in 1971 and carries Malvern Studiomark Number 2003 and makersmark L. This pink rose is native to the beautiful hills where the English studio is located. The edition was closed in 1972.

RPS-8802 ICEBERG ROSE (7″ x 3½″) English bone porcelain, decorated, nonlimited edition closed in 1972

The Iceberg Rose (called Bridal Rose on the 1971 Announcement) is a white rose with long stem and leaves. Like the Malvern Rose, it proved difficult to ship and was closed in 1972. The sculpture carries Malvern Studiomark Number 2004 and makersmark L.

RPS-8803 YELLOW ROSE (6″ x 3½″) English bone porcelain, decorated, nonlimited edition closed in 1972

The Yellow Rose (sometimes called Tea Rose) was announced as a nonlimited sculpture by the Malvern Studio in 1971. It closed the following year. The piece carried Malvern Studiomark Number 2005 and makersmark L.

RPS-8804 SWAN CENTERPIECE (22″ x 6″) English bone porcelain, decorated, L.I.G. 350. Closed in 1974, 133 made

Announced in 1971, the Swan Centerpiece carries Malvern Studiomark Number 3001 and makersmark K. The piece was discontinued in 1974, because despite extra precautions taken in packing, a high percentage of the pieces were damaged in shipment. This was evidently a major cause of its lessened edition size.

The Swan Bowl was designed by Helen Boehm as part of her Year of the Swan. That,

RPS-8804

of course, was the year the great Mute Swans were developed for presentation to the People's Republic of China. The Centerpiece bowl has swans at either end of the sculpture, which is filled with peonies.

The European formality of this piece did not find favor among collectors. It was a strangely atypical image for Boehm to produce, and stands alone as an example of decorative porcelain—as contrasted to the more natural replications for which Boehm is known.

RPS-8805 YELLOW DAISIES (8″ x 8″) English bone porcelain, decorated, L.I.G. 350

Introduced in 1971, the Yellow Daisies carry Malvern Studiomark Number 3002 and makersmark K. When Helen Boehm first saw the work of the young men who were in charge of what was to become the Boehm Malvern Studio, they were doing floral sculptures under the name of Cranleigh Art Ceramics. These very attractive flowers attracted Helen's attention, and it was not long after the Malvern Studio opened that Helen, in association with the two young men, Terry K. Lewis and Richard Lewis, produced floral pieces that were to become a very important part of the Boehm repertoire. As of February 1, 1976, 323 sculptures had been completed.

RPS-8806 SWEET VIBURNUM (12″ x 13″) English bone porcelain, decorated, L.I.G. 350, closed after 35 were made

The Sweet Viburnum, announced in 1971, was to be a limited edition of 350. But the length and delicacy of the stems of this piece made it impossible to ship, and it was closed in September 1972 after only 35 were made. The piece carried Malvern Studiomark Number 3004 and makersmark K. The sculpture depicts the long-stemmed sweet viburnum with an iceberg rose. It is rare and valuable today, for very few of the 35 made survived shipment.

RPS-8805

RPS-8806

RPS-8807 CLEMATIS (6″ x 21″) English bone porcelain, decorated, L.I.G. 350 but apparently only one was made

This was announced in 1971 by the Malvern Studio with a L.I.G. of 350.

RPS-8808 CHRYSANTHEMUM AND BAMBOO (9″ x 12″) English bone porcelain, decorated, L.I.G. 350, but only 5 made

The Chrysanthemum and Bamboo was issued and discontinued in the same year, 1971. The piece was simply too difficult to ship, and only five were made. It is a very rare and important piece. I called the Studio to get a Malvern Studiomark Number for it and was told that both the Chrysanthemum and Bamboo and the Chrysanthemum with Butterfly issued in 1972 (RPS-8813) carry number 3005 with makersmark K. The sculpture depicts a cluster of chrysanthemums with the Bamboo in a dish.

RPS-8809 QUEEN'S MASTERPIECE ROSE (8″ long) English bone porcelain, decorated, nonlimited edition still in production

The Queen's Masterpiece Rose was announced in 1972 along with several other flower sculptures. It is a long yellow bloom with leaves and thorns. It carries Malvern Studiomark Number 2006 and makersmark L.

RPS-8810 PEACE ROSE (8″ long) English bone porcelain, decorated, nonlimited edition still in production

This is the second rose issued by the Malvern Studio in 1972 and bears Malvern Studiomark Number 2008 and makersmark L. This is a large yellow rose tipped with pink.

RPS-8811 IRIS, BLUE (12″ long) English bone porcelain, decorated, nonlimited edition still in production

RPS-8808   RPS-8809

RPS-8810   RPS-8811

289

RPS-8812

RPS-8813

RPS-8814

RPS-8815

RPS-8816

RPS-8817

Another flower entry of 1972, the Blue Iris carries Malvern Studiomark Number 2009 and makersmark L. The iris is the State Flower of Tennessee. The Boehm Studios' control of color is nowhere better exhibited than in this piece. The blues and purples approach that softest iridescence so typical of the iris.

RPS-8812 PAT NIXON CAMELLIA (7″ x 5″) English bone porcelain, decorated, nonlimited edition still in production

The Pat Nixon Camellia was announced in 1972. It carries Malvern Studiomark Number 200-12 and makersmark L. The sculpture is of a pale pink camellia with two buds. The petals of the flower are hand-cut and shaped, then joined together. Following a drying period, the second layer of petals is similarly formed and applied. With intermittent drying periods the build-up of as many as eight layers of delicate petal groups is finally achieved. Mrs. Boehm noticed a picture of the First Lady planting the Pat Nixon Camellia and decided to make her a replication.

RPS-8813 CHRYSANTHEMUM WITH BUTTERFLY (8″ x 9½″) English bone porcelain, decorated, L.I.G. 350

This sculpture was announced in 1972; it carries Malvern Studiomark Number 3005 (same as RPS-8808) and makersmark K. The Malvern Studio's skill in the creation of porcelain flowers has contributed a major element to the Boehm story. The flowers are all done individually by hand. In this sculpture are four large chrysanthemum flowers, each of which contains from 80 to 90 petals, and a beautiful life-size replica of a Clouded Swallowtail butterfly. As of February 1, 1976, 260 sculptures had been completed.

RPS-8814 SINGLE PEONY (10″ x 5¼″) English bone porcelain, decorated nonlimited edition still in production

This single pink peony was introduced in

1973. It carries Malvern Studiomark Number 200-14 and makersmark L.

RPS-8815 DOUBLE PEONY (12″ x 6″) English bone porcelain, decorated, nonlimited edition closed in 1973

The beautiful pink double peony was issued and closed in the same year. The piece was extremely difficult to handle and only 132 were made. The flower was too heavy for the stem, and there was heavy breakage in shipping. The piece carries Malvern Studiomark Number 200-15 and makersmark L; it was redesigned and brought out as a limited edition of 500 (RPS-8818) in 1974.

RPS-8816 CORNUS NUTTALI DOGWOOD (4¾″ x 8″ x 12½″) English bone porcelain, decorated, L.I.G. 500

Introduced in 1973, this piece carries Malvern Studiomark Number 3003 and makersmark K. Large, creamy involucral bracts make the flower heads, which can be up to six inches in diameter, splendid in the late spring, while its red autumnal leaves and gaudy fruiting heads are equally attractive. As of February 1, 1976, 182 sculptures had been completed.

RPS-8817 STREPTOCALYX POEPPIGII (19″ x 12″) English bone porcelain, decorated, L.I.G. 200, cut to 50

This sculpture shows a beautiful flowering plant of the Bromeliaceae "Pineapple" family with a life-size male Morpho Cypris butterfly, a native of Colombia, resting on the plant. It was issued in 1973 as a limited edition of 200, but was cut to only 50 in 1976. It is certainly the finest of all Boehm flower sculptures and perhaps the finest flower sculpture ever done in porcelain by anybody. The overwhelming complexity involved in hand-sculpting over 600 parts makes this piece of special interest to those concerned with sophisticated technical porcelain problems. It is obvious that the cutback took place for this reason. I feel that the Streptocalyx was not fully appreciated during its issue period but will achieve eventual recognition.

The sculpture carries Malvern Studiomark Number 3006 and makersmark K. As of February 1, 1976, 40 sculptures had been completed.

RPS-8818 DOUBLE PEONY (3½″ x 8½″) English bone porcelain, decorated, L.I.G. 500

RPS-8818

The Double Peony (tree peony) was reintroduced by the Malvern Studio in 1974. It replaces the nonlimited Double Peony which was discontinued because of breakage problems. The sculpture carries Malvern Studiomark Number 3007 and makersmark K. As of February 1, 1976, 137 sculptures had been completed. The floral presentation features a substantial pink bloom. The Boehm artisans have captured every important detail, so much so, in fact, that it seems to exude the rich roselike fragrance characteristic of this flower. This piece was presented to the People's Republic of China in 1975 by President Ford.

RPS-8819

RPS-8819 DEBUTANTE CAMELLIA WITH VIBURNUM (3½″ x 8½″) English bone porcelain, decorated, L.I.G. 500

The Debutante Camellia was introduced in 1974. It carries Malvern Studiomark Number 3008 and makersmark K. As of February 1, 1976, 198 sculptures had been completed.

RPS-8820 GENTIANS WITH BUTTERFLY (3″ x 7″) English bone porcelain, decorated, L.I.G. 750

Introduced in 1974, the Gentians with Butterfly carries Malvern Studiomark Number 3009 and makersmark K. It presents a cluster of blue gentians with a small yellow butterfly. As of February 1, 1976, 182 sculptures had been completed.

RPS-8820

291

RPS-8821

RPS-8823

RPS-8824

RPS-8821 WATERLILY WITH SWAMP FLY (3½" x 8") English bone porcelain, decorated, L.I.G. 750

Introduced in 1974, this sculpture depicts a large blue waterlily with a swamp fly. The piece carries Malvern Studiomark Number 300-10 and makersmark K. It is one of the relatively few pieces that includes an insect. As of February 1, 1976, 167 sculptures had been completed.

RPS-8822 CARROLL WALLER CAMEL-LIA (3½" x 8½") English bone porcelain, decorated, 3 made

The Carroll Waller Camellia was created by the Malvern Studio and named after the First Lady of Mississippi to commemorate a Boehm exhibition held at the State Historical Museum on May 1, 1974. Two were made for presentation to Mrs. Waller and the Museum and one for Mrs. Boehm's private collection. It is one of those rare presentation editions with which Boehm commemorates important Studio events.

RPS-8823 EMMETT BARNES CAMELLIA II (4" x 9") English bone porcelain, decorated, L.I.G. 750

This semi-double white camellia with several buds was announced by the Malvern Studio in 1975. Emmett Barnes is a member of the American Camellia Society and there is an actual hybrid camellia named in his honor. The porcelain carries Malvern Studiomark Number 300-11 and makersmark K. As of February 1, 1976, 124 sculptures had been completed.

RPS-8824 EMMETT BARNES CAMELLIA II (3" x 6") English bone porcelain, decorated, nonlimited edition still in production

In 1975 the Malvern Studio also announced this smaller version of the limited Emmett Barnes II Camellia. This sculpture is just

the white camellia. It carries Malvern Studiomark Number 200-20 and makersmark L.

RPS-8825 PINK ROSE (10¼" x 5") English bone porcelain, decorated, nonlimited edition still in production

The Pink Rose was issued in 1975. It carries Malvern Studiomark Number 200-25 and makersmark L. Including the stem, the rose is 10¼" inches long. The Pink Rose is pictured with the long and short pussywillow also announced in 1975 (RPS-8828 and 8829).

RPS-8825
RPS-8828
RPS-8829

RPS-8826 BLUE POPPY (10¾″ x 4½″) English bone porcelain, decorated, nonlimited edition still in production

The Malvern Studio announced the Blue Poppy (Meconopsis) in 1975. It is pictured here with the pussywillow that was also introduced in 1975. The piece carries Malvern Studiomark Number 200-26 and makersmark L.

RPS-8827 PINK ROSE BUD (7″ x 3″) English bone porcelain, decorated, nonlimited edition still in production

Introduced in 1975, the Pink Rose Bud carries Malvern Studiomark Number 200-27 and makersmark L. The Pink Rose Bud is pictured here with one of the Pussywillows announced in 1975.

RPS-8828 PUSSYWILLOW, LONG (13¾″ long) English bone porcelain, decorated, nonlimited edition still in production

The Pussywillow, Long was issued in 1975. It carries Malvern Studiomark Number 200-28 and makersmark L. This is one of the few times Pussywillow has ever been attempted in porcelain.

RPS-8829 PUSSYWILLOW, SHORT (11″ long) English bone porcelain, decorated, nonlimited edition still in production

The Pussywillow, Short, was also introduced in 1975. It carries Malvern Studiomark Number 200-29 and makersmark L.

RPS-8830 MAGNOLIA GRANDIFLORA WITH MONARCH BUTTERFLY (6½″ x 13″) Trenton hard porcelain, decorated, L.I.G. 750

Announced in 1975, the Magnolia Grandiflora carries Malvern Studiomark Number 300-12 and makersmark M. The sculpture depicts a Monarch butterfly perched on the flower. As of February 1, 1976, 101 sculptures had been completed.

RPS-8831 SWAN LAKE CAMELLIA (5¾″ x 10½″) English bone porcelain, decorated, L.I.G. 750

The 1976 introduction of the Swan Lake Camellia by the Malvern Studio is an outstanding addition to the increasingly popular floral collection. Its variegated shape, chiffon-soft petals and plump honeybee give it both beauty and realism. The piece carries Malvern Studiomark Number 300-13 and makersmark K. As of February 1, 1976, one sculpture had been completed.

RPS-8830

RPS-8831

RPS-8832

RPS-8834
RPS-8828
RPS-8829

RPS-8832 QUEEN OF NIGHT CACTUS
(10½″ x 6¼″) English bone porcelain, decorated, L.I.G. 500

Only the desert could be so mysterious. From out of the decay of a cactus a new flower blooms. There is also a small lizard. The sculpture carries Malvern Studiomark Number 300-14 and makersmark K. As of February 1, 1976, one piece had been completed.

RPS-8833 ORCHID CACTUS (7¾″ x 9″) English bone porcelain, decorated, L.I.G. 500

Introduced in 1976, this delicate pink cactus flower is a welcome addition to the floral collection. The artists from the Malvern Studio have heightened its realism with the addition of a small desert lizard beneath the bloom. The piece carries Malvern Studiomark Number 300-15 and makersmark K. As of February 1, 1976, one piece had been completed.

RPS-8834 PEACE ROSE IN VASE (11″ x 4″) English bone porcelain, decorated, nonlimited edition still in production

This rose is an exact replica of the original Boehm Peace Rose with but one exception—the stem has been lengthened so it may be placed in a vase. It carries Malvern Studiomark Number 200-34 and makersmark L.

RPS-8835 PINK PERFECTION CAMEL-LIA (5½″ x 3¼″) English bone porcelain, decorated, nonlimited edition still in production.

One of the smallest Boehm floral creations but certainly to be included among the most popular. It carries Malvern Studiomark Number 200-35 and makersmark L.

RPS-8836 SUPREME PEACE ROSE (approximately 12″ x 5½″ x 6″) English bone porcelain, decorated, L.I.G. 250

RPS-8833

RPS-8835

294

A lush, magnificent bloom of the very popular Peace Rose, piled high with petals, whispered with color. A stunning addition to the limited floral collection from the Malvern Studio, the piece carries Malvern Studiomark Number 300-16 and makersmark K.

RPS-8837 SUPREME YELLOW ROSE (approximately 10″ x 5″ x 6″) English bone porcelain, decorated, L.I.G. 250

Another superb rose, sunny and perfect in form. A winning candidate for any flower show, this piece carries Malvern Studiomark Number 300-17 and makersmark K.

RPS-9000

RPS-8836

RPS-8837

VIII. Malvern Birds

Although Cranleigh Art Ceramics, the precursor of the Boehm Malvern Studio, had never worked directly in bird sculptures, it was obvious when Helen Boehm became involved that these young men would have to add to their earlier interest in flowers the production of birds. Their first pieces were not very good. Nuthatch, Little Owl and the Winter Robin were not up to the standards of the Trenton Studio, which caused many people to prejudge the validity of Malvern. As we can see now, these 1971 pieces were only a hint of what was to come. The first fruits were just that. They were awkward,

the decoration was not first-rate, but the Studio was learning its trade. By the second and third year it had become evident they were learning well. Now one is hard put to determine which of the Studios, the English or the American, is turning out the better work.

RPS-9000 NUTHATCH (8″ x 8″) English bone porcelain, decorated, L.I.G. 350

The Nuthatch was issued in 1971. It carries Malvern Studiomark Number 1001 and makersmark K. The sculpture also depicts a large

295

RPS-9001

RPS-9002

toadstool known as Fly Agaric, of the Amanita family. The edition was completed in January 1975.

RPS-9001 LITTLE OWL (6″ x 9″) English bone porcelain, decorated, L.I.G. 350

The Little Owl, perched on a branch, was issued in 1971, the second bird brought out that year by the Malvern Studio. It bears Malvern Studiomark Number 1002 and makersmark K. The edition was completed in January 1973.

RPS-9002 WINTER ROBIN (10″ x 12″) English bone porcelain, decorated, L.I.G. 350

The winter robin (not to be confused with the American robin) is a familiar bird in the English countryside. This sculpture was introduced in 1971, among the very first pieces to come out of Malvern, and reveals some of the immaturity of the Studio at that time. The sculpture depicts the Winter Robin among holly branches. The edition was completed in January 1975. The piece carries Malvern Studiomark Number 1003 and makersmark K.

RPS-9003 JENNY WREN (4″ x 6″) English bone porcelain, decorated, nonlimited edition still in production

This small sculpture was issued in 1971. It carries Malvern Studiomark Number 2001 and makersmark L. It was the first of the Malvern nonlimited editions and was enthusiastically received. It depicts a tiny wren perched on a pile of rock and has wide appeal for collectors. This is in fact a perfectly contained sculpture and, although unlimited, could very well have served as a small limited edition.

RPS-9004 GOLDCREST (8″ x 10″) English bone porcelain, decorated, L.I.G. 500

The Goldcrest was introduced in 1972. It carries Malvern Studiomark Number 1004 and makersmark K. The edition was completed in November 1974. The sculpture features a male Goldcrest, Britain's smallest bird, in characteristic activity among larch.

RPS-9005 BARN OWL (21″ x 27″) English bone porcelain, decorated, L.I.G. 350*

The Barn Owl was announced in 1972. It bears Malvern Studiomark Number 1005 and makersmark K. As of February 1, 1976, 292 sculptures had been completed. The Barn Owl is shown with wings outspread, claws hooked as if preparing to snatch a morsel of food. The original sculpture was 21 inches high and 21 inches wide, but the Boehm Studio decided to redesign it to bring the size more to scale. This is one of the few times a major change in a sculpture was made after its introduction. The redesigned Barn Owl has a wing span of approximately 27 inches and is the largest bone porcelain composition ever made. Its creation was equivalent in difficulty to that of the hard porcelain Ivory-Billed Woodpecker Ed Boehm and his craftsmen in Trenton made in 1964. The Woodpecker also had a wing-spread of 27 inches.

RPS-9006 BLACK GROUSE (13″ x 15½″) English bone porcelain, decorated, L.I.G. 350

The male, or Blackcock Grouse, as presented in this sculpture, is easily distinguished by its glossy blue-black plumage and lyre-shaped tail, conspicuous white under tail coverts and white wing-bar, whereas the female, confusingly known as the Greyhen, is about 7 inches smaller, with chestnut and buff plumage and a long notched tail. This piece was introduced in 1972 as a limited edition of 350, but the edition size was reduced and in January 1975 the piece was completed with only 175 made. This large and important sculpture bears Malvern Studiomark Number 1006 and makersmark K.

*See page 39

RPS-9007 TREECREEPERS (17″ x 9″) English bone porcelain, decorated, L.I.G. 350, cut to 200

The Treecreeper, like the Nuthatch, is an oddity among British birds, for although its typical mode of progress — up, around or along the trunk and branches of trees, pressing its still tail against the bark — suggests some relationship to the Woodpeckers, it is in fact a highly adapted member of the perching-birds family. The sculpture shows five adult Treecreepers in identical plumage with elder and mistletoe, and a fledgling peeking from its hold.

The Treecreeper was announced in 1972. This is another of those expensive, complicated pieces to make, and in early 1976 the Malvern Studio decided to reduce the edition size rather than raise the price. The edition was cut to 200, and as of February 1, 1976, 196 sculptures had been completed. They bear Malvern Studiomark Number 1007 and makersmark K.

RPS-9003

RPS-9004

RPS-9005

RPS-9006

RPS-9007

297

RPS-9008

RPS-9008 CUCKOO (YOUNG FEMALE)
(4″ x 5″) Trenton hard porcelain, decorated, nonlimited edition still in production

The Cuckoo (Young Female) was announced in 1972. It is a small sculpture depicting a fledgling, mouth wide open awaiting food. The piece carries Malvern Studiomark Number 2007 and makersmark N.

RPS-9009 BLUE TITS WITH APPLE BLOSSOMS (9¼″ x 11½″) English bone porcelain, decorated, L.I.G. 400, cut to 350

Blue Tits with Apple Blossoms was announced in 1973 with a limited issue goal of 400, but because of the cost factor the number was cut in 1975 to 350. As of February 1, 1976, 165 sculptures had been completed. The Blue Tit is one of Britain's best-known garden birds. It sports an attractive cap of cobalt blue, sometimes with a kingfisher-like sheen of silver blue. The sculpture depicts a pair of Blue Tits amid Apple Blossoms. It bears Malvern Studiomark Number 100-8 and makersmark K.

RPS-9009

RPS-9010 YELLOWHAMMERS WITH HAWTHORN (11″ x 11″) English bone porcelain, decorated, L.I.G. 400, cut to 350

The Yellowhammers was announced in 1973 as a limited edition of 400 carrying Malvern Studiomark Number 1009 and makersmark K. Primarily because of cost, the Studio in 1975 cut the edition size to 350. As of February 1, 1976, 210 sculptures had been completed. The male has a characteristic yellow head and dark-streaked chestnut upper parts; the female is somewhat duller in color and more heavily streaked. The plumage of both is muted in winter. The sculpture depicts a family scene with the parents feeding the three fledgings among the branches of hawthorn.

RSP-9011 SCREECH OWL (10½″ x 6″)

RPS-9010

English bone porcelain, decorated, L.I.G. 500

The Screech Owl was introduced in 1973, carrying Malvern Studiomark Number 100-10 and makersmark K. Characteristic ear tufts are typical of the smaller owls, such as the Screech. Other distinctive aspects are its bright yellow, forward-facing eyes and a large head that can twist 180 degrees. It is common to the continental United States, extending into central Mexico and parts of southern and western Canada. The sculpture depicts the Screech Owl perched on a rock, with its head slightly tilted. As of February 1, 1976, 343 sculptures had been completed.

RPS-9012 LONG-TAIL TITS WITH GORSE (14″ x 10½″) English bone porcelain, decorated, L.I.G. 400, cut to 350

The Long-Tail Tit, found throughout Eurasia, is a tame and confiding little bird that inhabits woodland thickets and hedgerows. Its black-and-white plumage is tinged with pink, and, as its name suggests, it has a conspicuous three-inch tail of black and white outer feathers. The sculpture features both male and female subjects amid gorse, a particular nesting favorite of the species.

In 1975, because of the increasing costs in manufacturing, the Malvern Studio decided to cut the limited issue goal to 350. The piece carries Malvern Studiomark Number 100-11 and makersmark K. As of February 1, 1976, 162 sculptures had been completed.

RPS-9013 PEREGRINE FALCON (20″ x 21″) English bone porcelain, decorated, L.I.G. 400, cut to 350

The Peregrine is one of the noblest of falcons. For centuries it has been the falconer's favorite bird. The Peregrine is now a rare and endangered species. An interesting thing about it is that during World War II the Ministry of Defense of Great Britain ordered

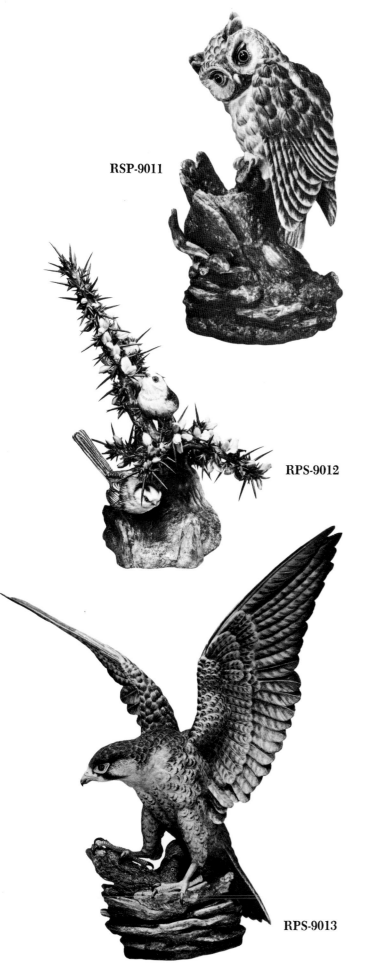

RSP-9011

RPS-9012

the destruction of the peregrine falcon because the birds were destroying the carrier pigeons that were delivering messages from Great Britain to the front lines. By the time the war was over the Peregrine was very rare indeed, and the species has not made a comeback.

The porcelain sculpture depicts the Peregrine Falcon with wings outspread on a rock base. The Malvern Studiomark Number is 100-12 and the makersmark K. It was introduced in 1973 in a limited issue goal of 400, but the following year the edition size was reduced to 350. As of February 1, 1976, 181 sculptures had been completed.

RPS-9014 BLACKBIRDS WITH CHERRY BLOSSOMS (pr.) (Male 17″ x 12″, Female 16″ x 12″), English bone porcelain, decorated, L.I.G. 250, cut to 75

This formal sculpture was introduced in 1973 under Malvern Studiomark Number 100-13 and makersmark K. The Blackbirds is one of the more complicated of the English bone porcelains. Its engineering is difficult and it is my feeling that the cutback that the Studio made in 1976 to only 75 was due to problems encountered in making the piece. As of February 1, 1976, 70 sculptures had been completed. The distinctive pitch-black plumage of the male Blackbird makes it unmistakable, but the same cannot be said of the female with its uniform brownish plumage, or of the juvenile with its patched coat. The sculpture shows the Blackbirds amid Cherry Blossoms.

RPS-9015 LAPWING WITH DANDELIONS (18″ x 19″) English bone porcelain, decorated, L.I.G. 400, cut to 100

The Lapwing, with its long curved crest, olive-green back and green wings shot with metallic iridescence, is unsurpassed in beauty and charm by any of the English shore birds. The sculpture was announced by the Malvern Studio in 1973 with a limited issue

RPS-9014

RPS-9015

RPS-9013

299

RPS-9016

RPS-9017

RPS-9018

goal of 400, but this was cut to 300 in 1974 and then cut again to 100 in 1976 because of the complicated design of the piece and the cost to produce it. The sculpture depicts the Lapwing, with wings outspread, landing in a clump of dandelions. It bears Malvern Studiomark Number 100-14 and makersmark K. As of February 1, 1976, 97 sculptures had been completed.

RPS-9016 GREEN WOODPECKERS WITH MORNING GLORIES (21" x 15"), English bone porcelain, decorated, L.I.G. 250, cut to 50

The Green Woodpeckers was introduced in 1973 as a limited edition of 250. It carries Malvern Studiomark Number 100-15 and makersmark K. Because of its size and structural complications, the edition size was cut back in 1976 to only 50 pieces. The firing of this piece requires excellent control and care.

The porcelain sculpture portrays a male and female in their best finery examining a tree trunk for the larvae of bark insects. Winding round the trunk and forming a pleasing complement to their brilliance are delicate handcrafted morning glories and vines.

As of February 1, 1976, 48 sculptures had been completed.

RPS-9017 BABY PUFFIN (4½" x 4½") Trenton hard porcelain, decorated, non-limited edition still in production

The Baby Puffin was introduced in 1973. It carries Malvern Studiomark Number 200-13 and makersmark N.

RPS-9018 SONG THRUSHES WITH CRABAPPLE (17" x 13") English bone porcelain, decorated, L.I.G. 350, cut to 200

Song Thrushes with Crabapple was issued in 1974 with a limited issue goal of 350. This is one of the pieces whose cost of manufacture in 1976 forced a reduction of edition size— to 200 pieces. The sculpture depicts male

RPS-9019

RPS-9020

RPS-9021

RPS-9022

RPS-9023

and female thrushes perched on the branches of a crabapple tree. The piece carries Malvern Studiomark Number 100-16 and makersmark K. As of February 1, 1976, 72 sculptures had been completed.

RPS-9019 STONECHATS WITH BLACK-BERRY AND BRAMBLE (12″ x 8½″) English bone porcelain, decorated, L.I.G. 350

Announced in 1974, the Stonechats carries Malvern Studiomark Number 100-17 and makersmark K. It depicts male and female stonechats perched on a stump entwined by blackberries and bramble, perhaps in search of their favorite foods—insects and spiders. As of February 1, 1976, 73 sculptures had been completed.

RPS-9020 CRESTED TIT WITH KERRIA JAPONICA (9½″ x 7¼″) English bone porcelain, decorated, L.I.G. 500

Announced in 1974, the Crested Tit carries Malvern Studiomark Number 100-18 and makersmark K. The sculpture depicts a Crested Tit with wings outspread on a Kerria Japonica tree. As of February 1, 1976, 161 sculptures had been completed.

RPS-9021 SWALLOWS WITH MARSH MARIGOLDS AND REEDS (18″ x 11½″) English bone porcelain, decorated, L.I.G. 350

The Swallows were introduced in 1974 and carry Malvern Studiomark Number 100-19 and makersmark K. The sculpture depicts a pair of Swallows—one perched atop a marsh reed has just captured an insect in its beak; the other, wings outspread in easy flight, seems to be searching for food. Also featured in this sculpture are the colorful Marsh Marigolds at the bottom. As of February 1, 1976, 68 sculptures had been completed.

RPS-9022 CHAFFINCH WITH DOUBLE

CHERRY (8″ x 14″) English bone porcelain, L.I.G. 350

The Chaffinch with Double Cherry was announced in 1974. It carries Malvern Studiomark Number 100-20 and makersmark K. The sculpture depicts a Chaffinch with wings outspread among pink flowering double cherry blossoms. As of February 1, 1976, 74 sculptures had been completed.

RPS-9023 RUBY-THROATED HUMMING-BIRD WITH CROCUS AND FORSY-THIA (10¾″ x 6¾″) English bone porcelain, decorated, L.I.G. 300

The Ruby-Throated Hummingbird was announced in 1974. It carries Malvern Studiomark Number 100-21 and makersmark K. As of February 1, 1976, 90 pieces had been completed. The sculpture shows the Hummingbird perched atop a floral grouping of crocus and forsythia. There is also a moth.

RPS-9024

RPS-9025

RPS-9026

RPS-9027

RPS-9028

RPS-9029

RPS-9024 FLEDGLING PEREGRINE FALCON (6″ x 5″) Trenton hard porcelain, decorated, nonlimited edition still in production

Introduced in 1974, the Fledgling Peregrine Falcon carries Malvern Studiomark Number 200-10 and makersmark N.

RPS-9025 FLEDGLING COMMON TERN (5″ x 5″) Trenton hard porcelain, decorated, nonlimited edition still in production

Announced in 1974, the Fledgling Common Tern carries Malvern Studiomark Number 200-17 and makersmark N. The sculpture depicts the Baby Common Tern with awkward wings and chubby neck standing on a small rock.

RPS-9026 EUROPEAN GOLDFINCH (9″ x 6¾″) English bone porcelain, decorated, L.I.G. 500

Announced in 1975, the sculpture depicts a male resting on a bough of flowering Mock Orange. The piece carries Malvern Studiomark Number 100-22 and makersmark K. As of February 1, 1976, 78 pieces had been completed.

RPS-9027 GENTOO PENGUIN (6″ x 5½″) Trenton hard porcelain, decorated, nonlimited edition still in production

Introduced in 1975, this piece carries Malvern Studiomark Number 200-11 and makersmark N. It shows a Gentoo Penguin whose curiosity has been aroused by a shimmering silver fish.

RPS-9028 YOUNG BONAPARTE'S GULLS (6″ x 6″) Trenton hard porcelain, decorated, nonlimited edition still in production

Introduced in 1975, this sculpture shows

RPS-9030

RPS-9031

two young Bonaparte's Gulls sitting on a piling; one is clearly ready for another meal. It carries Malvern Studiomark Number 200-18 and makersmark N.

RPS-9029 LITTLE BLUE HERON (6½″ x 5½″) Trenton hard porcelain, decorated, nonlimited edition still in production

Issued in 1975, this sculpture shows an awkward little fledgling wih a caterpillar-hunter beetle. The Heron's recently opened eyes seem almost afraid to focus on the strange creature which has chosen to violate its oversized foot. The piece carries Malvern Studiomark Number 200-19 and makersmark N.

RPS-9030 BRIDLED TITMOUSE (10½″ x 5″) Trenton hard porcelain, decorated, nonlimited edition still in production

Introduced in 1975, the Bridled Titmouse carries Malvern Studiomark Number 200-21 and makersmark N. The sculpture depicts the Bridled Titmouse in a branch with bracket fungus and metallic beetle.

RPS-9031 CHESTNUT-BACKED CHICKADEE (10″ x 4½″) Trenton hard porcelain, decorated, nonlimited edition still in production

The Chestnut-Backed Chickadee was issued in 1975. It carries Malvern Studiomark Number 200-22 and makersmark N. The sculpture presents the Chickadee at the top of a stump which is entwined by foliage and berries of Virginia creeper. The piece replaces the Black-Capped Chickadee with Holly, Boehm Studiomark Number 438, RPC-1034-01.

RPS-9033

RPS-9034

RPS-9032

RPS-9032 CAROLINA WREN WITH MUSHROOMS (7½″ x 7″) Trenton hard porcelain, decorated, nonlimited edition still in production

The Carolina Wren, official State Bird of South Carolina, was announced in 1975. It depicts the bird singing atop a clump of mushrooms. The piece carries Malvern Studiomark Number 200-23 and makersmark N.

RPS-9033 TREE SPARROW WITH JA-PONICA (6″ x 8″) English bone porcelain, decorated, nonlimited edition still in production

Issued in 1975 by the Malvern Studio, the Tree Sparrow carries Malvern Studiomark Number 200-30 and makersmark L. The sculpture depicts the Tree Sparrow sitting on a spray of flowering Japonica.

RPS-9034 PIED WAGTAIL (8″ x 7½″) Trenton hard porcelain, decorated, non-limited edition still in production

The Pied Wagtail was issued in 1975, and carries Malvern Studiomark Number 200-31 and makersmark N. The sculpture depicts a male Wagtail on a rock, with fringed water lilies at its feet.

RPS-9035 CROSSBILLS WITH BEECH

RPS-9035

RPS-9036

RPS-9037

(13½" x 13") English bone porcelain, decorated, no edition size announced

The Crossbills with Beech was announced as a 1975 limited sculpture carrying Malvern Studiomark Number 100-23 and makersmark K. No edition size was given and in June of 1975 the Studio canceled the sculpture because of the extreme difficulty of engineering such a large and heavy piece in porcelain. The sculpture was to depict a pair of Crossbills frolicking in a Beech.

RPS-9036 RIVOLI'S HUMMINGBIRD WITH HIBISCUS (8¼" x 8") English bone porcelain, decorated, L.I.G. 500

Issued in 1976, this sculpture is in the category of the bird-with-floral group. The piece carries Malvern Studiomark Number 100-23 and makersmark K. As of February 1, 1976, only one of these sculptures had been completed.

RPS-9037 KINGFISHERS (9¼" x 9¾") English bone porcelain, decorated, L.I.G. 350

This sculpture features two adult Kingfishers, one perched and the other just returning from flight. On its underside the sculpture carries Malvern Studiomark Number 100-24 and makersmark K. As of February 1, 1976, one piece had been completed.

Appendix A
Makersmarks

Until early in 1959, the makersmarks were not carefully regulated, and Studio records fail to be specific in their use. It is, therefore, impossible to be absolutely certain of the use of a particular makersmark on all —or even most—of any of the early editions. In this listing, we have assigned to the pieces only those makersmarks that we *know* they bear because we have seen examples.

In general, the dates assigned above are correct. However, because of the lack of control, makersmarks often overlapped each other. The Boehm signature, although introduced in 1954, may also have been used earlier.

We are certain only that the OSSO CERAMICS (makersmark A) was the first used and that makersmarks E and F were adopted in early 1959 and were used until 1970. These latter makersmarks were more carefully controlled, with makersmark E being used for limited editions and makersmark F for all other sculptures.

The Fondo Marino was the last subject to bear makersmark E. It was the last piece to have been done by Mr. Boehm.

With the Junco, makersmark I was adopted for use on all future Trenton limited editions. The single feather makersmark G will be used on all Lenox collector's plates and makersmark H will be used for limited edition porcelain paintings and will be visible through a window on the reverse of each plaque. Makersmark J is used for the nonlimited sculptures produced in Trenton. Limited edition bone porcelain

sculptures created in Malvern carry makersmark K, while the nonlimited bone porcelain sculptures bear makersmark L. Malvern Studio limited edition sculptures made of Trenton hard porcelain bear makersmark M, and the nonlimited pieces made of Trenton hard porcelain carry makersmark N. Makersmark O is on the back of all of the one-of-a-kind porcelain paintings. The limited issue decorative art plates (paintings in the round) bear makersmark P.

The feather used in the new 1970 makersmarks, which signals the passing of Ed Boehm, was, curiously enough, designed by Mr. Boehm himself many years earlier.

NOTE: On some *very* rare hand-painted pieces such as vases and plates, the makersmark appears as "Boehm" in script followed by the word "Handpainted."

OSSO CERAMICS

A

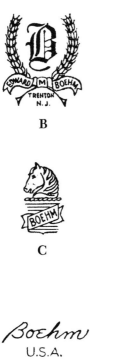

B

C

D

E

F

G

H

I

J

K

L

M

N

O

P

BACKSTAMP: This inscription is carried in 24-karat gold on the back of each Cardinal plate.

GIFT BOX: Of further interest to the consumer, each plate will be individually packaged in a handsome gold and green gift box, the perfect way to present this unique collector's item.

Appendix B Reassignment of Catalog Numbers

Old RP No.	Item	New RPC No.	Old RP No.	Item	New RPC No.
	Dog Subjects		143	Dachshund	117-01
101	Boxer, small	101-01	144	Dachshund	117-02
102	Boxer, small	101-02	145	Dachshund	117-03
103	Boxer, large	101-03	146	Dachshund	117-04
104	Boxer, large	101-04	147	Greyhound, Reclining	120
105	Scottish Terrier	102-01	148	Collie	119-01
106	Scottish Terrier	102-02	149	Collie	119-02
107	American Cocker	103-01	150	Collie	119-03
108	American Cocker	103-02	151	Collie	119-04
109	American Cocker	103-03	152	Whippet (unique)	121
110	American Cocker	103-04	153	Whippets	122-02
111	American Cocker	103-05	154	Whippets	122-01
112	American Cocker	103-06	155	Pomeranian	123
113	American Cocker w/Pheasant	105	156	King Charles Spaniel	124-01
114	Wire-Haired Terrier	106-01	157	Skye Terrier	125
115	Dane, Reclining	107-01	158	Dalmatian "Mike"	126-01
116	Dane, Reclining	107-02	159	Dalmatian "Mike"	126-02
117	Dane, Reclining	107-03	160	Basset Hound	127-01
118	Dane, Reclining	107-04	161	Basset Hound	127-02
119	Great Dane	108-01	162	German Shepherd	128
120	Great Dane	108-02	163	Pug	129-01
121	Great Dane	108-03	164	Pug	129-02
122	Great Dane	108-04	165	English Bull Dog	130
123	Doberman Pinscher	109-01	166	Sheep Dog Pup	131
124	Doberman Pinscher	109-02	167	Labrador Retriever	118-01
125	Doberman Pinscher	109-03	168	Labrador Retriever	118-02
126	Standing Foxhound	110	169	Large Cocker	104-01
127	Reclining Foxhound	111-01	170	King Charles Spaniel	124-02
128	Reclining Foxhound	111-02			
129	Reclining Foxhound	111-03		**Cat Subjects**	
130	French Poodle, Standing	112-01	201	Cat w/Two Kittens	202-01
131	French Poodle, Standing	112-02	202	Cat w/Two Kittens	202-02
132	French Poodle, Standing	112-03	203	Cat Playing w/Ball	201-01
133	French Poodle, Standing	112-04			
134	Poodle, Reclining	132		**Horse Subjects**	
135	Springer	113-01	301	Belgian Stallion	302
136	Springer	113-02	302	Percheron Stallion	305-02
137	Beagle	114-01	303	Percheron Stallion	305-04
138	Beagle	114-02	304	Percheron Stallion	305-05
139	Pointer	115-01	305	Percheron Stallion w/Roses	305-01
140	Pointer	115-02	306	Percheron Mare	306-01
141	Bull Terrier	116-02	307	Percheron Mare	306-02
142	Bull Terrier	116-01	308	Percheron Mare & Foal	301

Old RP No.	Item	New RPC No.
309	Colt	308-01
310	Colt	308-03
311	Colt	308-02
312	Colt	308-07
313	Colt	308-08
314	Arabian Stallion	309-03
315	Arabian Stallion	309-01
316	Thoroughbred w/Blanket	303-03
317	Thoroughbred, saddled w/Ex. Boy	303-07
318	Thoroughbred, saddled w/Ex. Boy	303-08
319	Thoroughbred w/Ex. Boy and Jockey	303-10
320	Thoroughbred, racing w/jockey	304-02
321	Thoroughbred, racing w/jockey	304-03
322	Hunter	307-04
323	Hunter	307-03
324	Polo Player	310
325	Thoroughbred w/Ex. Boy & Jockey	303-11
326	Colt	308-06
327	Thoroughbred, racing w/jockey	304-01
328	Hunter	307-01
329	Adios	311-02

Livestock Subjects

Old RP No.	Item	New RPC No.
401	Hereford Bull	402-03
402	Hereford Bull	402-02
403	Hereford Bull	402-01
404	Angus Bull	404-02
405	Angus Bull	404-01
406	Shorthorn Bull	406-01
407	Shorthorn Bull	406-02
408	Shorthorn Bull	406-03
409	Brahman Bull	407-01
410	Brahman Bull	407-03
411	Brahman Bull	407-02
412	Brahman Bull	407-04
413	Lamb	408
414	Holstein	401
415	Quad. Black Angus Calves	409
416	Hereford Bull	402-04

Wildlife

Old RP No.	Item	New RPC No.
501	Red Fox	502-01
502	Male Bunny	503
503	Female Bunny	504
504	Fawn	505
505	Squirrel	506-01
506	Cub	507-01
507	Cub	507-02
508	Lion	509
509	Tiger	508
510	Rabbit w/flowers	510-02
511	Rabbit w/flowers	510-01
512	White Mouse, Preening	511-01
513	White Mouse, Preening	511-02
514	Field Mouse w/Vetch	512-01
515	Newborn Rabbits	513-01
516	Chipmunk, Standing	514-01
517	Chipmunk, Standing	514-02
518	Chipmunk, Preening	515-01
519	Chipmunk, Preening	515-03
520	Red Fox	502-02
521	Squirrel	506-02
522	Cottontail Bunny	501
523	Rabbit Without Flowers	510-03
524	Field Mouse w/Vetch	512-02

Religious Subjects

Old RP No.	Item	New RPC No.
601	Madonna La Pietà, Large	605-01
602	Madonna La Pietà, Large	605-02
603	Madonna La Pietà, Med.	605-05
604	Madonna La Pietà, Small	605-07
605	Madonna Bust, Medium	603-02
606	Small Madonna Bust	606
607	Saint Maria Goretti	608-01
608	Saint Maria Goretti	608-02
609	Pigtail Angel	609-01
610	Lady of Grace	610-01
611	Lady of Grace	610-02
612	Saint Joseph	611-02
613	Saint Joseph	611-01
614	Guardian Angel	612-04
615	Angel on Pillow	612-02
616	Sister Angel	613-03
617	Sister Angel	613-04
618	Brother Angel	614-03
619	Brother Angel	614-05
619A	Brother Angel	614-04
620	Alba Madonna and Child	615-03
621	Alba Madonna and Child	615-02
622	Saint Francis of Assisi	616
623	Immaculate Conception	617-02
624	Immaculate Conception	617-01
625	Infant of Prague, Latin	618
626	Infant of Prague, Byzantine	619
627	Crucifix, Modern	622
628	Madonna and Child, Della Robbia	623
629	Pope John XXIII Bust	624
630	Pope Pius XII Bust, Large	620-01
631	Pope Pius XII Bust, Small	620-02
632	Madonna	604
633	Alba Madonna and Child	615-01
634	Small Saint Francis	601
635	Medium Madonna La Pietà	605-03

Figurine Subjects

Old RP No.	Item	New RPC No.
701	Neptune w/Seahorse	707-01
702	Neptune w/Seahorse	707-02
703	Diana w/Fawn	708-01
704	Diana w/Fawn	708-02
705	Venus	709-01
706	Venus	709-02
707	Mercury	710-01
708	Mercury	710-02
709	Apollo	711-01
710	Apollo	711-02
711	Quan Yin	712-01
712	Quan Yin	712-02
713	Cupid w/Flute	713-01
714	Cupid w/Flute	713-03
715	Cupid w/Flute	713-02
716	Cupid w/Harp	714-01
717	Cupid w/Harp	714-03
718	Cupid w/Harp	714-02
719	Cupid w/Horn	715-01
720	Cupid w/Horn	715-03
721	Cupid w/Horn	715-02
722	Ballerina, Swan Lake	716-03
723	Ballerina, Swan Lake	716-02
724	Ballerina, Swan Lake	716-01
725	Cherub on Pedestal	718
726	Beau Brummell, Old	720-03
727	Beau Brummell, Old	720-01
728	Gay Nineties	719-01
729	Gay Nineties	719-03
730	Mischief	706-01
731	Innocence	706-02
732	Ballerina, Pinky	703-01

Old RP No.	Item	New RPC No.	Old RP No.	Item	New RPC No.	Old RP No.	Item	New RPC No.
733	Ballerina, Pamela	703-02	835	Tulip Vase	950-03	883	Muffineer	810-02
734	Dutch Boy and Girl, Large	704-01	836	Fruit Pyramid	906-02	884	Muffineer	810-03
735	Dutch Boy and Girl, Small	704-02	837	Fruit Pyramid	906-01	885	Muffineer	810-01
736	Ichabod Crane	717	838	Plain Urn	930-01	886	Clover Ash Tray	868-02
737	Susie, Lipstick Girl	700-01A	839	Plain Urn	930-02	887	Clover Ash Tray	868-01
738	Kneeling Nude (Bathing Beauty)	702	840	Plain Urn	930-03	888	Acorn Ash Tray	870-03
739	Gay Nineties	719-02	841	Fluted Urn	931-02	889	Acorn Ash Tray	870-01
740	Choir Boy	705-01	842	Fluted Urn	931-01	890	Tulip Bowl	811-03
741	Beau Brummells, I	720-04	843	Fluted Urn	931-05	891	Tulip Bowl	811-04
742	Beau Brummells, II	720-07	844	Fluted Urn	931-03	892	Tulip Bowl	811-01
	Shriner	721-01	845	Small Fluted Ash Tray	864-02	893	Tulip Bowl	811-02
	Shriner	721-02	846	Small Fluted Ash Tray	864-01	894	Fluted Candlesticks	933-01
Dinnerware & Decorative Accessories			847	Small Fluted Ash Tray	864-03	895	Fluted Candlesticks	933-02
801	Service Plates	801-01	848	Clover Cigarette Box	869-01	896	Shell Nut Dish	830-05
802	Demi-Tasse Cup and Saucer	801-02	849	Clover Cigarette Box	869-02	897	Shell Nut Dish	830-02
803	Demi-Tasse Cup and Saucer	803-01	850	Acorn Cigarette Box	871-01	898	Shell Nut Dish	830-03
804	Demi-Tasse Cup	803-02	851	Acorn Cigarette Box	871-02	899	Shell Nut Dish	830-04
805	Demi-Tasse Cup	803-03	852	Round Fluted Ash Tray	851-09	900	Rose Pitcher	812-02
806	Small Swan	901-03	853	Shell Flower Holder	951-02	901	Rose Pitcher	812-03
807	Small Swan	901-02	854	Shell Flower Holder	951-01	902	Tulip Pitcher	816-02
808	Large Swan	901-03	855	Half-Fluted Ash Tray	865-01	903	Tulip Pitcher	816-03
809	Large Swan	902-02	856	Half-Fluted Ash Tray	865-02	904	Grape Pitcher	820-05
810	Fluted Grecian Vase	929-01	857	Chinese Vase	952-03	905	Grape Pitcher	820-03
811	Ming Bowl Centerpiece	928-03	858	Chinese Vase	952-01	906	Grape Pitcher	820-02
812	Ming Bowl Centerpiece	928-04	859	Grape Candlesticks	949-01	907	Grape Pitcher	820-01
813	Ming Bowl Centerpiece	928-02	860	Grape Candlesticks	949-02	908	Holly Pitcher	821-01
814	Oval Fluted Centerpiece	934-01	861	Maple Leaf Ash Tray	866-03	909	Holly Pitcher	821-02
815	Oval Fluted Centerpiece	934-02	862	Maple Leaf Ash Tray	866-01	910	Holly Cup	822-01
816	Oval Fluted Centerpiece	934-03	863	Grape Leaf Ash Tray	867-02	911	Holly Cups	822-02
817	Oval Fluted Centerpiece	934-04	864	Grape Leaf Ash Tray	867-01	912	Holly Nutmeg Shaker	823
818	Cigarette Box	853-02	865	Large Lotus Bowl	805-04	913	Rose Coffee Pot	813-01
819	Cigarette Box	853-03	866	Large Lotus Bowl	805-03	914	Rose Coffee Pot	813-02
820	Cigarette Box	853-04	867	Small Lotus Bowl	805-07	915	Rose Sugar Bowl	814-01
821	Hexagonal Ash Tray	854-01	868	Small Lotus Bowl	805-06	916	Rose Sugar Bowl	814-02
822	Hexagonal Ash Tray	854-02	869	Bunny Box w/Carrot	855-01	917	Rose Creamer	815-01
823	Dolphin Shell Vase	946-01	870	Tall Egg	904	918	Rose Creamer	815-02
824	Dolphin Shell Vase	946-02	871	Grape Jewel Box	856-03	919	Fluted Shell	832-02
825	Bee Hive	862	872	Grape Jewel Box	856-02	920	Fluted Shell	832-04
826	Grecian Candy Box	863-02	873	French Cachette	857-02	921	Grape Box w/Two Cupids	856-01
827	Bee Basket	808-01	874	French Cachette	857-01	922	Fruit Bowl Set	826
828	Bee Basket	808-03	875	Fluted Perfume Bottles	858	923	Horn of Plenty	905-02
829	Oval Grape Centerpiece	948-01	876	Fluted Candy Box	861	924	Horn of Plenty	905-01
830	Oval Grape Centerpiece	948-03	877	Corinthian Candlesticks	936-01	925	Bunny Milk Mug	807
831	Tulip Dinner Bell	809-02	878	Corinthian Candlesticks	936-02	926	Ming Candlesticks	955
832	Tulip Dinner Bell	809-01	879	Bud Vase	945-02	926A	Large Candlesticks	956
833	Tulip Vase	950-01	880	Bud Vase	945-01	927	Large Tulip Vase	939-04
834	Tulip Vase	950-02	881	French Fluted Vase	932-03	928	Large Tulip Vase	939-01
			882	French Fluted Vase	932-01	929	Lotus Candelabra	961-02

Old RP No.	Item	New RPC No.	Old RP No.	Item	New RPC No.	Old RP No.	Item	New RPC No.
930	Cherub Nut Dish	833	978	Gravy Boat	806-03	1040	White-Throated Sparrow	1027-01
931	Portrait Head	700-03	979	Gravy Boat	806-04	1041	White-Throated Sparrow	1027-02
932	Flower Vase	940-01	980	Gravy Boat	806-05	1042	Yellow-Throated Warbler	1028-01
933	Flower Vase	940-03	981	Phrenology Head	700-04	1043	Yellow-Throated Warbler	1028-02
934	Flower Vase	940-02	982	Percheron Stallion Bookends	903-02	1044	Baby Cedar Waxwing	1029-01
935	Ornate Urn	944				1045	Baby Cedar Waxwing	1029-02
936	Bird Urn	953-01		**Bird Subjects**		1046	Baby Blue Jay	1032-01
937	Bird Urn	953-02	1001	Canvasback Ducks	1001-01	1047	Baby Blue Jay	1032-02
938	Bird Urn	953-03	1002	Canvasback Ducks	1001-03	1048	Baby Robin	1033-01
939	Swan Cake Plate	700-02b	1003	Canvasback Ducks	1001-02	1049	Baby Robin	1033-02
940	Percheron Stallion Bookends	903-01	1004	Green Winged Teal	1002-01	1050	Black-Capped Chickadee	1034-01
941	Crimped Bowl	825-02	1005	Green Winged Teal	1002-03	1051	Black-Capped Chickadee	1034-02
942	Crimped Candy Dish	828	1006	Green Winged Teal	1002-02	1052	Hummingbird	1035-01
943	Crimped Vase	941-02	1007	Wood Duck	1002-04	1053	Hummingbird	1035-02
944	Oval Fluted Candlestick	935	1008	Wood Duck	1002-05	1054	Baby Bluebird	1038-01
945	Flower Vase	940-04	1009	Wood Duck	1002-06	1055	Baby Bluebird	1038-02
946	Thin-Necked Vase	942	1010	Leghorns	1003-01	1056	Baby Woodthrush	1040-02
947	Fluted Urn	931-04	1011	Leghorns	1003-03	1057	Baby Woodthrush	1040-03
948	Demi-Tasse Cups	801-03	1012	Red-Breasted Grosbeaks	1004-02	1058	Prothonotary Warbler	1041-01
949	Teacup and Saucer	801-04	1013	Red-Breasted Grosbeaks	1004-05	1059	Prothonotary Warbler	1041-02
950	Tulip Pitcher	816-01	1014	Red-Breasted Grosbeaks	1004-04	1060	Baby Goldfinch	1044-01
951	Rose Pitcher	812-01	1015	Evening Grosbeaks	1004-01	1061	Baby Goldfinch	1044-02
952	Shell Platter	827-01	1016	Gosling Duck	1009	1062	Fledgling Kingfisher	1045-01
953	Three-Section Nut Dish	831	1017	Gun Stock Box w/Mallards	1010	1063	Fledgling Kingfisher	1045-02
954	Large Tulip Pitcher	817	1018	Chick	1011	1064	Owls	1048-01
955	Ribbed Vase	943	1019	Golden Oriental Pheasant	1013-02	1065	Owls	1048-02
956	Fluted Grecian Vase	929-02	1020	Golden Oriental Pheasant	1013-01	1066	Baby Crested Flycatcher	1051-01
957	Large Round Ash Tray	860-02	1021	Macaws	1015-01	1067	Baby Crested Flycatcher	1051-02
958	Round Fluted Ash Tray	851-10	1022	Macaws	1015-04	1068	Baby Chickadee	1054-01
959	Round Fluted Ash Tray	852-02	1023	Macaws	1015-02	1069	Baby Chickadee	1054-02
960	Holly Tray	824	1024	Black-Tailed Bantams	1021-01	1070	Tree Sparrow	1059-02
961	Fluted Nut Dish	829-04	1025	American Eagle, 18″	1025-02	1071	Tree Sparrow	1059-03
962	Fluted Nut Dish	829-01	1026	American Eagle, 18″	1025-01	1072	Nuthatch	1060-01
963	Small Perfume Bottle	859	1027	American Eagle, 15″	1025-04	1073	Nuthatch	1060-02
964	Modern Centerpiece	959-01	1028	American Eagle, 15″	1025-03	1074	Fledgling Magpie	1066-01
965	Bell Candlestick	938	1029	Ruby-Crowned Kinglet	1036	1075	Fledgling Magpie	1066-02
966	Large Plain Urn	930-04	1030	Fledgling Purple Finches	1046-01	1076	Fledgling Blackburnian Warbler	1067-01
967	Planter	954	1031	Fledgling Purple Finches	1046-02			
968	Tulip Candlestick	937	1032	Woodthrush w/Crab Apple	1000	1077	Fl. Blackburnian Warbler	1067-02
969	Round Fluted Ash Tray	851-07	1033	Blackburnian Warbler w/Mountain Laurel	1037-01	1078	Song Sparrows	1019-01
970	Round Fluted Candlesticks	960				1079	Song Sparrows	1019-02
971	Easter Egg Paperweight	907-01	1034	Canada Geese	1007-03	1080	Cedar Waxwings	1017-01
972	Candy Egg	900	1034A	Canada Geese	1007-02	1081	Cedar Waxwings	1017-02
973	Oval Grape Centerpiece	948-02	1035	Canada Geese	1007-04	1082	Cerulean Warblers	1022-02
974	Bunny Box w/Carrot	855-02	1036	Tumbler Pigeons	1014-01	1083	Cerulean Warblers	1022-03
975	Shell Platter	827-02	1037	Tumbler Pigeons	1014-02	1084	Meadowlark	1031-02
976	Acorn Ash Tray	870-02	1038	Indigo Bunting	1026-01	1085	Meadowlark	1031-03
977	Ring Top Vase	925	1039	Indigo Bunting	1026-02	1086	Eastern Bluebirds	1047-01

Old RP No.	Item	New RPC No.	Old RP No.	Item	New RPC No.	Old RP No.	Item	New RPC No.
1087	Eastern Bluebirds	1047-02	1121	Mockingbirds	1052-01	1153	Green Jays	1075-01
1088	Mallards	1005-03	1122	Mockingbirds	1052-02	1154	Rufous Hummingbirds	1076-01
1089	Mallards	1005-02	1123	Sugarbirds	1053-01	1155	Wood Thrushes	1074-01
1090	Mallards	1005-04	1124	Sugarbirds	1053-02	1156	Macaws	1015-03
1091	Bob White Quail	1006-02	1125	Ptarmigan	1055-01	1157	Meadowlark	1031-01
1092	Bob White Quail	1006-03	1126	Ptarmigan	1055-02	1158	Canada Geese	1007-01
1093	Ring-Necked Pheasants	1008-02	1127	Lesser Prairie Chickens	1056-01	1159	Black-Tailed Bantams	1021-02
1094	Ring-Necked Pheasants	1008-03	1128	Lesser Prairie Chickens	1056-02	1160	Fledgling Canada Warbler	1080-01
1095	Woodcock	1012-01	1129	Blue Jays	1057-01	1161	Northern Water Thrush	1079-01
1096	Woodcock	1012-02	1130	Blue Jays	1057-02	1162	Crested Flycatcher	1077-01
1097	Cardinals	1016-01	1131	Mearns Quail	1058-01	1163	Blue Grosbeak	1078-02
1098	Cardinals	1016-02	1132	Mearns Quail	1058-02	1164	Fledgling Red Poll	1084
1099	Golden-Crowned Kinglets	1018-01	1133	Mountain Bluebirds	1061-01	1165	Fledgling Western	1083
1100	Golden-Crowned Kinglets	1018-02	1134	Mountain Bluebirds	1061-02		Bluebirds Group	
1101	Carolina Wrens	1020-01	1135	Towhee	1062-01	1166	Hooded Mergansers	1085-01
1102	Carolina Wrens	1020-02	1136	Towhee	1062-02	1167	Common Tern	1086-01
1103	Red-Winged Blackbirds	1023-01	1137	Robin	1063-01	1168	Kestrels	1081-01
1104	Red-Winged Blackbirds	1023-02	1138	Robin	1063-02	1169	Road Runner	1082-01
1105	Downy Woodpeckers	1024-01	1139	Killdeer	1064-01	1170	Western Bluebirds	1088-01
1106	Downy Woodpeckers	1024-02	1140	Killdeer	1064-02	1171	Verdins	1089-01
1107	California Quail	1030-01	1141	Bobolink	1065-01	1172	Black-Headed Grosbeaks	1090-01
1108	California Quail	1030-02	1142	Bobolink	1065-02	1173	Young American Bald	1087-01
1109	Black-Throated Blue Warbler	1037-02	1143	Ivory-Billed Woodpecker	1069		Eagle	
1110	Black-Throated Blue Warbler	1037-03	1144	Azuli Bunting	1059-01	1174	Orchard Oriole	1092-01
1111	Mourning Doves	1039-01	1145	Baby Woodthrush	1040-01	1175	Slate-Colored Junco	1094-01
1112	Mourning Doves	1039-02	1146	Leghorns	1003-02	1176	Oven Bird	1091-01
1113	Nonpareil Buntings	1042-01	1147	Tufted Titmice	1071-01	4001	Fondo Marino	1093
1114	Nonpareil Buntings	1042-02	1148	Parula Warblers	1073-02		Terrazzo Floor	2006
1115	American Redstarts	1043-01	1149	Varied Buntings	1070-01			
1116	American Redstarts	1043-02	1150	Catbird	1072-01			RPS No.
1117	Ruffed Grouse	1049-01	1151	Fledgling Great Horned Owl	1068-02	5001	Mockingbirds, pr.	2007
1118	Ruffed Grouse	1049-02	1152	Fledgling Great Horned Owl	•1068-03	5002	Song Sparrows	2010
1119	Goldfinches	1050-01		• This number was also used erroneously		5003	Meadowlarks, pr.	2009
1120	Goldfinches	1050-02		for the Red-Breasted Grosbeak #1004-03.		5004	Eastern Bluebirds, pr.	2008

Appendix C   Boehm Works in Public Collections

International

Canada: Royal Ontario Museum, Toronto

Denmark: American Embassy, Copenhagen

England: Liverpool Museum; American Embassy, London; Buckingham Palace, London; City Museum and Art Gallery, Stoke-on-Trent; City Museum and Art Gallery, Worcester

France: American Embassy (Rothschild Mansion), Paris; Palais de l'Elysée, Paris

Israel: Ha'aretz Museum, Tel Aviv

Japan: National Museum, Tokyo

Monaco: The Royal Palace

People's Republic of China: The Imperial Palace, Peking

South Korean Republic: The Blue House (Presidential Mansion), Seoul

Sweden: The Royal Palace, Stockholm

U.S.S.R.: Moscow (whereabouts uncertain)

Vatican City: Vatican Museum